Canada's
Natural Environment

Canada's Natural Environment
essays in applied geography

edited by

G.R. McBoyle
University of Waterloo
and
E. Sommerville
University of Waterloo

Methuen
Toronto • London • Sydney • Wellington

Canadian Cataloguing in Publication Data

Main entry under title:

Canada's natural environment

Includes bibliographical references.
ISBN 0-458-91930-6 pa.

1. Environmental policy — Canada.
2. Natural resources — Canada. 3. Man —
Influence on nature — Canada. I. McBoyle,
Geoffrey R., 1942-   II. Sommerville,
Edward, 1940-

HC120.E5C35   301.31'0971   C76-017017-7

51, 403

Printed and bound in Canada

1 2 3 4 5   10 9 8 7 6

Contents

PART 6. ENSURING THE FUTURE OF THE CANADIAN NATURAL
ENVIRONMENT: POLICY PRIORITIES 241

The editors and authors thank the following for permission to reproduce artwork:
Figure:
1.2   National Council for Geographic Education, *Journal of Geography*
2.1   Atmospheric Environment Service
2.2   Atmospheric Environment Service
2.3   Atmospheric Environment Service
2.4   Atmospheric Environment Service
2.5   Atmospheric Environment Service
2.6   Atmospheric Environment Service
3.1   R. W. Kates and *Natural Hazard Research*
3.2   Department of Geography, University of Toronto, *Research Publications*
3.3   Department of Energy, Mines & Resources, *National Atlas of Canada*
3.4   Canadian Committee for Geography, Department of the Environment
3.5   *The Canadian Geographer*
3.6   L-E. Hamelin and the Royal Society of Canada
3.7   *Natural Resources Journal*
4.1   Inland Waters Directorate
4.2   Inland Waters Directorate
4.3   Inland Waters Directorate
4.4   Inland Waters Directorate
4.5   Inland Waters Directorate
4.6   Inland Waters Directorate and Information Canada
4.7   Manitoba Hydro
4.8   Société d'énergie de la Baie James
5.1   University of Chicago Press, *The Theory of Groundwater Motion*, M.K. Hubbert
5.2   D.D. Brown
5.3   J.T.G. Andrew and J.M. Rigney
5.4a   Inland Waters Directorate and Information Canada
5.4b   National Research Council of Canada and Information Canada
5.6   Canadian Institute of Mining and Metallurgy
7.1   Associate Committee on Geotechnical Research, National Research Council
        of Canada
7.4   John Wiley and Sons, *Foundation Engineering*, R. Peck, W. Hanson, T. Thorburn
7.5   *Journal of National Buildings Organisation*
7.6   Acres Consulting Services
8.1   Information Canada
8.2   Parks Canada
8.3   Parks Canada
8.4   Parks Canada
9.1   Ecoplans
9.2   G. Brannon
9.3   Ecoplans
9.4   Ecoplans

Preface

During the last few years a number of books and anthologies have appeared dealing with the subject matter of this collection, Canada's Natural Environment. These earlier works seem to fall into one or other of two main types: (1) academic treatises, synthesizing what is known about the structure and function of the various natural subsystems (weather and climate; water; landforms; soil; biota) that collectively constitute the environmental resource base of the country; (2) popular consciousness-raising volumes focusing upon the problems associated with the exploitations of this resource base in the course of national growth and development.

We believe that this book comprises a third approach to the subject which combines elements of each of the above classes. Like the consciousness-raising works, the book is problem oriented rather than discipline oriented. Its tone and style, however, are academic. The book is concerned with the definition of the nature and scope of problems stemming from man-nature interactions within the contemporary Canadian ecumene, but its focus is upon actual and/or potential applications of the concepts, methods, tools and techniques developed by the family of academic specialities which may be grouped under the broad umbrella of environmental studies. In short, the book is not (except in flashes) yet another environmental polemic. It assumes an audience who, having listened to and largely accepted the basic premises and aims of the pre-election campaigners on behalf of the environmental cause, are now ready and waiting to hear about strategies and tactics from its post-election functionaries.

The book consists of ten specially commissioned essays. Two of these, the first by Krueger and the last by Jackson, are broad-ranging in scope. While the former summarizes the role of a specific discipline in applied environmental work, the latter provides an account of the response of the federal authorities to the environmental issue over the past decade. The remaining eight essays address themselves to four categories of natural environmental elements. A pair of articles on the atmospheric environment is succeeded, in turn, by pairs of essays on surface and underground water resources; soil in relation to agricultural and urban development; and the biotic components of natural ecosystems in the context of two extremes — wilderness environments and rapidly urbanizing ones.

After determining the conceptual structure and tone of the volume and providing guidelines with respect to length and level of difficulty, we left decisions about the details of content and approach to each of the individual contributors. This editorial policy was basically dictated by our perception of the current stage of development of applied environmental work in Canada. We believe this to be beyond the period of early childhood but far short of maturity, when established procedures of diagnosis and prescription and hence a common format would be appropriate. Adolescence is perhaps the best metaphor to characterize the present stage of evolution of this type of work. Hence the essays employ the diverse styles of approach and emphasis associated with an age of uncertain experimentation.

Some aim at comprehensive coverage and are essentially state-of-the-art reviews. McKay's essay on Climatic Resources and Economic Activity is perhaps the clearest example of this genre. Others are very specific, concerned mainly with illustrating the application of principles and methods by means of case studies. Kitchen's article on Ecoplanning is an example of this type. Several pieces focus almost exclusively on techniques; such as Hoffman's discussion of soil capability analysis and White's summary of soil engineering methods. Others, again, are more theoretically or even philosophically oriented. Examples of these approaches are Gardner's account of natural hazards research and Theberge's prescription for national parks planning. Finally, the importance of basic information is not neglected and, while stressed in several essays, is particularly evident in the pair of articles on surface and subsurface water resources by Quinn and Spence, and Parsons respectively.

While the essays are deliberately varied in their approach, they are quite uniform in their level of difficulty. Our instructions in this regard were to ask our contributors to write for a potential audience made up of students taking introductory level university and college courses in the various subject matter disciplines and professional training programmes dealing with all or parts of Canada's natural environment. Upper-level high school students, particularly in geography, may also benefit from this volume. Outside of educational establishments we hope that the book may be of some value to members of the general public, especially those interested in assessing the ability of technicians to respond to the challenges posed during this post-hysteric age of the environmental movement in Canada.

PART 1
THE CANADIAN
NATURAL ENVIRONMENT:
GEOGRAPHIC CONTRIBUTIONS

1

The Role of Geography in Environmental Research, Action and Education

Ralph R. Krueger, Department of Geography, University of Waterloo

THE CHANGING NATURE OF GEOGRAPHY

In explaining to students the nature of the discipline of geography and its relevance to current environmental problems, I find a simple diagram showing three major thrusts in geography to be very useful. There is nothing particularly novel in this illustration. Each thrust has a long history behind it. However, the emphasis placed on each has varied from time to time in a rather regular almost cyclical way.[1]

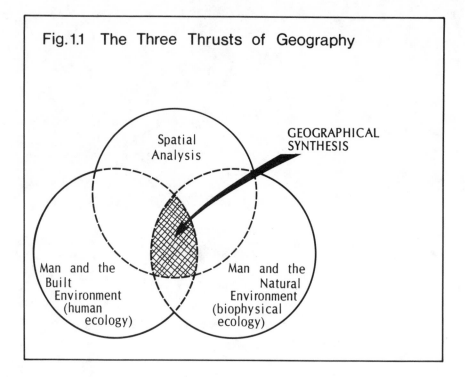

Fig.1.1 The Three Thrusts of Geography

Spatial Analysis

GEOGRAPHICAL SYNTHESIS

Man and the Built Environment (human ecology)

Man and the Natural Environment (biophysical ecology)

The man-natural environment (or, man-land) thrust in geography has its origins in the writings of the Ancients who emphasized physical geography and its impact on man. By the turn of the twentieth century, this man-land tradition had evolved into the doctrine known as environmental determinism, which is perhaps best exemplified by the writings of the American geographers Ellsworth Huntington and Ellen Semple. Because of the dogmatic nature of determinism (the environment was said to govern all manner of things, even the intelligence and industriousness of nations) geography lost a great deal of credibility in the eyes of other disciplines. In reaction, geographers themselves began to back away from the man-land emphasis. As a result, physical geography fell into relative neglect, at least in the United States. In Canada, however, partly because of the influence of British geographers, who did not disregard physical geography, and partly owing to the presence of the influential environmental determinist, Griffith Taylor (who was instrumental in establishing Canada's first university geography department, and who was a prolific and persuasive writer) physical geography remained strong in most university geography programmes. This, in turn, explains why physical geography has long been emphasized in the curricula of Canadian secondary schools.

Physical geography in Canadian universities has, until quite recently, consisted primarily of geomorphology and climatology. Biogeography and ecology were neglected, and the study of landforms and climate tended to be conducted independent of each other rather than as parts of the natural system which comprises "the earth as the home of man." Nowadays, physical geographers are paying much greater attention to biogeography and to ecological relationships, and are using an ecosystem approach to their subject.[2] This new emphasis has made it possible for geographers to cooperate more effectively with biologists and other scientists in tackling environmental problems in which ecological factors are important.

Because of their disenchantment with environmental determinism, many geographers adopted a philosophical position that has been termed possibilism: the freedom of man to choose from a range of possibilities within a given natural framework.[3] Those holding this viewpoint tended to ignore the role of the natural environment and in so doing created a second thrust, namely a human geography that concentrated on the study of man's relationship to the built environment. This shift brought the subject close to the human ecology being developed by sociologists and anthropologists. As geographers attempted to explain the processes that led to patterns of settlement, land use and economic activity, they began to draw upon theories and research methods developed by other social scientists. Many began to specialize in subfields of the discipline such as urban geography, rural geography and industrial geography. This development added greatly to our understanding of the man-made environment.

The third thrust in geography, that of spatial analysis, encompasses the idea of location or "whereness" which has always been a central component of geography. It is this thrust which has led to comments like "if you can map it, it is geography" or "history is to time what geography is to place."

Hartshorne[4] has used the terms *areal differentiation* or *area interrelationships* to describe the way in which geographers deal with both physical and human factors which exist in an area, and which serve to distinguish it from other areas. However, since the late 1950's the emphasis has been on the development of an abstract theoretical approach to an understanding of the spatial organization of society. This approach has resulted in more cumulative generalizations and has led to more rigorous testing of hypotheses. A corollary of the new theoretical approach was a rapid increase in the use of statistical and mathematical techniques in geographical research.[5] Although the theoretical-quantitative approach is not necessarily restricted to spatial analysis, it is in this thrust where it has been most often applied.[6]

The theoretical-spatial emphasis in geography has led to overlap with work being done by other social scientists. For example, location theory, based on the assumption of "economic man," is of equal interest to both the economist and the theoretical-spatial economic geographer. Spatially-oriented sociologists have much in common with many modern social and urban geographers. The work of environmental psychologists is useful to geographers who use a behavioural approach to the study of topics such as environmental hazards, recreational resource use or the utilization of urban space. Thus, the theoretical emphasis within the spatial thrust of geography has led to valuable interdisciplinary research efforts.[7]

Weaknesses in the theoretical-spatial approach in geography have been forcefully expressed recently by Taafe:

> The progressive abstracting of spatial patterns brought with it the danger of an over-concern with sterile geometric patterns. . . . A disproportionate share of research might be allocated to problems which are as socially trivial as they are theoretically tractable. . . . All too often, laboring mountains of technique . . . produce a few intellectual mice, and formidably complex articles . . . triumphantly produce more parsimonious ways of doing things which probably weren't worth doing in the first place.[8]

In the past, unfortunately, there was a tendency for geographers to become so immersed in one thrust of geography that they totally neglected the others. All three make a major contribution towards the ultimate goal of geographical synthesis (Figure 1.1) which is required to understand "the earth as the home of man."

The serious societal concern about environmental problems in the late 1960's and early 1970's has been, I believe, chiefly responsible for a new concern among geographers to adopt a more holistic approach to geographical research and teaching, i.e. an approach that encompasses all three thrusts of geography.

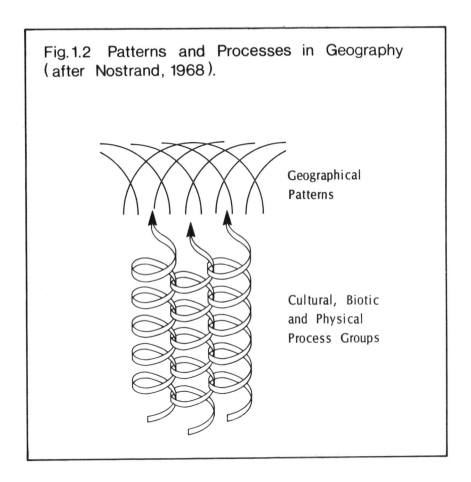

Fig. 1.2   Patterns and Processes in Geography (after Nostrand, 1968).

Geographical
Patterns

Cultural, Biotic
and Physical
Process Groups

The diagram in Figure 1.2 illustrates that geography is monistic, i.e. it is not divided between physical and human, between regional and systematic, or between man-environment and spatial. The diagram defines geography in terms of patterns (natural and man-made) and the processes which create the patterns. The three groups of processes (cultural, biotic and physical) are shown as being intertwined and interrelated. It suggests that not only can the spatial and ecological views co-exist, but that a comprehensive geographical synthesis is not possible without both of them.[9]

THE RELEVANCE OF GEOGRAPHY

Geography by its very nature *is* relevant. We do not have to make it so. In fact, one has to work very hard at doing any geographical study which is not directly relevant to contemporary environmental concerns. It is true that some geographers appear to have spent a great amount of effort on trivial things, but it is more than likely that ultimately these geographers will develop theories and methods which will greatly enrich our understanding of man's environment.

The rapid rise of public concern about environmental problems in the past decade has led to an increasing recognition of the usefulness of a geographical approach to environmental investigation. A geographical study provides the kind of information often required by the decision-maker, i.e. a balanced and integrated assessment of the natural and built environment from a spatial point of view.

As an example of the relevance and applicability of geographic research to environmental issues, I should like to turn to my own work on the Niagara Fruit Belt of southern Ontario. Even back in the 1950's it was recognized by academics and some government people that unplanned urban development was a threat to the prime fruit lands in the Niagara Peninsula. However, when I began my investigations, I discovered that basic geographical knowledge about the region was lacking. There was not even a detailed map showing the precise limits of different intensities and different kinds of fruit growing. Furthermore, although public concern had been expressed about the disappearing Niagara Fruit Belt, no one knew how quickly fruit land was being converted to urban uses nor how long it would last. So I began to address myself to some basic geographical questions:

1. Where is the Fruit Belt?
2. How does the physical resource (climate, land-type and soils) compare with other parts of Ontario, Canada and the United States?
3. How does the quality of the fruit-growing land differ from place to place within the region?
4. How economically viable is the fruit-growing industry?
5. What are the industrial and general urban locational factors that are leading to urbanization in the area?
6. Where is most of the urban development going and what are the likely future directions of growth?
7. What are the social, economic and environmental consequences of urban sprawl?
8. Could Niagara fruit production be replaced by production in other places?
9. Are there feasible alternative directions and patterns of urban growth?

10. What are the attitudes of the various groups of people towards the issue — the fruit growers, the fruit processing industry, the urban people, local and provincial government?
11. What planning and governmental machinery is required to solve the problem?

To answer these questions, a relatively comprehensive geographical synthesis of a region, which focused upon a central environmental problem, had to be undertaken. Geographers of an older vintage would call it a study in thematic regional geography. Although most of the information was obtained from census records, air photographs and interviews, significant data was obtained from the work of other scientists and social scientists. But, the resulting synthesis was truly geographical and included elements of all three thrusts of geography (Figure 1.1).

Government agencies began using my Niagara study in various reports on the Niagara region. It was quoted widely in the press and in the Ontario Legislature, in efforts to convince the provincial and local governments that they should take some action. Many other studies were conducted by both academics and government personnel. But progress is often slow in a democratic society. Virtually no action was taken until 1970, when the Regional Municipality of Niagara was formed. By the time a master land-use plan was formulated only about one-third of the prime fruit land was left to preserve.[10]

However, the point of this story is not that government action is often tardy, but that geographical studies can be useful inputs to the solution of environmental and resource use problems. For example, the Policy Plan adopted in 1974 by the Regional Municipality of Niagara has land capability maps that can be traced back to maps in my study of 1959.

It is not my contention that only regional syntheses are useful. Geographical studies of specific resources, of a particular aspect of the natural or cultural environment or analyses of networks and flows can also be valuable. Likewise, I do not mean to suggest that only the work of geographers is required; the know-how of many other specialists is essential. I merely wish to point out that regional studies can be very rewarding and useful. This needs to be said because in the last couple of decades regional geography has fallen into disrepute amongst professional geographers (and consequently amongst geography students).

I am not alone in calling for more emphasis on synthetic regional studies. Kerr did so in his presidential address to the Canadian Association of Geographers back in 1960:

In Canada I can envisage a programme, among others, of studies on selected regions leading towards an understanding of the economic geography of the country as a whole. In eastern Ontario, for example, the theme of stagnation of economic growth could be selected and vigorously prosecuted, bringing into focus significant changes in agriculture, manufacturing, and related industries within a regional framework. Such research properly placed upon problems and oriented towards historical changes should produce, in the place of tedious regional compilations, monographs, which would attest to the contribution that geography can make towards understanding some aspects of the Canadian economy.

More recently, two geographers working for Environment Canada emphasized the usefulness of regional geographical studies in solving environmental problems:

The Windsor-Quebec axis is the demographic and economic heart of Canada. If the improvement of the human environment of Canada is a major national goal, then what happens . . . along this axis must be of central importance in the strategy to attain that goal. . . . We believe, therefore, that it would be difficult to conceive of a single more useful geographical contribution to the solution of Canada's environmental problems that an assessment of the major dimensions, implications, opportunities and constraints that influence the . . . human environment of the Windsor-Quebec axis. We would prefer to say "than a good regional geography of the axis", but the alternative jargon is likely to be more palatable, unfortunately, even among geographers. [11]

The geographer also has certain special research techniques that are often under-valued, because, on the surface, they seem so simple. Yet, techniques such as field observation and recording, air photo interpretation and mapping can be very useful in many environmental studies. Mapping, which is central to the discipline of geography, is often vital in environmental research, both as a research method that can reveal new spatial interrelationships and as a medium for presenting results in a useful form. For example, discussing the implementation of land-use regulations in the Canadian North, Hare and Jackson had this to say about the utility of maps:

1. They are integrative; they seek to assemble within the framework of a common spatial context, information concerning a wide variety of topics that interact with each other and together represent a major part of the environmental situation that is the basic subject of study.
2. Maps are a rapid means of identifying gaps in knowledge, at least where such gaps have a spatial component.
3. Drawing maps is often one of the quickest ways to contribute to the solution of environmental problems. . . . Compiling a map which conveys an accurate and balanced representation of a variety of disparate elements is a thoroughly professional occupation. [12]

GEOGRAPHY AND ENVIRONMENTAL ACTION

For many years, the most important criteria for choosing geographical research topics were: "Will it add to our store of empirical knowledge? Will it add to the development of theory or method? Will it enhance the researcher's professional reputation?" Although these are still important, in recent years a new criterion has been added: "Will the research make a contribution to the understanding and solution of social and environmental problems?"

As early as 1964, Hare, in a presidential address to the Canadian Association of Geographers, commented on the desirability of choosing research topics on the basis of their applicability to society's needs:

> *How is the subject of our research chosen? Do our choices make sense in the present state of national development? And is our work making its mark on the national life? The purist can answer, of course, that such questions are improper. He will say that research justifies itself; that one cannot choose a topic on any other basis than one's personal curiosity; and that it is no part of our business to ensure that our work is in the national interest. Such arguments impress me only when they are applied to the fundamental, primary sciences, such as molecular biology and particle physics, which have some chance of answering root questions. Geography is the scientific study of a highly evolved complex – the man-land relationship; and such a study is so intimately bound up with social and economic structure that relevance to national needs ought to be a major determinant in one's choice of research.*

In the above quotation, Hare singles out the man-environment thrust of geography and indicates that research in this direction is of importance to social and economic public issues. In a later statement (with Jackson) he comments on the usefulness of the spatial analysis thrust to the solution of environmental problems:

> *For the community as a whole, we see the need for recognition that spatial questions are among the major elements in the environmental problem, and among the least considered. It is the distribution of population, the degree of its nucleation, the location of industry, and the layout of communications systems that create the pollution problem. If Canada's population and economic activity were thinly spread across her land surface the problem would not exist, though important questions of resource conservation and wise use would still remain. Although spatial organization is extremely complex, and never repeats itself precisely, it can still be meaningfully analysed. Such analysis is the prerequisite to wise planning and management. . . . Throughout this essay it must have seemed to many that we have been appealing to an older tradition of geography which is now very much out of fashion. To the extent that this is so, we are glad to make that appeal. With rare and outstanding exceptions, however, the older tradition was not activist; it was concerned with description rather than with problem-solving. So, unfortunately, has been much of the new geography that has tended to replace it during the last*

decade. Our purpose in this essay is wholly activist. We do not advocate mapmaking because it is the way geography should be done, but because there is a need for such maps if environmental management is to be effective. We do not seek a geographical perspective on Windsor-Quebec because the axis is there, but because the quality of life of the millions who live there will be affected by the availability or absence of that perspective. Geographers have taken the environment as their parish for more than a century, but it was ecologists, not geographers, who played a major role in causing the United Nations Conference on the Human Environment to happen. We believe it is time we redeemed our position, not out of concern for the status of our discipline, but because we have a necessary role to play.[13]

American geographers are also discussing the applicability of their research. White made the following statement at a session on Geography and Public Policy at the annual meeting of the Association of American Geographers in 1970:

It may be helpful . . . to consider . . . criteria for selecting research problems in the light of possible social implications. Beyond the conventional questions of what might contribute to theory or method, what would be practicable and what would be interesting, are questions such as these: What is the prospect that the results will help advance the aims of the people affected? To what extent is it feasible for those affected to join in or consent to the research? Is the design of the research pointed to applying the results? . . . Speaking as one individual, I feel strongly that I should not go into research unless it promises results that would advance the aims of the people affected and unless I am prepared to take all practicable steps to help translate the results into action.

The Association of American Geographers responded to this challenge by appointing an *ad hoc* Committee on Development and Planning to explore how the Association might respond to the perceived social and environmental needs of society.

It is interesting to note that both the Hare-Jackson and White statements call, not only for applied geography, but, for an advocacy role for the geographer. In other words, the geographer has a responsibility (if not as a professional, then as a citizen) to see that the insights gained from geographical study are applied to the solution of problems. There is a wide range of activist approaches including:

1. publishing in popular journals or news media so that the public and decision-makers will become aware of research results;
2. becoming involved in government mission-oriented research projects;
3. taking consulting jobs with government and private enterprise;
4. becoming involved in public debate over environmental issues; joining action-oriented groups such as Pollution Probe;
5. joining the decision-makers by accepting appointment to agencies such as planning boards or special environmental commissions or by running for elected office;

6. identifying with and assisting citizen groups in their efforts to improve environmental quality.

Let me again draw from my own experience to illustrate the way in which applied geography plus an activist approach can influence environmental decision-making. Some years ago, a research team, in the Faculty of Environmental Studies at the University of Waterloo, conducted a study of a 450-acre parcel of land in the city of Waterloo, Ontario, which was in the process of being developed into a housing subdivision. The study was designed to:

1. provide baseline inventory data on the environment before development proceeded;
2. determine the impact of the development on the environment;
3. determine the degree to which specific types and qualities of natural environment are adaptable to urban development;
4. test a methodology for this type of research;
5. develop principles that could be applied in the future to minimize bio-physical environmental damage and, at the same time, enhance the quality of the residential environment.

This was pure research in that it aimed at furthering knowledge and at developing principles and testing methodology; yet, it was also applied research, in that the researchers perceived the possible application of their findings.

The results of the research were disturbing. The vegetation in the swamp that was set aside for a park died; so did most of the trees in the woodlot area that was subdivided for housing. Houses built on organic soils suffered damage from subsidence. The natural stream was shifted from its original channel, and its potential for open-space use, as well as its aesthetic value, was thus completely negated. Because no preventative measures were taken during the development period, thunderstorms created serious erosion problems. In brief, a development had been imposed on the landscape without any consideration for what it would do to the bio-physical environment. The researchers concluded that ecological studies in advance of the design of the subdivision could have substantially reduced both environmental and financial losses.[14]

There is often a long time lapse between university research and the application of the research findings. The academic must take on the role of activist if he or she wishes to shorten the time between research and application in the community. In this instance I was able to play the activist role in my capacity as a member of both the Kitchener Planning Board and the Waterloo County Area Planning Board. The opportunity of carrying out an ecological study in advance of development came when a developer presented a housing subdivision plan for an area with a diversity of landscape to the Kitchener Planning Board. The Planning Board decided to postpone a decision on approval of the subdivision plan until an ecological survey had been conducted. When the developer saw the results of the survey, he agreed to change his plan in order to reduce the damage to the bio-physical environment and, concomitantly, to maximize the quality of the residential environment.[15] Subsequently, the Kitchener Planning Board established a policy requiring developers of substantial new areas to conduct ecological studies before plans of subdivision are submitted.

At the regional scale, the Waterloo County Area Planning Board requested the University research group to study the environmental impact of alternative strategies of urban growth. The results of these studies were used in the development of a strategy of growth for the region.[16] Some members of the research group were asked to serve on a continuing environmental advisory committee to the Planning Board and its successor, the Planning and Development Committee of the Regional Municipality of Waterloo.[17]

In emphasizing the value of applied geography and the role of the geographer as an activist, it is not my intent to downgrade in any way the value of "pure" research or theory-building. Relevance and problem-solving are not enough. Without cumulative generalizations we will merely jump from one problem to another armed with only a narrow set of solutions to what are very complex problems. We badly need cumulative generalizations about man's interaction with his environment. Yet, the acid test of the utility of theory is its ultimate usefulness to society. Fundamental geographic research on processes and relationships can have great long range impacts on numerous environmental problems and can bring about drastic changes in the kinds of solutions applied. However, is it not incumbent upon the geographer today, more than ever before, to express clearly what his findings are and how they may be useful in the immediate or more distant future?

GEOGRAPHY AND ENVIRONMENTAL EDUCATION

Because of its very nature it is obvious (to geographers at least) that the discipline of geography has an important role to play in environmental education. Brouillette talked about "Geography in General Education" in his presidential address to the Canadian Association of Geographers in 1955. From the following quotation it is clear that he feels that geography has an important educational role because of its integrative, synthetic approach:

> When geography borrows elements derived from the related sciences, it synthesizes those elements with its own particular methods and way of thinking, which is best

described as esprit géographique, *the geographical mind. It is something intangible and difficult to define. We are thinking geographically when we consider jointly man, environment and space. . . . Geography, understood in its full meaning and taught accordingly, has an educational value that permits it to be compared favourably with any other discipline in the curriculum of studies.*

The recent upswing in interest in environmental education has reinforced the importance of geography in the educational curriculum. Typical of the comments being made by geographers on this topic is the following statement by Elam:

. . . . Our discipline is the middle ground wherein the natural and social sciences meet. My point is that – it is our privilege, indeed our professional obligation, to bring both into focus on problems of environmental quality lying between the two – and our task is probably more important when it entails conflict resolution. [18]

Public statements such as these are being made by geography teachers from elementary to university levels because, in response to public and student demand for relevant environmental courses, a rash of new environmental programmes and courses is springing up across the country, and these often do not involve geography and sometimes overlap with geography courses already being given. This state of affairs may result partially from the lack of appreciation on the part of other disciplines of the nature of geography, but also from geographers' lack of emphasis on the man-environment thrust and the integrating role of the discipline. Likewise, there has been a decline in emphasis on the value of field work in geography at a time when outdoor activity is becoming a more important part of education concerned with environmental issues. Also, geography has not always been seen as a relevant discipline that leads to action relating to environmental issues. It seems clear to me that if geography wishes to achieve its potential in environmental education, it needs to adhere to its triple thrust (Figure 1.1), deal with explanatory processes in an integrated manner (Figure 1.2) and use a wide range of investigative and pedagogical techniques including things such as field studies, mapping raw and statistical data, systems modelling, simulation games and role playing. [19]

I do not wish to imply that only geography should be involved in environmental education programmes and courses. It is true that many academic disciplines tend to think they should be the focus of all environmental education, as is expressed by Francis in the following quotation:

Disciples of disciplines such as biology, geography or anthropology can, and regularly do, proclaim that theirs is the integrating discipline for "environment" around which presumably everyone else is qualified only to help fill in minor details. True believers of other disciplines, for example, economics, psychology, or geology readily suggest that the really "fundamental" aspects of "environment" are best embraced by them and the other things being talked about are at best peripheral or simply miss the point altogether. [20]

There is room for a wide range of approaches to environmental education and each discipline has its role to play. There is need for both broad integrative environmental programmes and very narrow specialist ones. The major point I am making in this essay is that geography, because of its nature, methodology and techniques, has a very important role and that its potential has not been generally achieved.

The role of geography in environmental studies programmes can be well illustrated by reference to developments at the University of Waterloo. Shortly after a Department of Geography was established in 1962, geography at Waterloo began to branch out into environmental planning. This was done because many geography graduates were finding employment as urban planners, regional planners or resource managers. Although their background in physical and human geography and in geographical research methods stood them in good stead, they were lacking in areas vital to planners such as ecology, environmental design and the decision-making aspect of the planning process. To accommodate students who wanted to become professionally involved in environmental planning, an urban, regional and resource planning option was added to the geography programme and professional planners, bio-physical ecologists and a sociologist, who specialized in rural development, were added to the faculty. Later, the planning programme was separated from the Department of Geography and became a professional School of Urban and Regional Planning. However, the undergraduate planning programme still retains a core of geography courses and several of the faculty members of the Planning School have a geographical academic background.

The geography-planning relationship has had a two-way advantage. Geography students have benefited by being able to take planning courses and by mixing with planning students. The geography faculty itself has been enriched by planning faculty with various disciplinary backgrounds having joint appointments in both Geography and Planning.

To further enhance the university's environmental studies efforts, in 1969 a new Faculty of Environmental Studies was created. It brought together Geography, Planning, Architecture and a new Department of Man-Environment Studies. The latter is composed of a group of faculty representing disciplines such as anthropology, resource economics, psychology, sociology, biology and geology. In addition to mounting an interdisciplinary undergraduate programme focusing on certain environmental themes, the Department of Man-Environment Studies greatly enriches the other disciplinary programmes in the Faculty.

Thus, at Waterloo, geography played a key role in the evolution of a broad interdisciplinary programme of environmental studies. By initiating and remaining at the centre of such an environmental studies programme, geography has made a major contribution to environmental education and has benefited greatly in return. This would not have been so had it remained on the sidelines as other disciplines organized to meet the environmental challenge in the university.

Regardless of administrative organization within an educational institution, there are several distinct contributions geography can make towards environmental education:

1. prepare geographers for professional geographical research.
2. contribute the man-environment and spatial point-of-view to other specialist programmes.
3. provide a broad environmental education for those intending to go on to graduate professional training, e.g. law, planning, business administration teaching.
4. make an environmental input to general education programmes.

Of these, it may be that in the long run the latter will turn out to be the most important. In our society the decision-makers are unlikely to (and in many cases unable to) succeed in substantially improving our environment unless there is a large proportion of the public which is well informed about the nature of our natural and man-made environment and the consequences of alternative courses of action. Because of its nature and philosophy, geography is well suited to play a major role in general environmental education.

NOTES

1. Pattison, W.D. (1964). "The Four Traditons of Geography." *Journal of Geography*, 63(5), 211-16.
   Taafe, E.J. (1974). "The Spatial View in Context." *Annals of the Association of American Geographers*, 64(1), 1-16.
2. Russwurm, L.H. and E. Sommerville, eds. (1974). *Man's Natural Environment: A Systems Approach*. North Scituate, Mass.: Duxbury Press.
3. Tatham, G. (1957). "Environmentalism and Possibilism." *Geography in the Twentieth Century*, edited by G. Taylor, London: Methuen.
4. Hartshorne, R. (1939). "The Nature of Geography: A Critical Survey of Current Thought in the Light of the Past." *Annals of the Association of American Geographers*, 29 (3, 4).
   Hartshorne, R. (1959). *Perspectives on the Nature of Geography*. Association of American Geographers, Monograph Series No. 1, Chicago: Rand McNally.

5. Burton, I. (1963). "The Quantitative Revolution and Theoretical Geography." *The Canadian Geographer*, 7, 151-62.

6. Haggett, P. (1965). *Locational Analysis in Human Geography*. London: Arnold.

7. Proshansky, H., W. Ittleson and L. Rivlin, eds. (1970). *Environmental Psychology*. New York: Holt, Rinehart and Winston.

8. Taafe, E.J. (1974). *op. cit.*

9. Clarkson, J.D. (1970). "Ecology and Spatial Analysis." *Annals of the Association of American Geographers*, 60 (4), 700-16.

10. Krueger, R.R. (1959). "Changing Land Use Patterns in the Niagara Fruit Belt." *Transactions of the Royal Canadian Institute*, 32(67), Part II, 38-140.
    Krueger, R.R. (1972). "Recent Land Use Changes in the Niagara Fruit Belt." *Applied Geography and the Human Environment: Proceedings of the Fifth International Meeting Commission on Applied Geography International Geographical Union* edited by R.E. Preston. Department of Geography, Publication Series No. 2, University of Waterloo, 164-82.

11. Hare, F.K. and C.I. Jackson. (1972). *Environment: A Geographical Perspective*. Geographical Paper No. 52, Ottawa: Department of the Environment.

12. *Ibid.*

13. *Ibid.*

14. Kitchen, C.M. (1971a). "Ecology and Urban Development." In *Urban Problems: A Canadian Reader*. edited by R.R. Krueger and R.C. Bryfogle, Toronto: Holt, Rinehart and Winston, 282-86.

15. —— (1971b). "Ecological Concepts in Subdivision Design." *The Waterloo County Area Selected Geographical Essays*, edited by A.G. McLellan, Department of Geography Publication Series No. 1, University of Waterloo, 255-65.

16. Coleman, D. (1974). *An Ecological Input to Regional Planning*. Ph.D. Thesis, School of Urban and Regional Planning, University of Waterloo.

17. Kitchen, C.M. (1975). "The Role of Ecological Appraisal in Urban Development." *Urban Problems* (revised), edited by R.C. Bryfogle and R.R. Krueger, Toronto: Holt, Rinehart and Winston, 254-63.

18. Elam, W.W. (1974). "Environmental Education and Its Influence on Geographic Education." *The Monograph*, No. 1, 29-31, 22.

19. Emery, J.S., C. Davey and A.K. Milne. (1974). "Environmental Education: The Geography Teacher's Contribution." Journal of Geography, 73(4), 8-18.

20. Francis, G.R. (1974). "An Overview of Post-secondary Environmental Studies." *The Bulletin of the Conservation Council of Ontario*, (April), 5-10.

PART 2
THE VALUE OF
CLIMATE AND WEATHER
IN CANADA

Introduction

That climate is a double-edged phenomenon, both resource and liability, emerges clearly in this section. Both authors, McKay and Gardner, address themselves to the socio-economic implications of Canada's climate — especially its vagaries.

McKay's paper begins by tracing the historical significance of climate in Canadian development, first its role in agriculture, later its impact on early air services and, still later, its input to site planning with respect to pollution dispersal. McKay calls our attention to the fact that this long history of interest in climate has bequeathed to us a legacy of excellent data records — a resource we are inclined to overlook — at a time when computerized usage could immeasurably aid in design and management operations.

Viewed as a resource, climate has an important support relationship to water resources, agriculture and recreation, and a potential future role in the search for new sources of renewable energy; the economic implications of which McKay ably demonstrates. No less significant are the economic losses and the human inconveniences resulting from the climate in its role as hazard. Commenting on the range of human adjustments to this phenomenon, McKay makes the case that passive acceptance is no longer necessary and he suggests several cases where pre-planning, with climate data as input, can greatly alleviate later financial loss and personal hindrance. This will be especially true, he feels, in the face of growing urbanization: one area of much-needed research is "the climate of the street".

Throughout his paper, McKay emphasizes that, to be of use in economic and environmental planning, the raw climate data available must be transformed into data sets relevant and comprehensible to the user.

Taking the theme developed in McKay's paper, Gardner points out that where adjustments to climatic hazards are concerned, pre-planning has rarely been evident. The traditional, and more costly, response has been the application of "band-aid" treatment after the event. Hazards research in geography, therefore, must take its directive from the need for preventative rather than curative measures.

Gardner's model of human adjustment to a specific hazard develops the concept of "threshold", i.e. delineating the hazard-resource character of a particular climatic phenomenon. Significantly, damage threshold levels may be altered through human intervention.

He points out that, although the bases of all the processes giving rise to natural hazards in Canada are geophysical — water and energy — the climatological event has meaning as "hazard" only in the context of people. Furthermore, the characteristics of those people affected — their density, culture, technology, economy, structures, etc. — all influence the felt impact of a natural hazard. Because North American cities are repositories of enormous amounts of wealth and technology, losses may be high economically but are also low in human life. As happens in Canada, those areas highly developed in terms of population and production are usually areas of high natural hazard potential. Gardner's ensuing analysis of specific natural hazard types (drought, storms and floods) in the light of socio-economic impacts and human adjustments are therefore of high significance to any serious student of applied geography. His is the man-land theme of traditional geography given the acumen of contemporary reality.

Thus, in this section, climate in Canada emerges as a geographical phenomenon of tremendous impact, long recorded but little used; a mixed blessing of resource and hazard. The need and potential for much better management of this resource is implicit in both papers in this section, data restructuring and pre-planning are but two suggestions. To both these writers, climate is clearly not only a subject of academic learning, but is also a human affair.

2
Climatic Resources and Economic Activity in Canada

G.A. McKay, Atmospheric Environment Service,
Environment Canada

CLIMATE AND CANADIAN ECONOMIC DEVELOPMENT

Since the time of Canada's discovery, climate has been inexorably linked with its development. Early explorers and traders endured the climate primarily because of the promise of wealth. As early as 1794-95 at Fort York, the air temperature was measured to determine the freezing point of (and thereby the possible hazard to) the supplies of rum, gin and brandy.

As Canada reached nationhood, the conquest of the wilderness and sovereignty through settlement was a major issue. But our stormy climate posed a major hazard for supply vessels at sea and on the Great Lakes. The Canadian Meteorological Service was formed in 1871 to help mitigate this hazard. Weather forecasting was commenced in 1876, and by 1877 climatic data were being published in a Monthly Weather Review to assist in determining what areas were most favourable for settlement.

With settlement, Canada acquired an agricultural economy which by 1921 was supplying 40 percent of the world's export wheat. The combination of rich soils and climate earned the prairies renown as a grain producer. There, precipitation is so distributed during the year as to be most abundant when needed for growth, while sunny and dry weather usually occurs at the time of ripening and harvest. On the other hand, drought, blizzards, dust storms and extremes of heat and cold take their toll from time to time.

Although climate dominated economic activities and resource use, there were few attempts made to use climate in planning, other than in a casual way. Early promotional efforts to induce settlement painted glowing pictures of our climate which could not be easily confirmed or refuted. Purposeful studies had to await adequate data. In 1915 Connor published "The Temperature and Precipitation of British Columbia," and in 1920 a similar study of Alberta, Saskatchewan and Manitoba was also published. Studies of the climates of the other regions of the country, although prepared, were never published. In 1936 Connor prepared "The Climate of Canada" as part of the *Köppen-Geiger Handbuch der*

Klimatologie. Other reports concentrated on climate and agriculture, particularly in the prairie provinces. These were, no doubt, of great assistance to agriculture in the selection of crop varieties, and to the planning of irrigation systems to achieve greater stability for Canada's agriculturally-dominated economy. Understanding, however, was insufficient to offset the effects of crop failures in the early thirties, a time of general economic recession.

About the time of the great depression, aviation was beginning to emerge as a major factor in our way of life. In 1925 the airplane was used in aerial photography and forest protection; by 1930 the bush pilots had made resource development in the hinterlands possible, and air mail service was inaugurated in the east. Airports and supporting weather services were quickly developed across Canada, and a national air service was inaugurated in 1937. With short-range aircraft and relatively primitive aids, the role of the meteorologist in flight safety was an important one which gradually became a major occupation. The British Commonwealth Air Training Plan of World War II exploited the sunny, dry weather of the prairies to accelerate training in relative safety.

In 1938 two Canadian meteorologists, Hewson and Gill, undertook for the International Joint Commission (IJC) a mesoclimatic study of wind, temperature and air pollution in the Columbia River Valley of British Columbia. Their report[1], which recommended the release of gases according to atmospheric conditions, was a milestone in the use of climate and weather in the siting of industrial plants and in emission control. These meteorologists established a model which has utility in environmental impact assessment procedures of our times and which, as part of the comprehensive, integrated planning process, is inseparable from economic issues.

But the extensive use of climatology in grappling with economic issues had to await the arrival of the electronic computer and the training of specialists who could use them in an inter-disciplinary fashion. At the end of World War II the processing of climatological records was about six years in arrears and the volume of data was growing exponentially. Unlike Europe, whose records were shattered by wars, Canada had long, unbroken series of homogeneous data which were highly amenable to exploitation. Fortunately, electronic data processing was also being developed at this time.

For most Canadians, exponential growth is a modern phenomenon. There were only eleven million Canadians in 1940. But our population-doubling time is about 30 years, and the doubling time of that measure of our economic productivity, the Gross National Product (GNP), has been about 15 years. The post-war era stands out as one of rapid industrialization, and of migration from the family farm. At the time of Confederation three out of four Canadians lived on farms, but by 1966 the ratio was one in four. Urbanization had arrived, and the labour force had shifted from the farms to the cities and to industry.

The post-war industrial boom, coupled with the introduction of the computer and an increasing trend towards inter-disciplinary training and understanding, made it both necessary and feasible to put climatology to work in achieving more rational decisions and greater efficiency and effectiveness in design, management and operations. Perhaps the greatest difficulty in this process has been that of problem recognition. From the purely climatological standpoint, Canada has an excellent data archive of approximately 100 million observations containing about a dozen elements each which are accessible electronically. The depth of record is varied, but is good by most standards; Toronto records, one of the best, extend back to 1841. Furthermore, the statistical and computer procedures for their analysis are well developed. Interpretation in terms of an effect on non-climatological entities poses a challenge, but the scientific methodology is generally not complex. The complacency of Canadians with their climate and the failure of the climatologist to acquire a sufficient understanding of the nature of the user's problem has been a formidable obstacle to advancement in using this archive.

Canadians have tended to accept their climate fatalistically. However, this attitude is no longer wise; a much more objective approach is essential. Our desire to remain both consumers in a modern society and custodians of ecological values poses a need for skill, efficiency and prudence with respect to using and living with climate. Sustained economic development is essential to provide an increasing population with the consumer goods desired. This demands greater efficiencies and effectiveness in the use of our limited resources than we now practise. On the other hand, our desire for a sustained high environmental quality demands that commerce, industry and social practices be within the restraints imposed by our climatically-controlled ecosystem. Failure to do so for short-term benefits, may at best require very costly corrective measures in the future, or at worst create irremedial problems.

Climate is both a resource and a liability. As a resource, it provides the heat and moisture that are essential for life. It makes agriculture possible. It provides warm lakes for swimmers and snow for skiers. It drives ocean currents. On the other hand climatic phenomena like droughts, floods and hurricanes are hazards that may destroy life, damage property, inconvenience people and often bring to a halt all normal economic activity within a community.

CLIMATE AS A RESOURCE

Climatic elements — heat and cold, rain, snow and wind — are exploitable resources. Definition of the nature of climatic resources has been a major occupation of geographers over the past century. Maps of temperature, precipitation, snow cover and evapotranspiration have been necessary for the planning of land use (particularly in agriculture), for the development of water and supplies, drainage, irrigation systems, etc. The trend to optimal productivity through fuller exploitation of climatic energy, light and moisture sources is increasing as natural resource supplies become more stringent. Several of the ways in which climate may be considered as a resource or a supply factor are noted below.

Water Resources

Precipitation is the primary source of surface water supplies, and evapotranspiration the major consumer. Planning, public and political conviction, and the economic decisions as to the viability of a hydrologic system are therefore frequently dependent upon climatology.

Annual expenditures in Canada on water control and conveyance structures designed in whole or in part on the basis of rainfall, snow melt and evapotranspiration data amount to about one billion dollars. Benefit-cost data for hydrometeorological studies in Canada are not readily obtainable, but it has been estimated that a one percent improvement in the spring flow forecast to the Portage Mountain Reservoir, for example, will yield $1 million per year in reduced operational costs.

Snow cover is the source of the bulk of the surface water resources which are readily managed in Canada. From simple water balance considerations it can be shown that most summer precipitation is returned to the atmosphere as evapotranspiration and that the melting snow in spring is the major source of surface water systems and replenisher of groundwater supplies. Definition of the snow resources and ablation, along with the development of management programmes, have been remarkably neglected by Canadians and measurement technology is so inadequate that we do not really know the magnitude of this precious resource.

Climatic probabilities are required for water resource development and other design problems. Average conditions are reasonably well known, but extreme floods and low flows are crucial in many instances. Mapping of return period values as well as specific occurrences of extremes of snow cover, snowfall, snow melt and rainfall for critical durations is a fundamental role for the climatologist in support of water resource planning.

Agriculture and Forestry

In 1968 the National Committee on Agrometeorology published a general study entitled *Climatological Services for Resource Development Planning in Agriculture*. This report stressed the need to know the climate as basic to understanding plant growth for the effective planning of land use and in raising animals. It recognized as major hazards: drought, frost, hail, excessive rainfall, flood, wind, snow, winterkill and indirect climatic effects on such matters as disease, epidemics and insect infestations. Recent major losses, based on assistance payments, are identified in the following table:

TABLE 2.1

Crop Losses as Identified by Assistance Payments

Year	Cause	Location	Estimated Loss (millions $)
1945	Low Temperatures	Nova Scotia	4.0
1954	Wheat Rust	Prairies	33.0
1959	Wet Harvest	Prairies	12.0
1964-65	Wet Weather	Quebec	1.5
1965	Drought	Eastern Canada	5.5

Losses paid by others, such as hail insurance companies, are not identified here.

The production of rapeseed, a $100 million business in 1971, illustrates the importance of climate in the agricultural economy. Rapeseed thrives in the prairie climate of hot, sunny days and cool nights, and its production is unique to this area. To the south, the amount of oil contained in the seed decreases so that its growth becomes uneconomic in the latitudes of Minneapolis. Delineation of the area where the climate is suitable for such crops as rapeseed has obvious economic value.

As pressures on agricultural lands increase, finer zonation according to soils and climate assumes increasing importance. Near urban markets where lands are hilly and topography complex, mesoclimatic studies are highly advantageous. Zonation studies have been used to define those areas in Quebec, Prince Edward Island, Nova Scotia and British Columbia where advantage can be taken of oceanic effects and landforms to obtain the best mesoscale climates for agriculture. In Ontario, as urbanization advanced over the Niagara peninsula, mesoclimatic studies were undertaken to define the lands most suitable for horticulture in the Georgian Bay area. Zonation studies undertaken by mobile survey or airborne sensors can be profitably increased in most areas in view of present urban trends.

In addition, climatic indices such as heat units, growing degree days, drying indices and fire hazard indices are also playing an increasingly important role. Heat units, for example, have been used to determine the best hybrids of corn for cultivation in specific localities of southern Ontario and are also used extensively in scheduling planting and ultimately the harvesting of vegetables for commercial canning.

Not only must the climate be suitable for growing, but it must also allow seeding, cultivating and harvesting operations to take place at the proper times. Climatological statistics have been used extensively to establish the risks of unfavourable weather during haying (for example) or the chances of getting favourable drying weather as the harvest season advances. Similar climatic statistics are also used in assessing the energy required for drying harvest grain,[2] the optimal size of implements for a specific field size and the tractionability of fields following rains and spring thaws.[3]

Since pests and disease also respond to climate, their occurrences are predictable from the study of climatic elements. The characteristics of the transport of spores of wheat rust are well documented, and the observations and predictions of the occurrence of weather favourable to tomato and potato blight can be used to control the outbreaks. The timing and feasibility of applying sprays and baits are also weather-dependent. Fungal diseases that afflict grasshoppers are weather-dependent, and cool, damp weather reduces hatching and increases mortality among hatchlings. Edwards[4] developed a grasshopper prediction method based mainly on the occurrence of precipitation and "population build-up".

Energy

The climatologist is involved in many phases of our energy problems. About one-quarter of the energy consumed in Canada is used to overcome the climate, primarily in the heating and air conditioning of homes and offices, as well as in snow removal and by stalled traffic during snow storms. Canadian use for these purposes probably exceed those found by Hirst and Moyers[5] in the United States (see Table 2.2). In the shift from an energy-intensive to an energy-efficient way of life, these percentages are of importance.

Fuel distributors have relied on climatic information in organizing their activities for many years, and the value of this information is becoming more important as supplies dwindle. In times of low inventories, excessive use of heating fuel usually requires cutbacks in industrial production. The use of heating degree days (Figure 2.1) provides the dispatcher with a view of areas of probable shortages and surpluses. Usually in a country the size of Canada the deficiencies and excesses are regional, so that it is possible to restrain production in one area and augment it in another to maintain desired national productivity levels.

TABLE 2.2

Energy used for specific activities expressed as a percentage of total consumption, U.S.A.

Use (1970)	% of Total
Transportation	24.7
Space Heating	17.7
Water Heating	4.0
Air Conditioning	2.9
Refrigeration	2.3
Other Uses	48.4
	100.0

Air temperature is accepted as the principal weather variable correlating with fuel consumption, and it has been the basis of both heating and refrigeration design and energy-use studies. The accumulation of degree days above or below 65°F (18°C) is most commonly used. Other factors such as solar radiation, wind, rainfall and air pressure are important, particularly when considering individual buildings. However, Murphy[6] obtained improved expressions and showed that air temperature and wind accounted for 90 percent of the variance and that air temperature alone accounted for 79 percent of the variance.

Development of Canada's energy resources in hinterland and frontier areas poses major environmental problems in which climatology must play a dominant role. The release of sulphur dioxide (SO_2) from refineries in the tar sands area of Alberta could destroy vegetation over vast areas of land if improperly controlled. The capacity of the atmosphere to disperse this contaminant is therefore a major concern. Should coal come back into prominence, then the dispersal of SO_2 and particulate matter may be a major problem. Also problems of offshore drilling, shipping in ice-congested waters, the need for storage systems at sea in areas of great fog frequency, and the development of deep-sea harbours require a large input from marine climatology.

Environmental concerns should force the use of renewable energy resources, which in turn will require much improved interpretation and understanding of the space and time variations of wind and solar radiation. Of particular importance is a better understanding of winds since records are highly biased by measuring methods and may not disclose the full potential for energy development at a specific site.

Climatology is also required in support of the planning and engineering required for exploration, conversion, transmission and conservation of energy. For example, the spatial variation of snow cover in

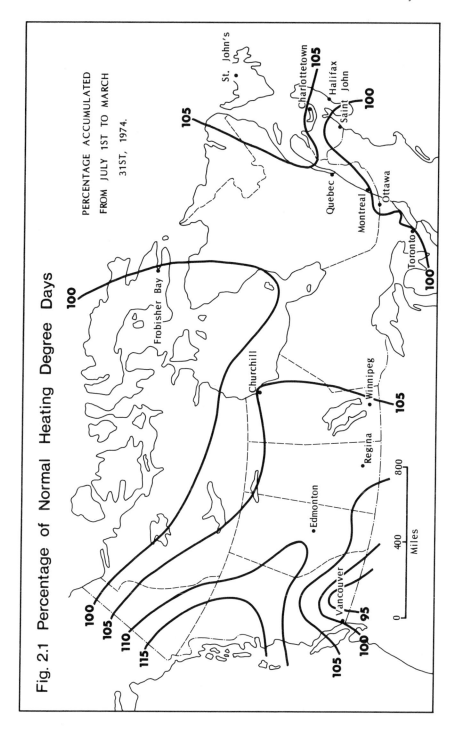

Fig. 2.1 Percentage of Normal Heating Degree Days

PERCENTAGE ACCUMULATED FROM JULY 1ST TO MARCH 31ST, 1974.

terms of topographic variables is being studied in support of pipeline construction in the Mackenzie Valley. The interest in snow stems primarily from the need for snow roads and for an understanding of heat flow in the atmosphere-snow-ground system since the duration and break-up dates of snow roads determine the length of the construction period in the North.

An understanding of snowfall and snow accumulation must be given to the planner by the climatologist when considering wintertime transportation. The proper use of landforms, trees and buildings to avoid accumulations of snow on roads, and of urban designs which avoid costly haulage and melting systems is an area of significant importance to Canadians in the interest of energy conservation. Removal and melting are both energy-intensive, and costs are rising rapidly as cities expand and environmental laws increasingly prohibit the use of conventional dumping areas.

Recreation and Tourism

For most Canadians, recreation is an out-of-doors activity and climate can dictate whether or not the outdoors experience is enjoyable. Recreation is highly oriented to renewable natural resources, and the state of the resources is climate-dependent. In some cases climate is the resource.

Recreation is "big business". In 1969 the average Canadian family spent about $14 on snowmobiles, $13 on trailers, $11 on boats and motors, $6 on water sports, and $5 on camping equipment. Also in that year Canadians spent their spare time as indicated in Table 2.3.

TABLE 2.3

Days Spent by Canadians on Specified Activities, 1969

Millions of Days (1969)	Activity
1,811	Water Sports
1,723	Passive Activities
1,634	Hiking
1,193	Fishing
883	Camping
618	Winter Sports
574	Hunting
442	Summer Sports

Source: *Statistics Canada*

In 1969 tourism and outdoor recreation was about a $5 billion business, and Canadians spent $15 billion on non-essentials highly related to leisure time. Recreation rated as the third largest industry in Quebec and Ontario in 1971, and in 1972 Americans visiting Canada spent an estimated $1.2 billion.

This level of spending is of great significance to national, provincial and local economies, and governments have immediate interests in the development of parks, lodges and other recreation areas. A rational approach to the development of tourism requires climatic inputs — even Niagara Falls is not too impressive when enshrouded by fog.

Recreation and tourism are highly weather-dependent from the viewpoint of travel as well as "pursuit satisfaction" at the recreation area. A suitable combination of temperature, humidity and sunshine is most important for enjoying the outdoor environment. Key components of that environment — water temperature, water state and the phenological state — are virtual products of the climatic regime.

Snow cover and ice are the basis of almost all Canadian outdoor sports in winter. Canadians made 9.4 million visits to ski areas in 1970-71 and spent $287 million on ski equipment and transportation to skiing areas. Furthermore, capital investments for ski facilities amounted to $12 million and operating costs totalled about $60 million. Snowmobiling now vies with skiing as a favourite winter sport and Canadian companies supply over 70 percent of the world market.[7] Revenues in the Province of Quebec from snowmobiling in 1970-71 were estimated at $10 million.

The need to consider climate in recreational planning has been recognized by most provincial governments. Climate-based recreation and tourism studies have been made for the Northwest Territories and are in progress for other regions of Canada. These employ daily and hourly weather information as well as snow cover data and water temperatures. Through the use of hourly weather data it is possible to use an "activity day" approach to outdoor recreation planning. For example, one can arbitrarily say that a day is suitable for skiing if there are six hours during the period 0800 to 1800 hours when there is at least one inch of snow on the ground, the winds are less than 15 mph, the temperature is in the range -5°F to 40°F, the visibility is better than a half mile and there is no liquid precipitation. It is a simple matter to compute the frequency of occurrence of such days, and thereby establish the time and quality characteristics of a skiing season for any locality (Figure 2.2).

Locations for which there are hourly records are not nearly as numerous as conventional climatological stations for which there are once or twice-daily observations. The two sets of data can be used corroboratively to develop decision information as shown in Figure 2.3.

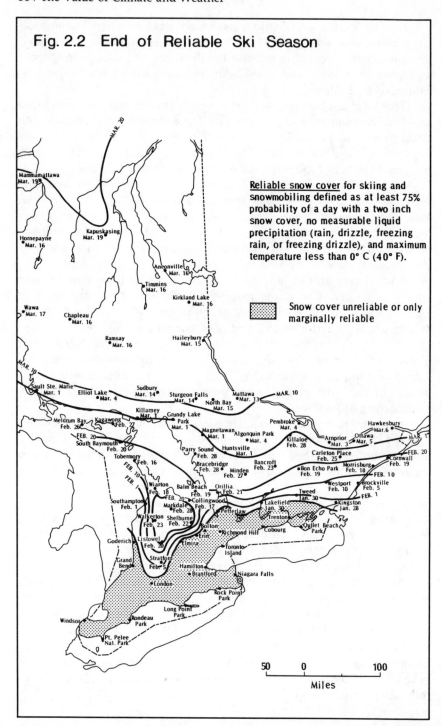

Fig. 2.2 End of Reliable Ski Season

Reliable snow cover for skiing and snowmobiling defined as at least 75% probability of a day with a two inch snow cover, no measurable liquid precipitation (rain, drizzle, freezing rain, or freezing drizzle), and maximum temperature less than 0° C (40° F).

Snow cover unreliable or only marginally reliable

50   0   100
Miles

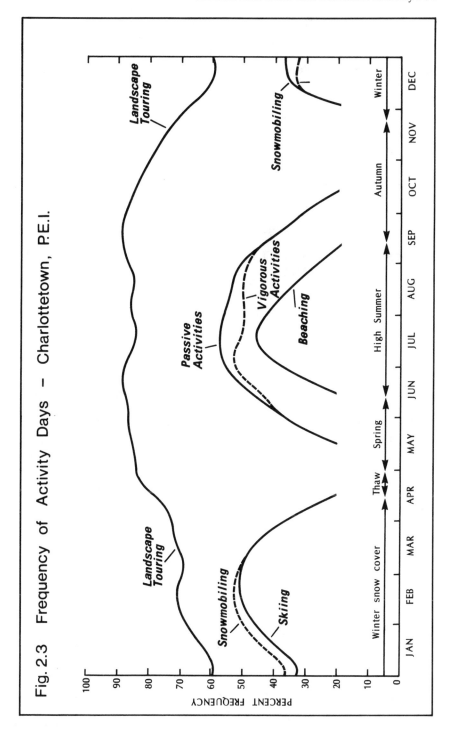

Fig. 2.3 Frequency of Activity Days — Charlottetown, P.E.I.

The development of a national park implies a major investment which warrants detailed planning in the placement of roads and facilities as well as deciding on possible recreational activities. Many new parks are being developed and others are being improved to meet the increased recreational demand and to preserve our national heritage. Topoclimatological analyses of the parks are needed for planning the placement of facilities, assessing seasonal lengths and quality, etc. Weather networks, if existent, are generally sparse in park areas, so that modelling is usually required to provide the needed planning information. In the case of Pukaskwa Park, Ontario, for example, water temperature, ice, wave and wind (lake and land breezes) data were interpreted to establish the most suitable locations for marinas, beaches, barbecue pits, etc. In the case of the Arctic parks their large extent makes mobile and remote survey techniques necessary.

CLIMATIC HAZARDS: ECONOMIC CONSEQUENCES AND HUMAN ADJUSTMENTS

Climatic hazards stand out in our memory because of their great impact on society and their newsworthiness. Direct economic losses caused by some of the more notable weather events in Canada are noted in Table 2.4. Included in the list are events which are historically recognized as major disasters, but for which there was no available estimate of the direct economic effects.

Losses due to storms are rarely easy to estimate quantitatively. The dollar value of cattle lost in a snow storm may be easy to define within certain limits, but it is difficult to place a dollar value on the weakened state of the remaining herd. The cost of replacing hydro wires is readily determinable, but the cost of the hardships experienced by the families and commercial establishments who were denied light, heat and water during the period of outage is virtually impossible to estimate.

Recent ice storms and storms of wet snow have caused remarkably great losses in terms of replacement as noted in Table 2.5. Damage to hydro and private property in the December 1973 storm in Quebec City was $2.2 million. But 250,000 people were deprived of electricity, heat and drinking water; freezers stopped operating; fire protection facilities were impotent during a period when the hazard was greatly increased by the use of camp stoves, etc.

While the economic consequences of major storms can be substantial, so are the cumulative effects of less spectacular weather. For example, the clearing of snow from roads, rails and airports is an energy-intensive operation on which Canadians spend over $200 million annually and the rate is increasing rapidly. The Canadian National Railway alone spends about $6 million annually and uses equipment valued at $15 million in keeping lines free of snow.

TABLE 2.4

Some Canadian Weather Disasters

Year		Estimated Loss	
		Life	Dollars (Millions)
1860's	Storms on the Great Lakes		
1868	Drought — Red River Settlement		
1885-96	Drought in Prairies		
1912	Regina Tornado	30	4
1917-21	Drought on Prairies		
1930-36	Drought on Prairies		
1935	Vancouver Snow Storm		
1944	Kamsack, Saskatchewan, Tornado (2,000 homeless)		2
1945	Nova Scotia Low Temperatures		4
1949	Ontario Drought		100
1950	Red River Flood		100
1953	Sarnia, Ontario, Tornado		5
1954	Hurricane Hazel, Toronto	100	252
1954	Wheat Rust — Prairies		33
1955	Ontario Drought		85
1957	Saskatchewan Hail Storm		17
1959	Wet Weather, Harvest Lost, Saskatchewan		12.5
1959	Snow Storm — Ontario		
1967	Alberta Snow Storm		10
1967-68	Forest Fires in Canada		100
1969	Glaze Storm near Quebec		30
1973	Drought — British Columbia		
1973	Glaze Storm — Sept Iles		10

Among the many other effects of adverse weather are:

Travel
— access restricted
— accident rate increased
— increased travel time, airline flight diversions, etc.
— energy consumption increased
— maintenance costs increased
— vehicle performance impaired
— tourism depressed

TABLE 2.5

Wet Snow, Freezing Rain and In-Cloud Icing Storms (October 1969 — May 1974)

Date	Location	Type of Storm	Thickness	Approximate Extent of Damage In Millions of Dollars
Nov. 1969	Quebec City — Saguenay River, Que.	In-cloud Icing	6-8"	30.0
Feb. 1970	Bay d'Espoir, Nfld.	Freezing Rain	5-6"	3.0
Sept. 1970	Churchill, Man.	Wet Snow	3-4"	0.5
Feb. 1971	Western Newfoundland	Freezing Rain	2-4"	0.5
Apr. 1971	Saskatoon, Sask.	Wet Snow	2-4"	2.0
Jan. 1972	Upper Fraser Valley — Squamish Area, B.C.	Wet Snow / In-cloud Icing	2-4"	3.0
Mar. 1972	North of Montreal, Que.	Freezing Rain	2-3"	4.0
Oct. 1972	Churchill, Man.	Wet Snow	4-5"	0.5
Nov. 1972	Come By Chance, Nfld.	Freezing Rain	2-4"	0.5
Feb. 1973	Calgary, Alta.	In-cloud Icing	2-4"	1.0
Apr. 1973	Sept-Iles — Manic 3, Que.	In-cloud Icing	7-10"	10.0
May 1973	Lake Louise, Alta.	Wet Snow	2-4"	0.5
Dec. 1973	Joliette — Matane, Que.	Freezing Rain	2-4"	4.5
April 1974	Calgary — Red Deer, Alta.	Wet Snow	2-4"	1.0
May 1974	Swift Current, Sask.	Wet Snow	2-3"	0.5
			TOTAL	61.5

Resources	— losses through frost, drought, floods, moisture excess, cold weather — increased pests and disease, forest fires
Property	— damage due to landslides, floods, avalanches — hurricane or tornadic wind damage — materials damaged as a result of soil shrinkage, frost heave, freeze-thaw cycling, rain penetration, excessive snow and wind loads
Utilities	— increased water and energy consumption — decreased effectiveness of sewage treatment systems — disruption of transmission
Shipping	— damage to perishables due to heat, cold — time loss in transit
Commerce	— altered demand and purchase patterns — insurance claims and rates increased
Construction	— crane operations risks increased — reduced soil tractionability — concrete quality reduced — working conditions
Manufacturing	— temperature and humidity-sensitive processes restrained

According to Hibbs:

Man may adapt his activities to this resource in five, not necessarily mutually, exclusive ways, namely:

1. passive acceptance;
2. avoidance of areas and actions unfavourable to effect use of resource conditions;
3. current operational and defensive actions based on assessment of meteorological information;
4. modification and direct control of the weather/climate;
5. structural and mechanical defences — i.e. capitalizing on climatological knowledge.[8]

We do not need to take our losses passively; there are alternatives.

Typical of the defensive actions are sanding and salting programmes for highways, switching from carbon to steel trolleys by transit systems, the operation of frost protection devices and evacuation of areas likely to be flooded.

An example of Hibbs' structural defence has been the contribution by climatologists by means of the National Research Council's Division of Building Research to Canada's largest industry — construction. They have attacked such problems as snow loads on roofs, wind loading, drainage and rain penetration of walls, etc. Climatologists have also been employed by hydroelectric agencies for work in hydrometeorology, while others have aided in the fields of agriculture and forestry. They have provided a broad service to highly weather-sensitive activities to assist in planning to overcome drought, periods of moisture excess, etc., so as to stabilize regional economies, and in the interest of achieving greater overall economies and efficiencies.

Typical of some of the design studies were those undertaken for the construction of dams along the Columbia and Saskatchewan river systems. Among the inputs to these studies were estimates of rainfall and snow melt for spillway design, and the estimated net water yield for the upstream area. Climatic data and meteorological expetise were used to assist in the prediction of "setup" and wave heights to allow for the design of shoreline protection.

Hydrometeorological studies have evolved steadily since the 1930's, attempting to ease the problems of low water levels during droughts and high levels during periods of moisture excess such as for water level control in the Great Lakes, to effect economies in spillway design, and to minimize flood damage along rivers such as the Saint John, the Red and the Fraser, as they arose.

There are many other areas of activity which are relatively new, such as airport climatology. The use of aviation has grown exponentially. Airport capacities have been repeatedly exceeded within short periods after construction, and the noise created by modern aircraft has been of increasing concern. To alleviate this growing problem, new airports have been proposed at some distance from the large cities of the country. The complexity of our times, especially land speculation and parliamentary "lobbying," has not permitted a relaxed, studied evaluation of specific local climates for this purpose. It has been necessary to synthesize the climates of proposed airport areas rather quickly, using available climatological knowledge, interpolating carefully with due consideration for topography and validating cautiously by field investigations.

For Mirabel Airport in Quebec, it was necessary to extrapolate Dorval and St. Hubert airport information outward over a 75-mile radius, using both topography and data from the basic climatological network as bases. The objective was to find, all other things being equal, the location having the most favourable takeoff and landing weather, and whose runway orientations would not cause conflict with Dorval Airport's traffic patterns. The organization of winds in each valley, the occurrence of fogs due to the presence of a river, the effect of the large urban area, had to be interpreted along with those conditions resulting from severe storms and stagnating or stationary fronts. The end product was expressed in a map which showed isolines of a simple suitability index (Figure 2.4).

In Ontario more data were available for assisting in the selection of a second Toronto airport. It was possible to develop relationships with weather conditions and topography for each wind trajectory and month, and thereby develop maps of frequencies of specific weather conditions as shown in Figure 2.5. Also wind directions and speeds were interpreted in terms of landform, to enable evaluation of runway layouts and possible traffic conflicts.

Similar studies are carried out for the development of Arctic airports. With even less information, the topography-climate relationships are the basis of Arctic site selection, and are therefore an important factor in northern resource development and supporting air, sea and land transportation. Shoreline and inland installations have been blown away or badly damaged by Arctic winds and thus shelter is all-important. On the other hand, unventilated areas allow air pollution and ice fog under the persistent cold and airmass inversions to accummulate with resulting hazards. The study of air drainage and wind is, therefore, most important in the location of facilities and habited areas. Ice-fog problems such as have existed at Fairbanks, Alaska could conceivably have been avoided had planners considered the characteristics of valley air-drainage patterns.

Insurance provides another means of defence, and insurance rates are set according to the frequency and extent of each climatic hazard. The Canadian Hail Underwriters have used climatology and topography relationships to set basic hail insurance rates. Wind and ice hazards are considered in the insuring of television and communication towers. Precipitation statistics are used in insuring against the "rain-out" of major sport events and outdoor festivals. The probabilistic approach used is basically the same as that implemented by an agricultural economist who recognizes that more than two drought years in ten may spell financial ruin for the farmer. This approach pays little attention to scientific causes, but it does produce very worthwhile results.

CLIMATE AND ECONOMIC DECISION-MAKING

Knowledge of the probability of occurrence of specific weather conditions has many other uses in the determination of economic decisions. Thompson[9] provides the example of the farmer who is advised there is a 20 percent chance of rain when his hay is ready for harvest. His economic decision is based on the cost/loss ratio as follows:

Fig. 2.4 Fog and Low Cloud Index — Mirabel

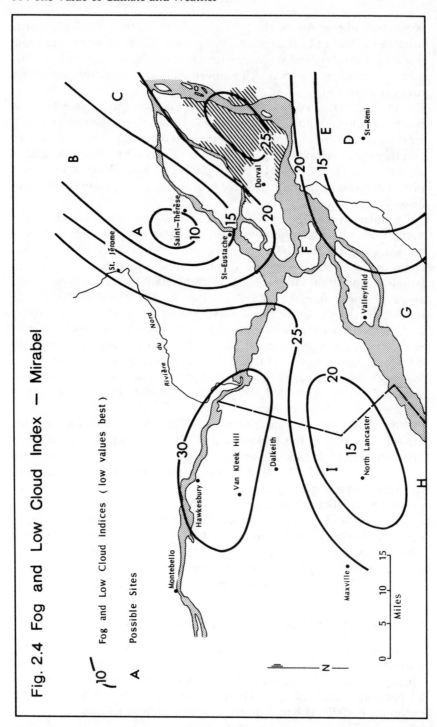

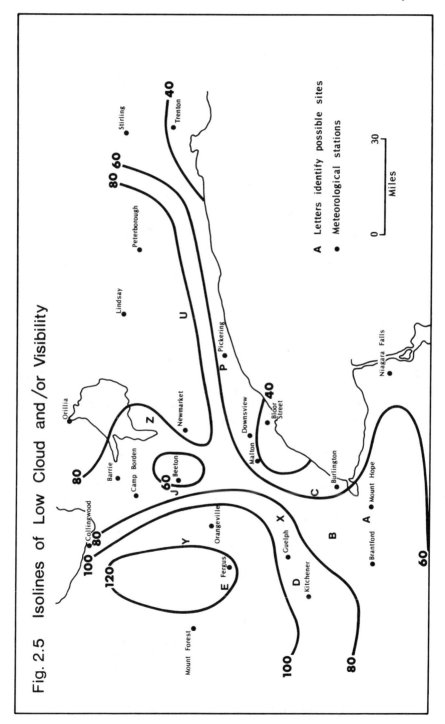

Fig. 2.5 Isolines of Low Cloud and/or Visibility

A Letters identify possible sites
• Meteorological stations

0   30
Miles

$$
\begin{array}{ll}
> & \text{Protect} \\
P = C/L & \text{Either course} \\
< & \text{Do not protect}
\end{array}
$$

where   P is the probability of adverse weather

C is the cost of protection for each adverse weather event

L is the loss suffered for each adverse event if no protective measures are taken

Used in this manner, climatological statistics can aid the farmer in the long run; however, he will experience individual losses that may be serious. Where there is forecasting skill he can further reduce his losses by taking protective measures as warranted by the accuracy of the forecasts although this usually varies for different precipitation types and amounts.

While in certain instances it is possible to show a positive financial benefit from the use of information, the actual economic cost of most weather events is difficult to establish with precision. In general, those processes, activities and services which are highly exposed or sensitive to weather stand to gain most from weather services. If the weather sensitivity is considered in conjunction with the total value, the overall benefit becomes much more apparent. Mason[10] showed benefits of 10 to 1 for services to British civil aviation which grossed £6 million compared to 200 to 1 for agriculture which grosses £10 million, suggesting a decided advantage in expanding services for agriculture. The overall support of agriculture was relatively small, however, and probably dedicated to a very sensitive sector. At any rate, the benefit-cost ratio cannot be assumed to apply to all aspects of agriculture.

With few exceptions, the use of climate by the business sector is on an *ad hoc* basis and is generally undertaken by climatologists. For example, the operators of outdoor enterprises such as Belmont Park near Montreal have used weather forecasts to determine if they should concentrate on hot dog or ice cream sales. Also major retailers have timed the sales of overshoes and other apparel to match public perception of need. Food distributors have adapted their distribution according to buying habits which are dictated by weather. Also the petroleum industry alters its additives to gasoline to suit seasonal and regional differences in climate, and both trucking companies and railways pay cautious attention to ice and snow storms when shipping produce.

But by and large, industry appears to accept climate as it is. Forecasts are listened to in the light of other circumstances but little attention is paid to the risks indicated by historical records. Contractors assume that summer weather will be average and tend to ignore the probabilities for long periods of unsuitable weather when placing bids for road construction or other earthwork. Snowmobile sales and ski lodges in southern Ontario had a disastrous season in 1972-73 due to a lack of snow — a risk which climatology shows to be common.

Maunder[11] provides a large list of activities for which useful relationships can be established between climate and industry. The transfer of this knowledge to the Canadian scene is obvious.

CLIMATE AND URBANIZATION IN CANADA

While urbanization is a global problem, it is particularly startling in Canada. About one-third of the world's population lives in towns of over 5,000 but in Canada over two-thirds of our population are so urbanized. Not only are Canadians leaving the farm for the towns, but they are abandoning the towns to concentrate in a few large urban centres. MacNeill[12] speculates that by the year 2000, 20 million Canadians (60 percent of our population) may live in 15 centres with populations over 300,000 and 17 million people in cnetres of a million or more population. This trend is of major socio-economic importance, and the problems created are formidable and complex. The associated climatological roles are equally numerous and complex.

Tomorrow's cities will require massive support systems and must therefore be considered in a regional context. Land use planning for cities and urban corridors must be a primary consideration, and the use of the land is contingent on climate. Climatic factors are very pertinent in determining what lands should be reserved for agriculture, green space, recreation, industrial parks, residential areas, infrastructures, etc. These factors are also of great importance in determining the most economic and efficient use of materials and space with a viewpoint of energy conservation and safety, as well as of minimizing management maintenance and operational costs. Furthermore, the urban and building climates must be controlled or modified, such as through the use of trees and materials to provide acceptable human environments.

The need to use climate is recognized today, but is difficult to find in practice. Climate was considered in the planning of Kitimat, B.C.[13] and in developing the townsite at Come By Chance, Newfoundland. It is being considered in the development of Saint John, N.B., and for local area studies elsewhere. One of the most progressive climatological Canadian studies for urban land use planning was that undertaken in *The Haldimand-Norfolk Environmental Appraisal*.[14] Climatic studies of the area led to recognition in the planning process of 1. mesoclimatic variations due to the Great Lakes, landforms and soil types, 2. climatological inputs to conserve health and to minimize economic loss, 3. the lake-induced air-temperature inversion and its role in photochemical reactions which damage urban environments and agricultural crops. A land use suitability map based on air quality issues was prepared as a result of the mesoclimatic investigations, showing areas suitable for heavy industry, a green belt, recreation, agriculture, residence, pollution-prone areas and parklands that should be protected.

Having decided about land use, there remains much to be said about the climate within the city. The climate within streets is one factor. Can we accept structures which cause very strong wind speeds at the street level? These have been shown to be dangerous to pedestrians and motorists. What about the pedestrian? Should he be a canyon dweller, tramping through snow which has been pushed off roads onto the only remaining space — the sidewalks — or should we use our knowledge of climate in relation to buildings, trees, pavement and grass to create a humane environment? And what about the pedestrian's taxes? Figure 2.6 shows the amount of money spent in snow removal in relation to the population of Canadian cities. As the city grows, haulage distances become very great and costs mount. Planners have allowed but a few disposal areas within the city cores, and even these cannot be used for environmental reasons. There are some alternatives, such as melting the snow in the streets, but this requires large amounts of energy. A better understanding of the properties of snow and of the meteorology of

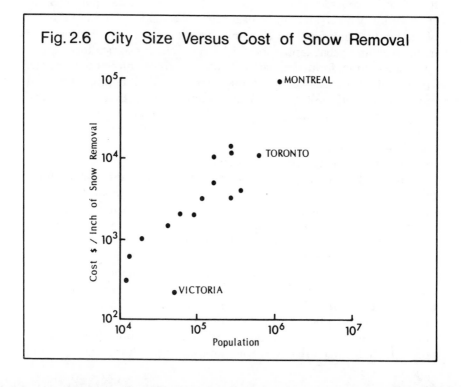

Fig. 2.6 City Size Versus Cost of Snow Removal

snowfall could help alleviate this major cost item which must continue to grow exponentially as urbanization increases and demands for snow control continue to increase. Snow removal is but one aspect of the problem; there remain traffic congestion, fuel consumption, time lost by people going to work, accidents, and loss of productivity. It has been found that the loss of income of the Toronto labour force due to snow-storms was as great as the dollar value spent in snow removal ($2 million (M) loss in 1967-68 compared to a Toronto budget of $2.5M). The town planner requires detail on radiation, wind stress, inversions, fog, pre-cipitation, snow, glaze icing, cold pockets, low clouds — in the general plan and within the street level. Our knowledge of the climate of Cana-dian streets is extremely limited.

Creation of climatically and aesthetically desirable surroundings within the city core could create an alternative to the mass evacuation of cities which occurs on summer weekends, creating massive demands for energy, roads, etc. This is yet another area of challenge in which the mesoscale climatologist can play a significant role.

CLIMATE AND THE PLANNING PROCESS

Because of its pervasive influence in economic as well as environmental and social matters, climatology has a major supporting role to play in comprehensive planning. The climatological data base is perhaps one of the best available to planners, yet surprisingly it remains virtually un-touched from the viewpoint of integrated planning.

Apart from acquiring the scientific expertise, one of the main obsta-cles to using climatological data in planning appears to be the lack of knowledge of physical and social responses to climate. The standard climatic data do not explain the microclimates, or even the mesoclimatic features displayed by vegetation and soils. They do not explain the variations in water temperature in a bay and why one bay differs mar-kedly from the next one. They do not explain the wide variation in popular and biological response to weather. Until these knowledge gaps are overcome, the integration of climatology into the planning process will remain inadequate.

The potential of climatological analysis is being recognized in a comprehensive approach to the economic development of Newfound-land. This started with an evaluation of the tourist climate, which is difficult enough for the interior, but more complex for coastal areas. The tourist climate is being considered along with the climatic aspects of inland and sea transportation, agriculture, forestry and industrial site location in an attempt to make optimal use of climatology for economic development.

The concept is simple, but rarely in the past have climatologists attempted to interpret climate in the user's terms. Traditionally that step has not been taken, with the result that knowledge was often poorly interpreted and frequently not used at all. The development of tourism and recreation climatology, and general development climatology is a healthy sign, in that it presages a more vigorous and positive approach to the application of climatology than heretofore. Its success is based on bridging a communication gap between scientist and the planner. This same problem must be overcome in the other areas of application if climatology is to fulfill its obligations to society.

APPLIED CLIMATOLOGY IN CANADA: THE FUTURE

What are the problems which should be tackled? Canada's probably do not differ significantly from those which have been identified by the World Meteorological Organization's Commission on the Special Application of Meteorology and Climatology. These are:

— housing and building for human settlements
— climatic fluctuations and man
— human biometeorology
— urban problems
— air pollution
— energy use, transmission and development
— land use planning
— economic modelling
— storage and transportation of merchandise
— outdoor recreation and leisure time

To this list must be added the concerns of other World Meterological Organization Commissions, e.g. water, agriculture and the meteorology involved in air and marine transportation. Their relative importance must be interpreted in terms of Canadian concerns, goals and aspirations, which from a political viewpoint can be quite variable. Of course, there are always new roles in the traditional areas of activity, such as renewable natural resources and transportation. These sectors can benefit by a more aggressive approach tuned to social, environmental and political concerns. In all instances the user must be *provided with information that he can easily comprehend and use directly* in the economic decision process. Most processed data and mean value maps for conventionally measured elements usually fall far short of this mark, being unintelligible or too inconvenient for the non-climatologist.

There is a need to distinguish between what should be done and what can be done. The potential for applying climatology in economic decisions is virtually infinite. Some applications have a high payoff, others a low payoff. In still other cases, the payoff may not be clearly definable because it is indirect. Naturally, the high payoff values will have precedence; but not always, because the climatological application may be part of a greater integrated or comprehensive plan of which it is an essential component. For example, the planning process may require that climate be understood as part of the environmental impact assessment. Two areas then are likely to receive support: 1. where the economics are irrefutably advantageous, and 2. where climatology is identified in a supporting role with other major issues.

NOTES

1. Hewson, E.W. and G.C. Gill. (1944). *Meteorological Investigations in Columbia River Valley, near Trail, B.C.* Report submitted to the Trail Smelter Arbitral Tribunal. Bulletin No. 453, United States Department of Interior, 23-228.

2. Treidl, R.A. (1974). "Corn Drying in Canada Using Ambient Air." *Canadian Agricultural Engineering*, 16(2), 96-102.

3. Selirio, I.S. and D.M. Brown. (1972). "Estimation of Spring Workdays from Climatological Records." *Canadian Agricultural Engineering*, 14, 79-81.

4. Edwards, R.L. (1960). "Relationship Between Grasshopper Abundance and Weather Conditions in Saskatchewan, 1930-1958." *The Canadian Entomologist*, XCII (8), 619-24.

5. Hirst, E. and J.C. Moyers. (1973). "Efficiency of Energy Use in the United States." *Science*, 179, 1299-1304.

6. Murphy, A.H. (1954). *An Analysis of the Influence of Wind on the Relationship Between Degree Days and Fuel Consumption.* B.Sc. Thesis, Massachusetts Institute of Technology.

7. Brack, D.M. (1973). "Living with Snow." *Canadian Geographical Journal*, 86, 106-17.

8. Hibbs, J.R. (1966). "Evaluation of Weather and Climate by Socio-economic Sensitivity Indices." *Human Dimensions of Weather Modification*, edited by W.R.D. Sewell, University of Chicago, Department of Geography, Research Paper No. 105, 91-109.

9. Thompson, J.C. (1968). "Potential Economic Benefits From Improvements in Weather Information." *The Economic Benefits of National Meteorological Services*. World Meteorological Organization, World Weather Watch Planning Report 27, 41-9.

10. Mason, B.J. (1966). "The Role of Meteorology in the National Economy." *Weather*, 21 (11), 382-93.

11. Maunder, W.J. (1970). *The Value of Weather*. London: Methuen

12. MacNeill, J.W. (1971). *Environmental Management*. Ottawa: Information Canada.

13. Landsberg, H. (1956). "The Climate of Towns." *Man's Role in Changing the Face of the Earth*, edited by W.J. Thomas, Chicago: University of Chicago Press.

14. Munn, R.E. and Associates. (1970). "Atmospheric Inventory and Air Pollution Analysis." *The Haldimand-Norfolk Environment Appraisal* directed by V. Chanasyk, Ontario Ministry of Treasury, Economics and Intergovernmental Affairs, Vol. 1, 23-53.

3

Natural Hazards of Climatic Origin in Canada

James S. Gardner, Department of Geography,
University of Waterloo

THE STUDY OF NATURAL HAZARDS: CONCEPTUAL FOUNDATIONS

Nearly everyone expresses concern when a major natural disaster occurs. When a drought causes famine and death in central Africa humanitarians from all around the world appeal for and send aid. When a flood sweeps away villages and towns in Brazil, people react with horror and then set about helping in whatever way they can. The International Red Cross, agencies of the United Nations, a variety of religious and secular humanitarian groups, as well as nation-states, rush to aid the victims of earthquakes, floods, avalanches, drought, hurricanes and storm surges. This type of activity is essential and well-meaning but it is nevertheless a form of "band-aid" treatment. It is an emergency form of adjustment to natural hazards. It is after the fact. It does not directly address the underlying reasons for the disaster and as such treats symptoms of the disease but not its cause. Natural hazards research in geography has been stimulated by the need to find alternative forms of adjustments and to develop an understanding of the underlying causes of disasters.

Natural Hazard Research and Geographic Traditions

As part of the discipline of geography, natural hazards research has a place and roots in some very old geographic traditions and schools of thought. The man-land or man-environment tradition in geography is reflected in natural hazards research. Quite simply, the concern is for the relationships between human activities and artifacts and the natural environment, and the impact of each on the other. Ecological concerns in geography also find expression in natural hazards research. The study of geography as human ecology was an important theme in the United States in the 1920's and '30's. Natural hazards and resource management research may be traced directly to this theme in geography as enunciated by Harlan Barrows and implemented by Gilbert White and his students.[1]

Natural Hazards: A Conceptual Model

Figure 3.1 is a systematic and sequential representation of a natural hazard and the human adjustments to it. The effects and impact of the hazard are a function of the characteristics of both the natural event and the human use component both of which differ from place to place and change through time. Important characteristics of the natural events component are: the type of event or process, its magnitude, the frequency and regularity with which it occurs, the speed or rapidity with which it affects an area, the size of the area it affects and the specific time when it occurs. Consider, for example, an area which experiences two sharply contrasting types of atmospheric hazard — tornadoes and drought. Tornadoes occur every year in spring and summer. Major droughts occur on the average once in 40 years. Short term mid-summer water shortages are counteracted by irrigation. People come to expect the regular (annual) occurrence of tornadoes and therefore develop relatively sophisticated forecasting and warning systems which create immediate awareness of the approaching hazard and provide the necessary lead time to allow escape or other precautionary measures to be taken. The drought may begin with little recognition or expectation and no warning, resulting in few adjustments. A single tornado or even a family of tornadoes directly affect relatively small areas although the indirect consequences may be regional and national in extent. On the other hand, a major drought may be sub-continental in extent. The timing of the events is critical. A tornado which sweeps through a busy downtown area in mid-afternoon may have a vastly different impact than one which occurs in late evening. The drought on the plains of North America in the 1930's had an enormous impact because of its timing. It happened at a time when areas of cultivation were expanded into marginal agricultural environments, when markets for produce became glutted and prices fell and when a world-wide economic depression occurred. The effects of less than normal rain were devastating.

The characteristics of the human use component: the number of people, their distribution and density, their culture, their technology, their economy and their structures and movements all influence the impact of the natural event. North American cities are characterized by vast material wealth and sophisticated technology. A tornado, therefore, may result in millions of dollars damage although loss of life is usually quite low as a result of early warning systems. In a different society, with less material wealth and little technology, structural damage may be less but loss of life greater.

The remainder of the conceptual framework depicted in Figure 3.1 follows logically. The occurrence or possibility of a hazardous situation gives rise to adjustments which may be of the rescue and relief variety or of a management and planning variety. Adjustment is simply an at-

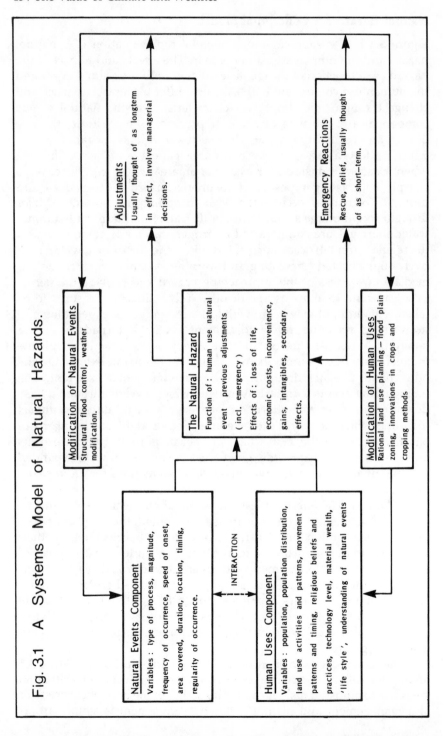

Fig. 3.1 A Systems Model of Natural Hazards.

Modification of Natural Events
Structural flood control, weather modification.

Natural Events Component
Variables : type of process, magnitude, frequency of occurrence, speed of onset, area covered, duration, location, timing, regularity of occurrence.

INTERACTION

Human Uses Component
Variables : population, population distribution, land use activities and patterns, movement patterns and timing, religious beliefs and practices, technology level, material wealth, 'life style', understanding of natural events

The Natural Hazard
Function of : human use natural event previous adjustments (incl. emergency) Effects of : loss of life, economic costs, inconvenience, gains, intangibles, secondary effects.

Adjustments
Usually thought of as longterm in effect, involve managerial decisions.

Emergency Reactions
Rescue, relief, usually thought of as short—term.

Modification of Human Uses
Rational land use planning — flood plain zoning, innovations in crops and cropping methods

tempt to change one or several of the characteristics of either the natural events or human use components with the objective of reducing loss of life and/or loss of property. Modification of the natural events system include such things as flood control dams and weather modification programmes. Rational land use planning is the basis of many modifications in the human use system. Examples include flood plain zoning and control or manipulation of cropping practices and patterns. Any adjustment should influence (reduce) the impact of future occurrences of natural hazards by diverting, buffering, preventing or controlling the collision between the natural and human components; in other words, adjustments attempt to raise the "threshold" at which that collision becomes destructive and negative.

Natural Hazards and the Concept of Threshold

The phenomena, processes and events in nature are bittersweet experiences in man-land affairs. They are at once and at different times hazards and resources. For example, the hurricane which devastates the coastline of Louisiana, Mississippi, Alabama and Florida may have been the sole source of fresh water to a small rocky island and its inhabitants off the east coast of Central America. Hurricanes have enormous value and yet impose tremendous costs. The point of division is a *threshold*. Figure 3.2 illustrates threshold and changing thresholds and uses these concepts to draw a distinction between hazards and resources. The illustration shows the erratic behaviour of a natural event variable over time. Rainfall would suffice as an example and the time period could be anything from a few months to several years. The characteristics of the human use component and the natural events component determine upper and lower thresholds. So long as the rainfall remains within the limits set by the threshold, it will be useful, i.e. a resource.

In Figure 3.2 the magnitude of the natural events variable (rainfall) below the lower threshold is shown at point A in time; this might be considered a drought and damage is done until point B in time when the rainfall is again within the thresholds. Between A and B is the realm of *hazard*. Between points B and C, the affected society takes some form of action to guard against deficiencies of rainfall in the future by attempting to modify the natural process, e.g. artificial rainmaking. The modification is reflected by a decrease in the downward fluctuations in the graph of the natural events variable. The threshold remains the same.

At point C, excessive amounts of rainfall occur; the upper threshold is exceeded and flooding results. Damage is done and the rainfall is again in the realm of hazard. At point D, the rainfall is again within the thresholds. This time the society does two things: first, measures to reduce the impact of downward fluctuations in rainfall are taken, such

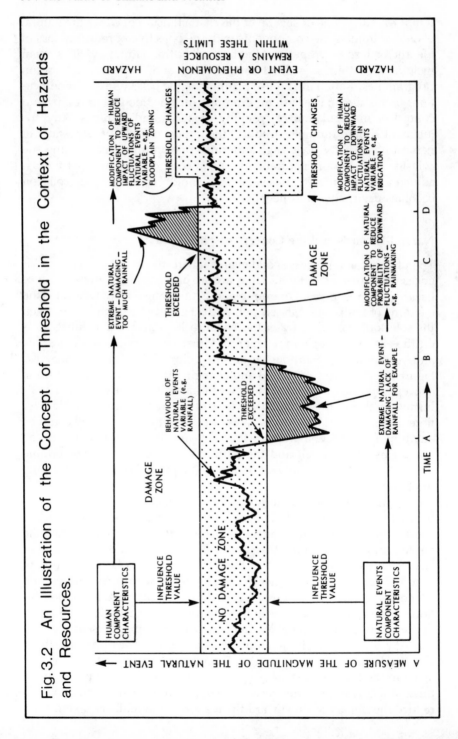

Fig.3.2 An Illustration of the Concept of Threshold in the Context of Hazards and Resources.

as the institution of irrigation and artificial water storage; and second, measures such as the restriction of building in flood-prone areas are taken to reduce the impacts of excessive rainfall and the resulting floods. In both cases, the damage thresholds are changed. It now takes a drier drought or a bigger rainstorm to cause damage to the human use component.

The concept of threshold may be applied to any natural event. While the illustration above has two thresholds, an upper and a lower, not all forces do. In the case of tornadoes, there is a single threshold of wind speed delimiting damage from no damage.

The concept of threshold is important in defining what constitutes an extreme event. In most regions some ongoing costs are imposed by the weather and climate. Occasionally they become so extreme that the system cannot cope with them and the threshold is exceeded. The following example describes the distinction between ongoing costs and hazard costs. We bear the costs of putting antifreeze in the radiators of our cars every winter. The antifreeze may be effective to -35°C. Should the temperature drop to -50°C, the threshold is exceeded and we may be looking for a new engine block.

NATURAL HAZARDS OF CLIMATIC ORIGIN IN CANADA: TOWARDS A GEOGRAPHY OF CAUSAL CONDITIONS

We do not fully understand what causes a tornado to form although we are aware of the atmospheric conditions that are associated with tornado occurrence. We know what drought is but the atmospheric processes that lead to it are poorly understood. We do not yet have a map of the hazard potential in Canada based on the geography of causal factors. However, we do know roughly where certain hazards of climatic origin are likely to occur because of our understanding of solar energy, moisture, air masses and the geography of the human component.

By their very nature, hazardous natural events are not average conditions. At a given point or area they are unusual and extreme in magnitude. Therefore, the data depicting certain atmospheric and hydrological variables (Figures 3.3, 3.4 and 3.5) are meant to provide a background and context in which the hazards occur. The data explicitly portray energy at the surface (net radiation), moisture deficits, positions of the Arctic front, thunderstorm days, runoff and river regimes. However, implicitly they portray much more.

The patterns of net radiation, which is a rough indicator of solar energy retained at the surface, and air temperature are generally similar, taking on a latitudinal distribution with the greatest inputs of energy over the course of a year being in southern Canada (Figure 3.3). Demands on environmental moisture through evapotranspiration are

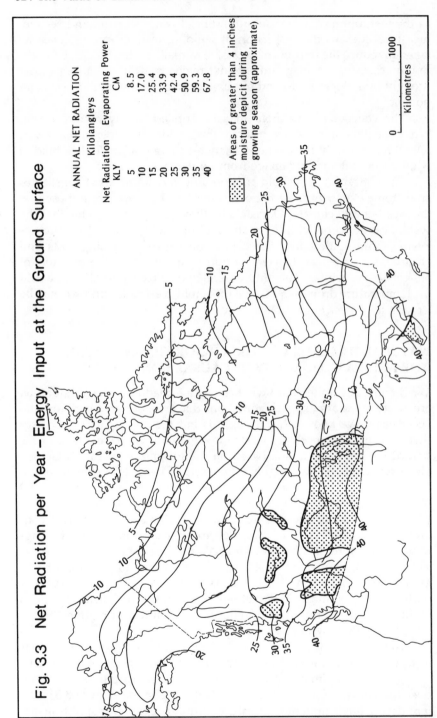

Fig. 3.3 Net Radiation per Year — Energy Input at the Ground Surface

ANNUAL NET RADIATION

Net Radiation KLY	Kilolangleys Evaporating Power CM
5	8.5
10	17.0
15	25.4
20	33.9
25	42.4
30	50.9
35	59.3
40	67.8

Areas of greater than 4 inches moisture depict during growing season (approximate)

0   1000

Kilometres

greatest where and when available energy is greatest. When coupled with the distribution and temporal patterns of moisture supply (precipitation), moisture demand is useful in showing areas of possible moisture deficit, as Figure 3.3 shows. The prairies, the interior of British Columbia and southern Ontario are the most notable moisture deficit areas. All three areas have relatively low summer precipitation which coincides with the time when moisture demands are greatest. It is reasonable then to expect that these areas would be most prone to damaging water deficits or drought.

Surface energy (net radiation) is an indicator of probable areas of intense ground surface and lower atmospheric heating which is one of several factors contributing to the development of intensive and localized storms. Indeed, the distribution of thunderstorm days partly reflects this fact (Figure 3.4) with thunderstorm activity being greatest in south-central Alberta and southern Ontario. However, other factors including the Rocky Mountains and the position of frontal activity are also reflected in thunderstorm distribution.

Figure 3.4 also shows the seasonal positions of the "Arctic front" over Canada. The Arctic front presents the generalized boundary between cold or cool, dry air masses of Arctic or polar origin and warmer and generally more humid air masses of Pacific, southwest United States, Gulf of Mexico or Atlantic origin. Cyclonic storms are known to develop in the frontal zones and to travel generally from west to east along them. As the Arctic front moves to the south during the winter months very cold, dry air covers much of Canada east of the Rockies, bringing with it the so-called "cold waves." During the summer, with the Arctic front over the subarctic-Arctic transition area, the southern part of Canada is under the influence of warm air with varying humidity, depending on its origin. Influxes of very humid and warm maritime tropical air from the Gulf of Mexico region give rise to the very uncomfortable "heat waves" in the Great Lakes and St. Lawrence regions.

Hot humid air is also a store of latent energy. Cooling of this air can set in motion extremely intense storms. Indeed, the pattern of tornado occurrence has been shown to coincide with distinctive frontal zones where hot humid air is forced aloft by more dense, colder and drier air.

Because of its location with respect to the Arctic front, southern Canada, particularly that part east of the Rockies, is subject to all the vagaries, extremes and dynamism that characterizes the mid-latitude "westerlies." We would therefore expect this to be an important factor in understanding the weather hazards of the Canadian environment.

The mean annual runoff and river regimes as depicted in Figure 3.5 are the outcomes of climatic and other factors. They provide a general basis for understanding some of the water hazards, floods in particular. Although low runoff areas coincide with areas of moisture deficit, low

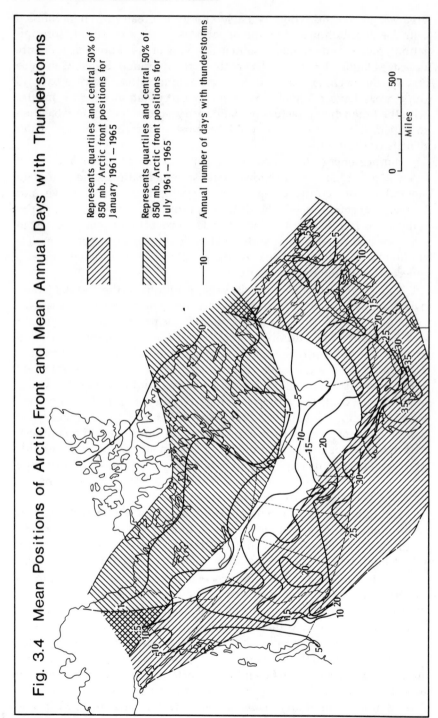

Fig. 3.4 Mean Positions of Arctic Front and Mean Annual Days with Thunderstorms

Represents quartiles and central 50% of 850 mb. Arctic front positions for January 1961–1965

Represents quartiles and central 50% of 850 mb. Arctic front positions for July 1961–1965

—10— Annual number of days with thunderstorms

0   500

Miles

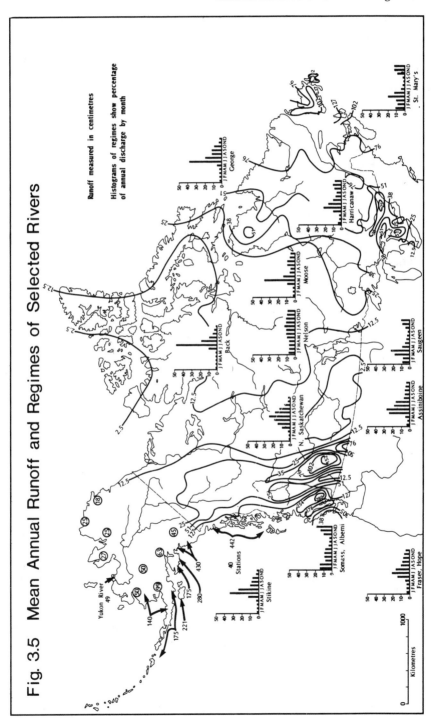

Fig. 3.5 Mean Annual Runoff and Regimes of Selected Rivers

precipitation and very cold temperatures, it cannot be said that low average runoff areas are also areas of low flood potential. Seasonality is evident in most of the regimes (Figure 3.5) and is marked in subarctic and Arctic rivers like the George and Back but occurring in most other Canadian rivers as well. The river systems including their channels and floodplains are therefore adjusted to great variations in their annual regime.

Variability of runoff is further complicated by the timing of peak runoff which usually follows or coincides with snowmelt, river and lake-ice break-up, and, in some cases, intense spring rainstorms or the annual peak precipitation periods. Rivers characteristically have difficulty handling both ice and large volumes of water. Ice-jam flooding is common throughout much of Canada. In other cases, flooding results simply from enormous volumes of water. The Fraser River provides a good example. A deep snow cover, rapid snowmelt and heavy rains all coinciding in late-April, May and early-June may result in large discharges. Much of the drainage basin lies in a high runoff region (Figure 3.5). In smaller drainage basins, such as the Saugeen in Ontario, very intense or prolonged rainstorms that cover the whole drainage basin are probably of greater importance in causing floods.

Water and energy are the bases of all the processes that give rise to natural hazards in the Canadian environment. Transformations and dissipation of energy within the atmosphere and between the atmosphere and the land surface give rise to excess of wind and water, or lack of the same. Out of this come: wind, rain, lightning, hail, glaze and snow storms, tornadoes, blizzards, heat and cold waves, droughts, floods, avalanches and storm surges along coastlines.

To have meaning as natural hazards, natural events must occur in the context of prople. To portray the geography of the human component in Canada, the concept of "ecumene" has been chosen. Hamelin[2], who studied the Canadian ecumene and produced the map shown in Figure 3.6, describes ecumene as referring to an ill-defined melange of habitation, utilization, organization and productivity characteristics of a territory.

The zones of "bloc" ecumene representing areas of large population, heavy utilization, continuous occupation and high productivity should indicate areas where both loss of life and property damage potential are high. The lower mainland of British Columbia, the prairies and the southern Great Lakes-St. Lawrence River region stand out as such areas. These regions also correlate with high surface energy areas, summer moisture deficit areas, zones of maximum thunderstorm occurrence and the area of Arctic front fluctuations. For our purposes, it is of interest that, in general, the developed areas are the zones of high hazard potential in both human and natural terms.

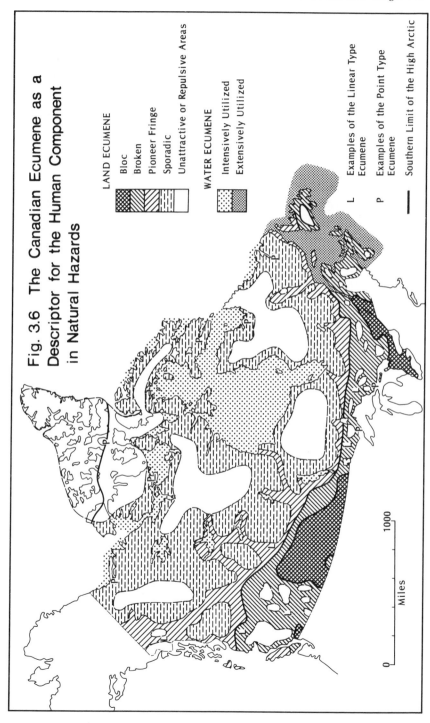

Fig. 3.6 The Canadian Ecumene as a Descriptor for the Human Component in Natural Hazards

LAND ECUMENE

Bloc
Broken
Pioneer Fringe
Sporadic
Unattractive or Repulsive Areas

WATER ECUMENE

Intensively Utilized
Extensively Utilized

L   Examples of the Linear Type Ecumene

P   Examples of the Point Type Ecumene

Southern Limit of the High Arctic

0   1000

Miles

NATURAL HAZARDS OF CLIMATIC ORIGIN IN CANADA: TYPES AND CASES

Natural hazards, which include a wide range of atmospheric, hydrological, geological and biological phenomena, may be classified in a number of ways. Possible criteria for classification include: 1. the principal causal agent, 2. the type of material involved, 3. the type of interference or disruption involved, 4. the type of energy loading involved and 5. the relative amount of damage done.[3] A number of damaging events involve more than one environmental element. Floods, for example, involve water, atmospheric processes, land surface morphology and vegetation cover. Thus it is difficult to distinguish mutually exclusive or unrelated hazardous events. Moving air and water are the two primary transportation media in nature and two important manifestations of potential energy in the environment. For these reasons they encompass directly or indirectly a number of the specific hazards noted in Figure 3.7. The specific hazards, severe storms of all sorts, drought and floods, most directly related to atmospheric conditions, will be discussed by way of specific examples.

Drought

Examples of damaging drought in Canada should come from one of three general areas: the southern interior of British Columbia, the southern prairies and southern Ontario (Figure 3.3). However, if drought is defined as a moisture deficiency, one might expect that drought could occur anywhere demands on water supply exceed the available water. This is an important concept because in recent times some damaging droughts have occurred in areas thought to be well-watered. The growth of cities and industry and the attendant demand on water supplies has led to water shortages in low rainfall years in humid regions. However, our best examples of damaging drought in Canada are from low rainfall agricultural areas.

Long term droughts in agricultural areas have led to some of history's great famines. This has been a recurring phenomenon on the Indian sub-continent. A current example is being enacted in a broad region south of the Sahara desert in Africa. The drought of the 1930's on the Canadian prairies and the Great Plains of the United States provides us with a disaster of equal magnitude but different consequences.

There are several types of drought and some of its physical characteristics make drought particularly hard to deal with. Saarinen[4] suggests four principal types of drought: permanent, seasonal, contingent and invisible. In areas of permanent drought the precipitation never meets

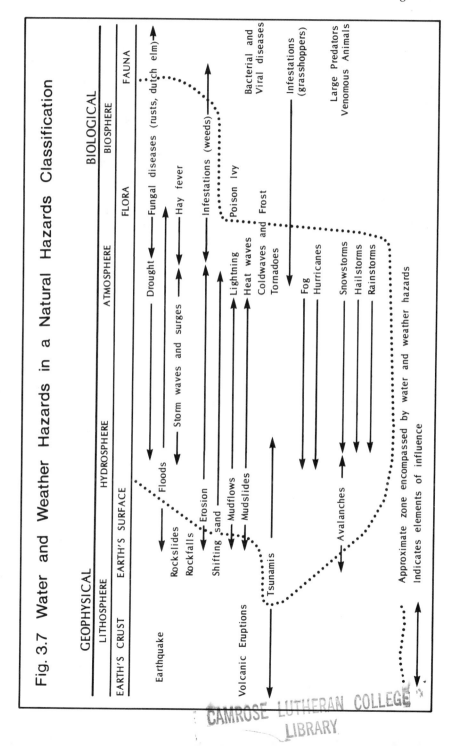

Fig. 3.7 Water and Weather Hazards in a Natural Hazards Classification

the demands of potential evapotranspiration. The prairies illustrate seasonal drought in that moisture is deficient during the growing season in most years. The period in the 1930's represents a contingent drought which refers to variations in precipitation from year to year. Invisible drought occurs within a given growing season when not enough moisture is available at critical times in plant growth. It is usually reflected in markedly lower crop yields at the end of the growing season.

Permanent drought and seasonal drought are features of the environment that can be recognized and to which the human use of an area can be adjusted. Dry farming techniques, irrigation and drought-resistant crops are examples of such adjustments. Contingent drought and invisible drought are recognized less easily. In fact, they are usually not recognized until well after onset when it is too late to make any adjustments. The onset of drought is slow and less easily recognized in comparison to other hazardous events. In addition, drought may cover a huge area which may mean a disaster of national or international scale which makes emergency adjustments particularly difficult. Timing may be important, too. The drought of the 1930's on the prairies was particularly damaging because it occurred at a time when markets were depressed, economic conditions were in a depressed state and grain farming was greatly expanded in response to wetter than average conditions and excellent market conditions in the previous 15 years.

Recognition of the permanent drought conditions on the prairies came as early as the 1850's when Palliser was commissioned to survey the area.[5] The heart of the area roughly depicted in Figure 3.3 as the moisture deficit region of the prairies has been termed "Palliser's Triangle" and its utility for agriculture long suspected on the basis of deficit moisture. Subsequently, the dry area has been defined more precisely by various researchers.[6]

The 1930's drought, although it may have been most extreme in the heart of the Palliser Triangle, affected the whole of the bloc and broken prairie ecumene depicted in Figure 3.6. Much of the 1930's drought reputation comes from the abnormally dry years of 1936 and 1937. The low precipitation coincided with higher than normal temperatures. The years 1931 through 1934 were characterized by warmer than average temperatures, strong winds and exceptionally violent summer storms. The years 1936 and 1937 established heat records that stand to this day. The winter of 1936-37 was amongst the most severe on record. High summer temperatures, low winter temperatures, lack of precipitation and violent winds were accompanied by huge infestations of grasshoppers and rust. When it did rain, it rained too much and too intensely, resulting in large amounts of runoff and soil erosion.

The overly expanded grain and livestock economy, the society and many individual's lives were decimated. In 1927 the wheat crop was valued at $90,000,000. In 1936 it was worth $3,000,000.[7] Fodder and feed crops failed as well. Farmers were unable to pay debts on land and machinery acquired during the lush 1920's. Prairie towns, being agricultural centres, lost their economic base and the welfare roll grew. Adjustments to the drought years were many — people moved, the federal government established rehabilitation programmes (Prairie Farm Rehabilitation Act), the Red Cross established emergency relief programmes, relatives in the east contributed to the welfare of their western relatives and the whole of the farming game on the prairies was reassessed and long term adjustments in methods were made.

The final adjustment was nature's. It came in 1938 with the return of moisture. Some of the moisture came in the form of a March blizzard in Alberta that left the coulees filled with snow and the remains of the livestock dead underneath. By July, one of the best wheat crops stood in Saskatchewan fields. By the end of the month 200 million bushels had been reduced to 132 million bushels by wind, rust and insects.

The prairie drought of the 1930's, coupled with economic conditions in general, left a strong imprint on Canadian and U.S. society, economics and politics. Droughts continue to cause damage, however. Research done in southern Ontario suggests that drought losses there can be expected once in seven years.[8] These are primarily crop and livestock losses but are increasingly evident in water supply and hydroelectric power generation as urban demands on water and energy increase.

Storms

Intense or excessive rainfall, solid precipitation, strong winds and/or lightning are the bases of damaging storms. Damage may be caused directly or indirectly. Forms of direct damage to structures, crops, trees, animals and people are caused by excessive loading or shear stress imposed by rain, hail, snow, ice and wind. Mechanisms of indirect damage include: river flooding from excessive rainfall, avalanches from excessive snowfalls, reduced visibility from intense rain or snowfall, and shoreline or coastline flooding from storm surges and waves on a large body of water.

It is not possible to discuss all these forms and mechanisms here. The Canadian environment, and particularly the bloc ecumene, provides examples of them all. Heavy rain and hail damages field crops in every agricultural area of Canada. While the grain crops on the prairies are not as susceptible to damage by hail as some of the soft fruit crops of other Canadian agricultural areas, the frequency and magnitude of hail storms in this area, particularly central Alberta[9], are a significant factor in the economy of the region. Heavy snowfalls occur throughout the southern part of Canada. In urban areas they disrupt the flow of information, goods, services and people.[10] Snowstorms and blizzards are an important hazard to agriculture on the prairies with calving damage in the livestock industry. Ice or glaze storms occur commonly in southern Ontario and Quebec where they overload and break power lines and trees, as well as making driving hazardous. Wind storms whether they be tornadoes or not are common occurrences winter and summer. Wind-driven waves and water cause damage and erosion on the windward shorelines of Lakes Erie, Ontario and Huron. Wind in combination with heavy rain or snow accompanies Atlantic storms that affect the maritime provinces. Occasionally the remnants of an Atlantic hurricane reaches southern Ontario to cause wind and flood damage. Heavy snow and rainstorms in coastal and interior British Columbia periodically disrupt rail and highway transport through the mudflows, landslides and snow avalanches they cause.

All these storms are in various ways related to the relative location of Canada with respect to major atmospheric patterns and flows. Being situated within the "westerlies" and in the zone over which the Arctic front seasonally oscillates makes the heavily populated and utilized part of Canada particularly subject to violent atmospheric events. Contrasts among Pacific air modified in its passage over the Cordillera, cold and dry Arctic air, and warm humid air masses from the Gulf of Mexico give rise to atmospheric conflicts that manifest themselves in violent storms of which the 1912 Regina tornado and Hurricane Hazel in 1954 are illustrations.

True tornadoes, depicted by the funnel cloud, are relatively rare in Canada, at least in relation to farther south on the Great Plains of the United States. About five tornado situations are reported each year in western Canada.[11] They also occur in southern Ontario where damage is caused and lives are lost, e.g. the April 1974 tornado at Windsor was responsible for eight deaths. Since tornadoes are usually associated with sharp frontal contrasts between cool dry air and very warm and humid air, we tend to associate them with southern Canada. Yet, on June 19, 1962, a true funnel cloud was sighted near Yellowknife in the Northwest Territories.[12]

The Regina tornado occurred on Sunday, June 30, 1912 at about 4:45 p.m. In all, 41 people died, 300 were injured and 3,000 were left homeless, all significant numbers for the small "Queen City." About six million dollars in damage resulted, an enormous figure at that time. The debt on a provincial rehabilitation loan of $500,000 was finally paid off by the city in 1959.[13] The tornado was unexpected and very unwelcome for it occurred at a time when local entrepreneurs were attempting to attract people and business to the region. Its occurrence on a Sunday afternoon was fortunate because the main path of the tornado concentrated on the central business and warehouse areas which surely would have been heavily populated on a business day. In many respects this was a local disaster. Even the provincial government, itself situated in Regina, provided little in the way of emergency financial aid and long term rehabilitation. Individuals were not compensated for financial losses. Hurricane Hazel in 1954 provides a marked contrast.

Hurricanes we associate with subtropical oceans and their adjacent land masses. Of those affecting the eastern half of North America, almost seven percent have been traced over or close to southern Ontario. The severity of most of these storms is greatly diminished by the time they reach this part of Canada. Hewitt and Burton[14], therefore, estimate a six-year recurrence interval for hurricane emergencies in southern Ontario. Hurricane Hazel, which occurred October 15 to 16, 1954 was one such emergency. Unlike the Regina tornado, Hurricane Hazel was expected, which is the case with most major and large scale storms today and is a reflection of modern weather forecasting technology. Hurricane Hazel was a disaster of regional proportions and national implications. Most of southern Ontario felt its winds and rains. Wind speeds as high as 70 mph were recorded. Strictly speaking, these winds are not of hurricane magnitude, the accepted minimum value being 75 mph. However, 7 inches of rain fell in 24 hours, the greatest recorded intensity in this region of Canada. In suburban Toronto, $25 million worth of property damage was done, primarily through flooding. About 81 people died as a direct result of the flooding. The Holland Marsh was inundated and $10 million worth of onions, cabbages and pumpkins were destroyed.[15] Had Hurricane Hazel occurred in early September or during the growing season, damage to crops probably would have been much greater. Hazel is amongst the most damaging of natural disasters in Canadian history.

Floods

Potential flood damage is primarily a function of the human use of the flood plains or flood zones of streams. The amount of flood damage from Hurricane Hazel reflects the fact that the storm occurred over a heavily populated and utilized region, namely Toronto. Other major flood disasters occurred in the lower Fraser River valley in 1948 and on the Red River in 1950 in the vicinity of Winnipeg. Burton[16] surveyed the potential for flood damages in Canada and listed 200 places with populations over 1,000 with such a potential. The geographical distribution of flood hazard in Canada correlates highly with the bloc ecumene regions of Figure 3.6. The prairie rivers, the small rivers of heavily populated southwestern Ontario and the lower Fraser valley from Hope to Vancouver are flood hazard foci. The lower Fraser is particularly worrisome[17] because of the extremely dense population in, and intense utilization of, the extensive flood plain, as well as the regime of the river which is known for very large spring discharges (see Figure 3.5).

The environment of Canada, particularly southern Canada, is characterized by a variety of flood generating processes. The occasional occurrence of severe tropical or Atlantic storms such as Hurricane Hazel may produce flooding in small and medium size drainage basins in the eastern half of the country. Intense orographic rainstorms on the windward slopes of the Cordillera may accentuate already large discharges during the spring in the major drainage basins of British Columbia. Intense summer storms of orographic, frontal or convective origin produce flooding in small watersheds throughout the country.

Taken as a whole, damaging floods can be expected every year in Canada. Data on flood frequency are slowly becoming available for many rivers in Canada.[18] For example, damaging floods have occurred once every one and a third years in Toronto over the last century[19], whereas a dangerous flood may be expected on the Thames River at London, Ontario once in four and a half years.[20]

Data on flood losses in Canada are scanty. Sewell estimates that $15 million on flood damage compensation and $155 million on flood control works were spent by the federal government between 1945 and 1965. On the basis of five year's data, the Quebec government estimates average flood damages of $2 million per year.[21]

The flood at Winnipeg in 1950 is perhaps the most spectacular example of flooding in Canada. The Red River flows northward from Minnesota across an extremely flat plain that was once a lake bottom. It flows directly through the centre of the Winnipeg metropolitan area. In the spring of 1950, snowmelt plus rain and sleet contributed to the flood. Unlike the Regina tornado, the rise of the Red River was expected. The river was closely watched and sandbagged in April 1950. However, strong winds on May 5 eroded and eventually breached the dykes, allowing the water to spread over 600 square miles of the old lake bottom land. Unlike the tornado and the Hurricane Hazel floods in Toronto, the Red River flood was of long duration. On May 18, the Red River finally crested at 30 feet above normal stage. Finally, on May 25 the waters began to recede slowly.

Great magnitude, very long duration, the huge area flooded and the fact that Canada's fourth largest city was virtually immobilized resulted in an event of national and international significance and interest. Over 107,000 people in a total population of 330,000 were evacuated from their homes. Over $100 million damage was done. The flood waters left a legacy of inconvenience, social dislocation and emotional upset for months afterwards. This is epitomized by a "for sale" sign which said "I paid $17,000 for this magnificent house overlooking the river. Will sell for $17."[22] Yet, only one person died in the flood waters.

The long term significance of the 1950 Red River flood is reflected in some of the long term flood hazard adjustments that have derived from it. A Royal Commission was established to investigate the disaster. Elaborate financial assistance, relief and compensation schemes were developed. Amongst these are the Manitoba Flood Relief Fund and a provincial government programme based on funds derived from the National Disaster Relief Fund, the province and the Red Cross. The Manitoba Emergency Measures Organization grew out of the 1950 disaster. Perhaps the most obvious adjustment and that most directly related to future flood damage reduction is a floodway that is designed to bypass flood waters around the city of Winnipeg. The floodway involves 32 miles of canals which cost almost $60 million. The diversity, extent, size and cost of adjustments are often a reflection of the severity of the hazard and in some cases stem from particularly disastrous events like the Winnipeg flood of 1950, at least in the context of a diversified, affluent and technocratic society such as that in Canada.

ADJUSTMENTS TO NATURAL HAZARDS

Adjustments to natural hazards are designed to reduce impacts of the natural events on society by some modification of the natural event and/or a modification of the human use of the area. The choice of adjustments is a complex process[23] related to such factors as perception of the hazardous process, beliefs, philosophies, technological level and financial means. The Winnipeg floodway is directed to diverting the impact of the natural process. Floodplain land use restrictions, such as those that exist along some Ontario rivers like the Grand,[24] are designed to reduce the impact of flooding by preventing the development of damageable property in flood-prone areas. In other words, they are directed at the human use of an area. The notion of "adjustment" brings us back to Figure 3.2. The adjustments to human use cause changes in the thresholds of damage. Adjustments to the natural system artificially change, contain, or buffer perturbations in the natural processes and phenomena.

It is impossible to estimate the expenditures made on hazard adjustments in Canada. Several adjustments to floods have been noted already. To this list could be added flood control dams and reservoirs, levees, channel dredging and straightening, flood insurance, flood proofing and building codes. The drought hazard has stimulated many adjustments, most of which are in evidence in moisture deficit areas. Included are: preventive measures like irrigation; conservation techniques such as summer fallow, strip cropping, drought resistant plants, dugouts, ponds and reservoirs; rehabilitation, education and assistance programmes like the Agricultural Rehabilitation and Development Act (ARDA); and crop insurance.

Too much snow is most disruptive to transportation, particularly highway and road transport, and it is there that we see the most significant adjustments. Legget and Williams[25] estimate that $250 million is expended annually on adjustment to snow. At least half this is devoted to clearance of roads while the rest is expended on equipment including tires and private snow clearance. Snow avalanches have taken a heavy toll in human lives and frequently disrupt transportation in mountainous areas like Rogers Pass.[26] Adjustments range from control measures such as: early release of avalanches with explosives, redistribution and stabilization of the snow cover with fences and baffles, and diversion of avalanches with dykes, mounds, snowsheds and walls; to preventive adjustments such as careful locational planning of highways and railroads and restricting the use of dangerous slopes by recreational skiers.

Hail presents a dilemma for the prairie farmer. While the southern Ontario farmer may have a wider choice of crops to grow, some of which are less susceptible to hail damage, the prairie farmer is more limited in his crop adjustments. Crop insurance is one form of adjustment. Another is suppression of the hail formation process through cloud seeding.

Weather forecasting specifically and the study of meteorology generally are in part directed to damage reduction. The forecasting of severe storms allows people to make adjustments before the advent of the storm. A forecast of hail does little for the farmer and his crop but he may be able to cover the plants in his garden. It also sets in motion a wide variety of practices and devices used by vegetable and fruit growers to protect their plants and trees from frost damage. Included are smudges, fans, oil burning heaters, electric heaters, flood lights and sprinkler systems. A storm warning in the heavily utilized coastal areas and on the many large lakes in Canada sends small fishing and recreational water craft searching for moorage and cover.

Conclusion

Many of these so-called hazard adjustments are things we take for granted. Some of them are not meaningful because they do not directly affect our livelihood. It is probably true that those most directly affected have the most sensitive appreciation and understanding of the hazards and the choice of adjustments to them. Yet, it is clear by the very nature of the Canadian environment that we are all directly and indirectly affected by hazardous events.

NOTES

1. Burton, I. and R.W. Kates. (1964). "Perception of Natural Hazards in Resources Management." *Natural Resources Journal*, 3, 412-41.
   White. G.F. (1973). "Natural Hazards Research." *Directions in Geography*, edited by R.J. Chorley, London: Methuen, 193-216.
2. Hamelin, L.E. (1968). "Types of Canadian Ecumene." *Readings in Canadian Geography*, edited by R.M. Irving. Toronto: Holt, Rinehart and Winston, 20-30.
3. Hewitt, K. and I. Burton. (1971). *The Hazardousness of a Place: A Regional Ecology of Damaging Events*. Toronto: University of Toronto, Department of Geography, Research Publications, No. 6.
4. Saarinen, T.F. (1966). *Perception of the Drought Hazard on the Great Plains*. Chicago: University of Chicago, Department of Geography Research Paper, No. 106.
5. Spry, I.M. (1963). *The Palliser Expedition: An Account of John Palliser's British North American Expeditions 1857-1860*. Toronto: MacMillan.
6. Laycock, A.H. (1960). "Drought Patterns in the Canadian Prairies." *International Association of Scientific Hydrology Symposium Proceedings*, (Helsinki), Publication No. 5, 34-47.
   Villimov, J.R. (1956). "The Nature and Origin of the Canadian Dry Belt." *Annals of the Association of American Geographers*, 46, 211-32.
7. Gray, J. (1967). *Men Against the Desert*. Saskatoon: Modern Press.
8. Hewitt, K. and I. Burton. (1971). *op. cit.*
9. Summers, P.W. and A.H. Paul. (1967). "Some Climatological Characteristics of Hailfall in Central Alberta." *Proceedings of 5th Conference on Severe Local Storms*. American Meteorological Society, St. Louis, Mo., 313-24.
10. Archer, P.E. (1970). *The Urban Snow Hazard: A Case Study of the Perception of Adjustments to, and Wage and Salary Losses Suffered from Snowfall in the City of Toronto, Winter 1967-68*. Unpublished M.A. Research Paper. Department of Geography, University of Toronto.
11. Lowe, A.B. and G.A. McKay. (1962). "Tornado Composite Charts for Western Canada." *Journal of Applied Meteorology*, 1, 157-62.
12. Burns, B.M. and C.E. Thompson. (1973). "A Tornado Funnel Cloud Near Yellowknife, N.W.T., Canada." *Musk-Ox*, 13, 12-21.
13. Rasky, F. (1961). *Great Canadian Disasters*. Toronto: Longman.
14. Hewitt, K. and I. Burton. (1971). *op. cit.*
15. Rasky, F. (1961). *op. cit.*
16. Burton, I. (1965). "Flood-Damage Reduction in Canada." *Geographical Bulletin*, 7, 161-85.
17. Sewell, W.R.D. (1965). *Water Management and Floods in the Fraser River Basin*. Chicago: University of Chicago, Department of Geography Research Paper, No. 100.
18. Collier, E.P. and G.A. Nix. (1967). *Flood Frequency Analysis for New Brunswick–Gaspé Region*. Ottawa: Department of Energy, Mines and Resources, Inland Waters Branch, Technical Bulletin No. 9.
   Durrant, E.F. and S.R. Blackwell. (1959). "The Magnitude and Frequency of Floods on the Canadian Prairies." *Spillway Design Floods*, Proceedings of Hydrology Symposium No. 1. Ottawa: Department of Northern Affairs and National Resources.
19. Burton, I. *et al.* (1972). *A National Review of Selected Natural and Man-Made Hazards in the Canadian Environment*. Prepared for the Commission on Man and Environment, 22nd International Geographical Congress, Calgary, Alberta.
20. Hewitt, K. and I. Burton. (1971). *op. cit.*
21. Burton, I. *et al.* (1972). *op. cit.*
22. Rasky, F. (1961). *op. cit.*
23. White, G.F. (1964). *Choice of Adjustment to Floods*. Chicago: University of Chicago, Department of Geography Research Paper No. 93.

24. Grand River Conservation Authority. (1966). *Resource Management Plan, Grand River Watershed.*
25. Leggett, R.F. and G.P. Williams. (1964). "Snow Removal and Ice Control in Canada with a Note on Snow and Ice Research." *Snow Removal and Ice Control.* Ottawa: National Research Council, Technical Memorandum No. 83.
26. Schaerer, P. (1962). *The Avalanche Evaluation and Prediction at Rogers Pass.* Ottawa: National Research Council, Division of Building Research, Technical Paper, No. 142.

PART 3
THE HYDROLOGICAL
RESOURCE BASE
IN CANADA

Introduction

The authors of this section, Quinn, Spence and Parsons, have succeeded in manipulating a wealth of data. The result is an excellent overview of Canadian water resources, both surface and subsurface, in geophysical terms and in relation to human use and human conservation.

Quinn and Spence remind us that no complete record of water resources in Canada yet exists — nor has any nation-wide water-use inventory yet been established. The data problem notwithstanding, the authors analyse the situation with respect to the surface water resources, pointing out that the vast area of lake surface in Canada belies the fact that the only measure of a country's renewable surface water supply is streamflow. Canada can claim about nine percent of the world's renewable water supply; yet much of this is seasonally "locked in" as snow, and most of it flows northwards away from the populous south.

The various types of uses for water — municipal, manufacturing, mining, energy, navigation, fishing and recreation — are all examined, and an assessment of the supply-withdrawal balance on a regional basis is made.

The problem of water quality impairment in and around cities, in inland and ocean waters, implies the need for much better management. In many cities this means beginning with waste treatment facilities for, despite heavy expenditures already made for such facilities, much more is needed to reduce the "urban backlog".

Finance, however, is not the only hurdle to be surmounted in improving water management: human attitudes and perceptions and government jurisdiction are equally problematical. The thorny tangle of Provincial-Federal responsibilities for water resources are carefully explained by the authors and then significant legislation is discussed. The changing tone of human perception and the use of the resource as outlined in Provincial-Federal water management agreements is covered by a four-fold classification; traditional, comprehensive, water quality, and the most recent, environmental impact. The authors' choice of three case studies, the Bennett Dam, the Churchill-Nelson development, and the James Bay project, illustrate all too clearly the highly politicized process of decision-making, and the widespread environmental, economic and sociological consequences of such projects.

Parsons expands on the theme of water resources by drawing our attention to the vast world of "subsurface space" whose waters comprise an intrinsic component of the hydrological cycle. Knowledge of this continuity of water movement between surface environment and subsurface space is essential to the understanding of the proper conservation of the resource as a whole.

A concise inventory of sources is provided: bedrock aquifers, still largely uncharted as to groundwater supply; drift aquifer, the focus of present development; permafrost areas, a relatively new focus of interest, gaining significance with increasing northern development.

The inventory continues with an overview of ground water quality in Canada, leading to the author's proposed model for ground water evaluation and development. Two case studies illustrate well the application of the model's principles in two contrasting situations; Shippegan, N.B. experiencing problems of saline water intrusion into the community's freshwater aquifer and Regina with a vast ground water resource constrained by its limited recharge potential.

These examples lead us into the topic of ground water development in general, and specifically to the problems of ground water contamination through waste disposal practices. Parsons warns us of the dangers of the use of sites unsuitable for solid waste disposal, especially in humid areas where relatively rapid infiltration of leachates may produce ground water contamination. Prevention, by use of protective clay liners for example, and monitoring are recommended by the author. Each method of liquid waste disposal, septic tanks, lagoons and effluent irrigation, requires a different set of conditions for safe usage. The conditions are not always met. More recent use of deep subsurface space for disposal of industrial and other liquid wastes presents another area of potential hazard of delayed, but perhaps irreversible, impact. Even modern agricultural practices present a potential danger to our ground water resources.

These facts, so clearly presented by the author, draw our attention to three related points: the resources of subsurface space are a function of surface conditions, including human activities; competent hydrogeological evaluation of waste disposal sites and efficient installations are essential for ground water conservation; the conditions and usage of subsurface space should be an integral part of land use planning. In making the case for an expanded conception of land use planning, Parsons' paper stands as a major contribution.

4

Canada's Surface Water Resources: Inventory and Management

F.J. Quinn, Inland Waters Directorate, Environment Canada and E.S. Spence, Department of Geography, York University

INVENTORY OF SURFACE WATERS AND THEIR USE

No really accurate measurement exists of the present extent, character, or distribution of Canada's water resources. Our lakes have not all been counted, much less measured for area or volume. Many rivers are still not gauged. Uniform criteria do not exist for groundwater resources to be evaluated on a consistent scientific basis from one region to another. Water quality and sediment transport information is available only at selected locations across the country.

Information gaps also exist on the many uses Canadians make of their water inheritance. Some data have been published on some uses or for some provinces, but until this year nothing approaching a nation-wide water use inventory has been established.[1] The inventory section of this chapter is therefore only a first approximation of Canada's current balance between water supply and water use. It is based on a survey of both published and unpublished sources undertaken by the Inland Waters Directorate, Environment Canada. Patterns of geographical variation are indicated by dividing the country (exclusive of the Arctic Islands) into 6 provincial/territorial and 26 drainage regions (Tables 4.1 and 4.2). The year 1970 was chosen as the most recent for which statistical data were available for most water uses.

Present Water Supplies

How well off are Canadians with respect to the distribution of the world's waters? Certain advantages are undeniable, but they are not without limit.

Washed by three *oceans*, Canada has the longest coastline of any country in the world. Most of it, however, is inaccessible to our population which continues to crowd the one continental boundary to the south. Withdrawal of water from the sea for use is, in any event, no-where significant. The principal uses of Canada's offshore waters are, of course, fishing and shipping. These waters remain open to all comers and pose continuing problems of international regulation of the fish

TABLE 4.1

Water Withdrawals by Provincial/Territorial Region, 1970
in million gallons per day

Region	Total Excluding Hydro	Municipal[a] and Rural Residential	Manufac- turing	Mining	Agriculture	Electrical	
						Thermal	Hydro
Atlantic	1,695	151	598	101	12	833	37,672
Quebec	2,502	521	1,823	53	67	38	449,975
Ontario	9,192	731	2,882	94	112	5,373	311,434
Prairies	3,901	211	613	253	1,061	1,763	91,902
British Columbia	2,240	189	1,028	64	284	675	64,031
Canada North	16	3	—	13	—	—	10,422
Totals	19,546	1,806	6,944	578	1,536	8,682	965,436

[a] Excluding manufacturers served by municipal systems; these have been transferred to the manufacturing column.
Sources: Canada, 1971; 1972a, b and c.

TABLE 4.2

Canadian Water Supplies and Withdrawals, 1970
in millions of gallons per day

Drainage Region	Supplies		Withdrawals					Electrical	
	Reliable Annual Runoff	Reliable Min. Monthly Runoff	Total excluding Hydro	Municipal[b] Rural Residential	Manufacturing	Mining	Agriculture	Thermal	Hydro
Fraser	56,800	13,452	403	128	116	10	134	15	5,016
Okanagan-Skagit	1,020a	242a	153	11	3	9	123	7	—
Columbia	30,700a	11,000a	287	15	233	10	17	12	36,234
Pac. Coastal	185,000	22,062	1,346	44	645	12	9	636	8,584
Yukon	37,000a	8,899a	8	2	—	6	—	—	10,293
Lower Mackenzie	103,000a	12,376a	12	2	—	10	—	—	129
Peace Athabasca	48,900	12,753	197	10	90	80	8	9	17,689
Arctic Coastal	37,800	13,614	—	—	—	—	—	—	—
Keewatin	53,900	12,914	—	—	—	—	—	—	—
Churchill	19,400	16,197	71	3	53	9	3	3	9,903
Lower Sask.-Nelson	8,670a	4,143a	322	10	262	24	13	13	56,949
North Sask.	3,320	398	1,043	52	85	20	32	854	110
South Sask.	2,750a	656a	1,567	75	53	56	926	457	3,305
Red-Assin.	630a	75a	720	72	100	73	43	432	—
Winnipeg	9,180a	7,695a	100	7	72	12	1	8	44,250
Milk	84a		48	1	—	11	36	—	—

Northern Ontario	85,200	20,448	119	8	82	8	1	20	37,938
Northern Quebec	204,000	48,967	20	4	1	15	—	—	10,032
Upper Gr. Lakes	38,500a	13,500	1,393	60	998	46	27	262	36,934
Southern Ontario	7,250a	2,600a	7,276	579	1,563	3	78	5,053	173,550
Ottawa	29,600	17,703	492	82	320	39	15	36	109,207
Mid. St. Lawrence	29,900a	14,313a	1,861	450	1,335	3	51	2	240,966
Quebec Coastal	134,000	32,400	371	40	274	21	6	30	127,545
Saint John-St. Croix	10,900a	5,004a	387	30	134	—	2	221	21,200
Maritime Coastal	34,400	12,323	1,078	83	384	17	10	584	4,422
Nfld. — Labrador	131,000	46,815	272	38	121	84	1	38	12,058
CANADA	1,302,904	350,549	19,546	1,806	6,944	578	1,536	8,682	965,436

a Excluding inflow contributions from the United States and/or from upper basin region(s).
b Excluding manufacturers served by municipal systems. These have been transferred to the manufacturing column.

harvest and of pollution which offset many of the opportunities traditionally enjoyed by this country.

Most of the world's water not found in the ocean reservoir is locked up in glacial ice or stored underground.[2] *Ice* caps are not likely to become a practical source of water supply in this or any other country, at least in the foreseeable future. The *groundwater* situation in Canada is a little more promising; but so much of this northern land is without soil cover, impregnated with permafrost and underlain with impermeable crystalline rock or saline formations that groundwater potential does not create great expectations other than on a local scale.

Canada probably has more *lake* area (which is not to say volume) than any other country in the world. Large and small, these surface waters dot the landscape from one end of the country to the other. Lakes perform an invaluable role in regulating the flow of rivers; they also provide a stable habitat for natural life and human enjoyment. But our lakes are the legacy of a recession of the ice fronts several thousand years ago. They are not renewable, except at a cost to the rivers which fill and drain them.

The only measure of a country's *renewable* water supply is *streamflow*. On an average annual basis, Canada's rivers discharge less than nine percent of the world's renewable water supply, roughly 3.5 million cubic feet per second (c.f.s.) (or 3.2 million if we exclude the Arctic Islands and flows entering the country from the United States). By comparison, the average annual runoff from the continental United States is about 2.7 million c.f.s. When set against a population which is less than one percent of the world's population, Canada's nine percent of the world's renewable water supply is a generous endowment indeed; however, when set against a territorial area which is almost seven percent of the world's landmass, our water supply is not so disproportionate.

National comparisons must be tempered with the knowledge that they usually disguise wide variations of water availability, in time and place, within the national boundaries. This is especially true in Canada where over one-third of total precipitation falls as snow and is held until spring runoff, and where almost two-thirds of total runoff flows away from the populous southern regions into the North.

Average annual surface runoff (Figure 4.1) varies greatly across the country, from over 100 inches in coastal British Columbia to less than five inches throughout the vast sweep of the prairies and northern territories. Average annual runoff is less than one inch over much of the southern prairies. Oddly enough, the prairie and northern regions are sometimes alluded to as a source of water "surplus" which could be readily exported.[3]

Average annual flow data represent a kind of theoretical water

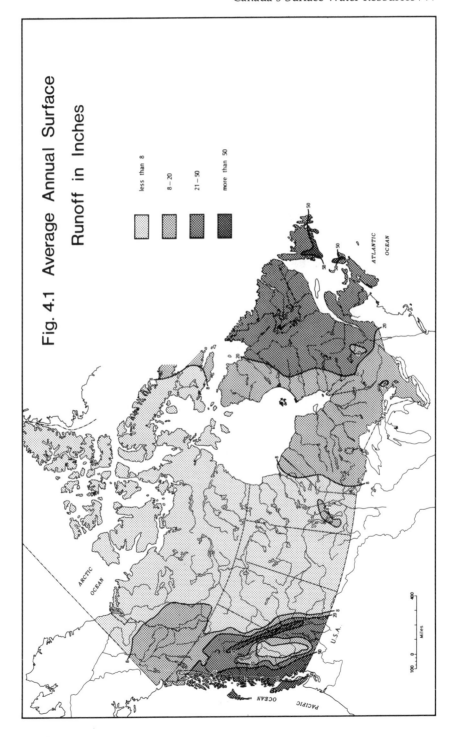

Fig. 4.1 Average Annual Surface Runoff in Inches

less than 8

8 – 20

21 – 50

more than 50

supply; they fail to indicate the fluctuations which normally limit that supply from year to year and season to season. For the purpose of this survey, "reliable" flow data have been estimated, both on an annual basis (available nine out of ten years) and on a minimum monthly basis (available in all except the lowest month in ten years). The effects of natural and artificial storage are much more important in the latter case. By showing both the reliable annual and reliable minimum monthly flows as a percentage of the average flow (Figure 4.2), the differences between theoretical and practical water supply availabilities across the country are seen to be striking.

In the northern and Pacific Coast regions, the reliable annual flow tends to be about 80 percent of the average, in the Ontario, Quebec and Atlantic regions about 60 percent to 80 percent of the average, but on the southern prairies only 30 percent to 40 percent of the average annual flow. On a minimum monthly basis the reliable flow in almost all basins is below 50 percent of the average, and in one-half the basins is below 20 percent of the average. The lowest percentages again occur in the southern prairies (Milk and Red-Assiniboine basins) where the minimum reliable monthly flow falls below five percent of the mean. It should be realized that these values of minimum flow are not unlikely possibilities but can be expected, on the average, to occur in a given basin once in ten years. Further, these percentages of the mean flow are calculated for the outlets of relatively large basins, where the extremes of low runoff in one area are often compensated for by moderating conditions in other parts of a basin. In a small basin, or portion of a basin, flows would be smaller and variations more extreme.

In relation to population, Canada appears to have a very abundant water supply, enough to provide, on the average, 90,000 gallons per person per day. But regional variations are important. The largest per capita supplies are in the north and in the sparsely settled areas on the eastern and western extremities of Canada. However, one-half of the drainage regions generate internally less than 50,000 gallons per capita per day of reliable annual flow. On the basis of a reliable minimum monthly flow, five drainage regions — North Saskatchewan, South Saskatchewan, Red-Assiniboine, Milk and Southern Ontario — have less than 100 gallons per capita per day available. This latter figure is less than what is used in the average urban household.

Present Water Uses

Water is used in Canada in a great variety of ways. The main categories of use include municipal/rural residential, manufacturing, mining, agriculture, electricity generation (all considered as withdrawals from nature) and navigation, fish and wildlife, and recreation (generally considered as non-withdrawal in-channel uses). A greater or lesser proportion

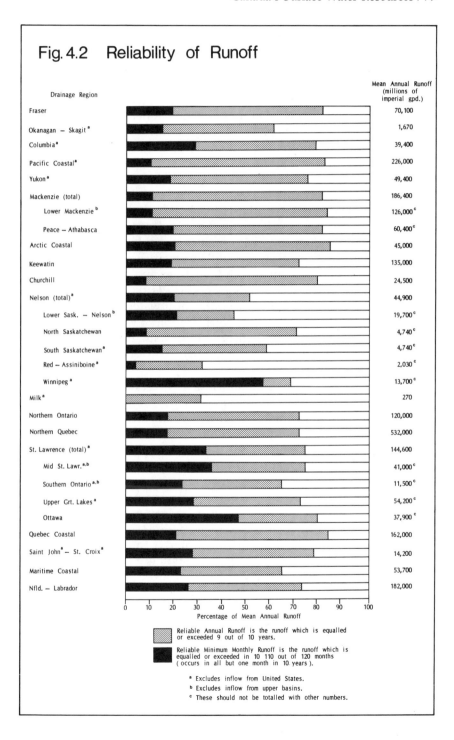

Fig. 4.2 Reliability of Runoff

of withdrawals are returned eventually to surface flows. What is not returned is said to be "consumed," or no longer available for use because it has evaporated from the surface, transpired from plants, been consumed by man or livestock, or otherwise removed from the water environment. Hydropower generation, which consumes almost no water, is here considered among the withdrawal uses even though the water used is not always taken out of the channel. Waste disposal is another important in-channel use of water, but is considered separately in a later section of the chapter. Summary data on withdrawal uses for 1970 have been aggregated[4] for provincial/territorial regions (Table 4.1) and drainage regions (Table 4.2 and Figure 4.3).

Coinciding closely with the distribution of population and economic activities, approximately two-thirds of all *municipal and manufacturing* water withdrawals are made in the Great Lakes-St. Lawrence Lowlands of Ontario and Quebec, with smaller concentrations in the Lower Mainland of British Columbia, the southern prairies and Atlantic region. Municipal and rural residential withdrawals (excluding those supplying industry) approach 1.8 billion gallons per day (g.p.d.). Manufacturing, at 6.9 billion g.p.d., withdraws by far the most water of any use excepting electric generation. The actual consumption of water for these purposes is only a small proportion of withdrawals; on the other hand, return flow is often so grossly polluted that it is in effect unavailable for subsequent use.[5]

Water withdrawal by the *mining* industry, estimated at 0.58 billion g.p.d., tends to be spread along the northern fringes of settlement for metallic extraction in Labrador, Quebec, Ontario and British Columbia, and centered in the prairies for petroleum recovery. Deep well injections in the petroleum fields of the prairies account for almost 44 percent of total mining water use and for an even greater proportion of what is lost or consumed.

Most of Canada's *agriculture* depends on the natural water supply through precipitation, but withdrawals for irrigation and stock watering are also important at 1.5 billion g.p.d. The prairies (mostly Alberta) lead in irrigated acreage and in irrigation water withdrawals (0.9 billion g.p.d.), followed by British Columbia and southern Ontario. Stock watering withdraws approximately 0.3 billion g.p.d. nationally. Unlike most other water uses, the greater part of agricultural water withdrawals are consumed and unavailable for subsequent use.

Hydro and thermal generating plants satisfy virtually all Canadian *electric energy* needs. More than 99 percent of all water used for this purpose in 1970 passed through hydro plants. The Great Lakes-St. Lawrence Gulf region accounts for two-thirds of the tremendous volume of water — 965 billion g.p.d. — used for electricity generation. Less than one percent of the water used, however, is actually consumed. It is

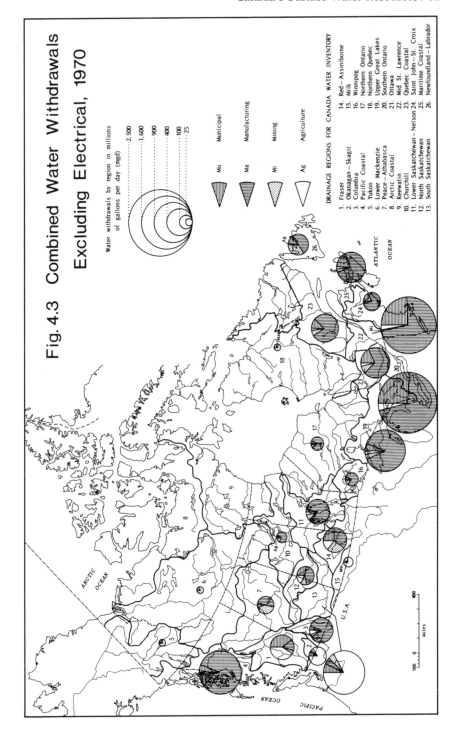

Fig. 4.3 Combined Water Withdrawals Excluding Electrical, 1970

Water withdrawals by region in millions of gallons per day (mgd)

- 2,500
- 1,600
- 900
- 400
- 100
- 25

Mu — Municipal
Ma — Manufacturing
Mi — Mining
Ag — Agriculture

DRAINAGE REGIONS FOR CANADA WATER INVENTORY

1. Fraser
2. Okanagan – Skagit
3. Columbia
4. Pacific Coastal
5. Yukon
6. Lower Mackenzie
7. Peace – Athabasca
8. Arctic Coastal
9. Keewatin
10. Churchill
11. Lower Saskatchewan – Nelson
12. North Saskatchewan
13. South Saskatchewan
14. Red – Assiniboine
15. Milk
16. Winnipeg
17. Northern Ontario
18. Northern Quebec
19. Upper Great Lakes
20. Southern Ontario
21. Ottawa
22. Mid St. Lawrence
23. Quebec Coastal
24. Saint John – St. Croix
25. Maritime Coastal
26. Newfoundland – Labrador

anticipated that the proportion of water withdrawn for thermoelectric generation will increase substantially in the next two decades.

Water *navigation* still remains the most economic means of transporting many bulky raw materials to market. Recent ocean port expansion near Saint John and Vancouver and increasing traffic along the Great Lakes-St. Lawrence deep waterway and on the Mackenzie River are impressive; while commercial traffic has declined on secondary inland waterways, pleasure boating is making strong gains.

The use of water by *fish and wildlife* is only partially explained by the exploitive aspects of the catch by the commercial fishery ($180 million) and the fur trade ($18 million). In many areas, however, these activities remain the major, if not sole, source of income. Fish and wildlife populations have evolved under specific conditions of the water regime where the extent and timing of level and flow changes and associated qualities are critical to survival. The loss of wetlands to drainage and filling poses a serious threat to waterfowl which is being counteracted, in part, by purchase and long term lease arrangements.

Outdoor *recreation* directly or indirectly related to water constitutes an important and growing use of leisure time by Canadians. One can estimate only with difficulty the real dollar value afforded by this use of the resource. Participation rates have been compiled, by province, on most forms of recreational activity; separate surveys indicate that 3.0 million anglers and 0.5 million waterfowl hunters were active about 1970.

Balance of Supplies and Withdrawals

Only a partial water supply-demand balance can be calculated at present for Canada and its drainage regions. On the supply side, information on source (fresh or saline, ground or surface) and quality is not available; streamflows are estimated for each region in terms of reliability, annually and monthly. On the demand side, withdrawals are the only water uses that can be quantified. But consumption data for these uses are not complete, and do not allow for the impact of use on the quality of the resource.

In Canada as a whole, the reliable supply-withdrawal balance is very favourable in quantitative terms (Table 4.2). The only regional exceptions to the national situation are the drainage regions of the southern prairies (Milk, North and South Saskatchewan, Red-Assiniboine), also southern Ontario and, to a lesser extent, the Okanagan Valley. The southern Ontario supply is much better than is indicated by the data because most of its large urban population depends, not on the region's tributary streams, but on the Lower Great Lakes, which receive the greater part of their inflow from the Upper Lakes and the United States (both outside the region). The Okanagan also appears to have sufficient water quantity, if not quality, for the immediate future.

That leaves the contiguous drainage patterns of southern Alberta, Saskatchewan and Manitoba as the only part of Canada with an emerging problem of water shortage. It is, however, hardly comparable to the hard core areas of water shortage in the U.S. Southwest. Low summer flows, on which the agricultural withdrawals in the prairies depend, can be increased by greater regulation of spring runoff, perhaps in combination with underground storage and/or small scale importation.

Dams, Diversions and Other Structures

In Canada, the principal means of regulating surface waters are channel improvements, dyking, dams and diversions. Channel changes and dykes are usually implemented on a local scale, often for flood control, with little impact on the overall water regime. Of much greater importance in modifying streamflow are surface storage and diversion projects (Figure 4.4). Peak spring-summer flows can be stored for use during other months. Canada is blessed with such abundance of natural water storage in lakes that man-made storage is, at present, very small in comparison; perhaps 250 million acre-feet, equal to the active storage provided naturally by the Upper Great Lakes. The effect of combined natural and man-made storage and subsequent regulation of rivers is apparent on the Ottawa and Winnipeg Rivers (Figure 4.2) where reliable minimum monthly flows are a relatively high proportion of the average flow.

If 10,000 acre-feet gross storage capacity is taken as the threshold requirement for a large dam, there are at present about 200 large dams either completed or under construction; 38 of these exceed one million acre-feet in storage capacity.[6] Most of this latter group have been constructed since 1950. Almost three-quarters of Canada's large dams have been constructed for hydroelectric power generation. Irrigation storage accounts for 10 percent, mainly on the prairies, and a few dams provide for municipal and industrial water supply. Of the 25 multi-purpose dams, some include flood control as a major function. Overall, Canada is still very much hydro country.

Given Canada's natural wealth in water resources, interbasin diversions have been few and recent. To date, some 13 interbasin diversions have been completed, mostly for power purposes, and others are under consideration. None of them, so far, cross provincial or national boundaries. However, the volume of water involved in one current diversion project (20 million acre-feet annually from the Churchill River at Southern Indian Lake into the Nelson for power purposes) will exceed the total of all existing diversions; indeed it will be the largest diversion on the continent.

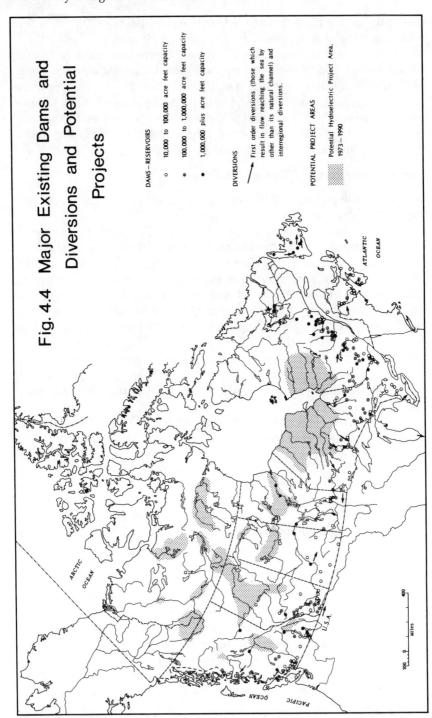

Fig. 4.4 Major Existing Dams and Diversions and Potential Projects

DAMS—RESERVOIRS

○ 10,000 to 100,000 acre feet capacity

● 100,000 to 1,000,000 acre feet capacity

● 1,000,000 plus acre feet capacity

DIVERSIONS

↗ First order diversions (those which result in flow reaching the sea by other than its natural channel) and interregional diversions.

POTENTIAL PROJECT AREAS

▒ Potential Hydroelectric Project Area, 1973—1990

Canadian dams and diversions are located mostly in an east-west band close to the southern border. Current investigations indicate that future dams and diversions will be built largely in the northern areas of the provinces and territories (Figure 4.4), and these programmes will be of major proportions. Surveys are underway or complete on the Stikine, Liard, Yukon and Fraser Rivers in British Columbia, on the Saskatchewan-Nelson, Peace and Churchill Rivers of the prairie provinces, in five basins of northern Ontario, and in the James Bay region of Quebec; likewise in the Yukon and Northwest Territories, where all promising hydroelectric sites are being inventoried. Considering the escalation in construction costs, however, and the fervour of environmentalists and native peoples to maintain the integrity of the Canadian North, new large scale projects are facing difficulties not encountered by those already in place.

Man-made structures not only affect water levels and flows, but have wide-ranging impacts on the channel, flora and fauna, and man himself. The effect of the Bennet Dam on the Peace-Athabasca Delta, discussed later in this paper, is a recent case in point. Detrimental effects must be weighed against the benefits of the project and adjustments made where possible to enchance the overall benefits.

Waste Loading and Treatment

Pollution of the water environment is primarily associated with concentrations of population and industrial activity. Three out of four Canadians now live and work in cities and towns that occupy less than one percent of our land area. In the vicinity of these urban complexes, the rivers, lakes and shorelines show marked evidence of impaired water quality. Abatement measures by some municipalities and industries have reduced the harmful effects somewhat, but much more remains to be done to restore the water to an acceptable level of quality.

Water quality is usually considered in terms of inland waters, but it should not be forgotten that the oceans are the ultimate receivers of Canada's water pollution. Man has regarded the sea and the estuaries leading to it as a perpetual sewage disposal system, only to find lately that these vast areas of salt water do not have an unlimited capacity for assimilating wastes. Our continued enjoyment of the coastal zone, and use of its resources, will call for management not unlike that applied to inland waters.

As of 1972, two-thirds of the urban population of Canada was served by sewage treatment facilities: 2.2 million by primary treatment only, and 7.4 million by primary through secondary. Of the remaining 42 percent of the urban population without treatment facilities, only 10 percent is without sewage collection. These figures represent "normal" operating conditions and do not account for the overflow of combined storm and sanitary sewer systems. Data on municipal waste treatment were derived from records of loans for sewage treatment systems made by Central Mortgage and Housing Corporation (CMHC) under Part VIII of the National Housing Act.

The regional pattern of municipal waste treatment facilities (Figure 4.5) reflects the degree of treatment provided by Canada's major urban centres. Three cities in Ontario (Toronto, Ottawa and Hamilton) treat 100 percent of domestic wastes, the first two to the secondary level. These and other communities are also undertaking a programme to curb algal growth by removing 80 percent of phosphorus wastes according to a provincial timetable. Other urban areas with over 90 percent of their populations served by treatment facilities include Calgary, Edmonton, Regina, Winnipeg and Fredericton. The rest of Canada's major urban concentrations have inadequate treatment facilities. Vancouver serves 49 percent of its population by primary systems but improvements are underway. Montreal, our largest city, serves only 12 percent of its 2.4 million population. The cities of Quebec and St. John's have no treatment facilities and Victoria has virtually none. This latter group has obviously relied on the disposal capacity of the ocean and estuaries to carry away waste without cost, a situation that cannot continue indefinitely. But plans for new facilities are underway.

Between 1961 and 1971, about $700 million was spent in establishing municipal waste treatment plants and collectors. Two-thirds of these costs were financed by CMHC.[7] Expenditures on treatment facilities are now growing at a rate of 10 percent per year nationally, much faster than population growth. Continued high levels of expenditure will be needed to catch up with the urban backlog and treat wastes to rising standards.

As with wastes produced by municipalities, approximately two-thirds of most waterborne wastes generated by Canadian industry enter the Great Lakes-St. Lawrence system, which also receives the proportionately heavier discharges into the Great Lakes from the U.S. side.[8] A distant second in waste loadings are the Pacific and Atlantic coastal regions. It is difficult to determine the precise extent to which each industry contributes to the loadings of various streams, as the information base is inadequate, particularly for the smelting and refining industries.

A cursory comparison of municipal and industrial waste loadings with respect to a limited number of parameters like biological oxygen demand (BOD) and suspended solids indicates that industrial wastes present by far the larger problem. Capital expenditures on construction by industry for treating effluent have so far been minimal, with other users suffering the effects. This in spite of the fact that industries installing pollution abatement equipment are eligible for accelerated tax write-offs under the Income Tax Act.

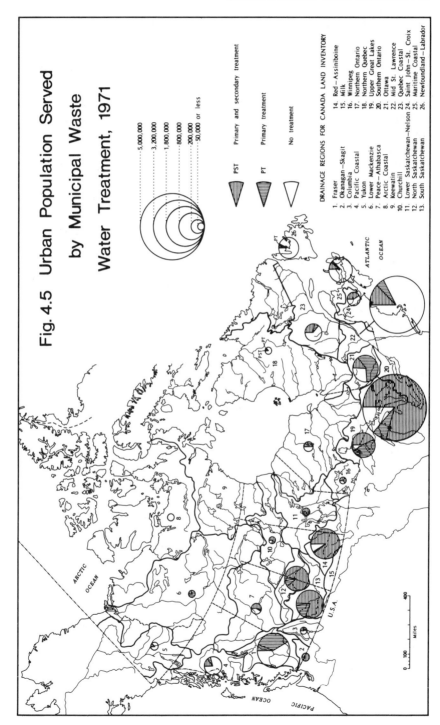

Fig. 4.5 Urban Population Served by Municipal Waste Water Treatment, 1971

5,000,000
3,200,000
1,800,000
800,000
200,000
50,000 or less

PST   Primary and secondary treatment

PT   Primary treatment

No treatment

DRAINAGE REGIONS FOR CANADA LAND INVENTORY

1. Fraser
2. Okanagan—Skagit
3. Columbia
4. Pacific Coastal
5. Yukon
6. Lower Mackenzie
7. Peace—Athabasca
8. Arctic Coastal
9. Keewatin
10. Churchill
11. Lower Saskatchewan—Nelson
12. North Saskatchewan
13. South Saskatchewan
14. Red—Assiniboine
15. Milk
16. Winnipeg
17. Northern Ontario
18. Northern Quebec
19. Upper Great Lakes
20. Southern Ontario
21. Ottawa
22. Mid St. Lawrence
23. Quebec Coastal
24. Saint John—St. Croix
25. Maritime Coastal
26. Newfoundland—Labrador

Subsurface loadings of industrial wastes amount to roughly 1,500 gallons per minute (g.p.m.). Some 31 industrial waste disposal wells located in southern Ontario, Alberta, Saskatchewan and Manitoba receive a variety of industrial wastes, including refinery wastes, potash brine and waste water.[9]

Section 33 of the Federal Fisheries Act provides for the development of national standards of quality in industrial effluent. Regulations have now been issued for the pulp and paper and the chemical industries; others are pending. These are for nationwide and immediate application. The Canada Water Act has a longer term objective of comprehensive water management which allows for the varying characteristics of water bodies and economic activities in developing water quality objectives from region to region. Part II of the Act provides for the establishment of regional Water Quality Management Agencies, but none has yet been established.

The preceding section of this paper, while based on the limited data available, represents a first approximation of Canada's current balance between water supply and use. Water supply has been considered both in terms of average annual run-off and in terms of reliable annual and monthly flows. The overview of water uses has included the consideration both of withdrawals from nature and on non-withdrawal in-channel uses. With respect to the balance of water supplies and withdrawals, it has been illustrated that while from a national viewpoint the reliable supply-withdrawal balance is quite favourable, regional shortages are already a problem in the southern prairies as a result of limited supply and, to a lesser extent, in southern Ontario, and in the Okanagan area of British Columbia as a result of water quality deterioration. The inventory section of this paper has also drawn attention to the increasing use of large dams and diversions in the management of Canada's surface waters and to the growing water quality problems associated with increased waste loading and inadequate treatment facilities. These latter two problems are considered in more detail in subsequent sections of this paper.

There is no doubt that the water inventory overview presented in this paper can be greatly improved upon review by licensing authorities and by water users themselves. The value of a more comprehensive inventory, periodically updated, should be apparent to governments with national and regional responsibilities in water management. Certainly, understanding present patterns is basic to anticipating future needs.

RECENT TRENDS IN CANADIAN WATER MANAGEMENT

A significant constraint on water management activity in Canada is the divided jurisdiction between the federal and provincial governments. To bridge this gap, almost all major water management programmes have involved some degree of federal-provincial cooperation and shared funding. Subsequent sections of this paper deal with the division of jurisdiction between the governments and a discussion of examples of different kinds of water management programmes involving inter-governmental cooperation.

Federal and Provincial Jurisdictions

The basic division of jurisdiction between the federal and provincial governments is set forth in the British North America Act (B.N.A. Act). While the Act does not contain any direct reference to water resources, aspects of water management are included under the various powers assigned to the federal and provincial governments. In discussing the division of jurisdiction with respect to water resources it is important to distinguish between proprietary rights and legislative rights.[10] With the exception of the Northwest Territories and the Yukon, where only the federal government has jurisdiction, the ownership of water and other resources generally falls to the provincial governments. Exceptions exist in the cases of Indian lands, national parks and other federally held territories.

The jurisdictional division with regard to legislative powers is considerably more complex. This division of powers is set out in Sections 91 and 92 of the B.N.A. Act.[11] Section 91 contains a list of 31 classes of matters which are subject to federal legislation; while Section 92 contains a list of 16 classes of matters subject to provincial legislation. Several of the classes of matters assigned to the federal government, including the regulation of Trade and Commerce 91(2), Navigation and Shipping 91(10), Sea Coast and Inland Fisheries 91(12), Indians and Lands Reserved for Indians 91(24), and the Criminal Law 91(27), are of some relevance with respect to water management. Of the classes of matters assigned to the provincial governments, the Management and Sale of Public Lands 92(5), Local Works and Undertakings 92(10), Property and Civil Rights in the Province 92(13), and generally all matters of merely local or private nature in the province 92(16), are of particular relevance to water management. In addition to the specific powers assigned to the federal and provincial governments, Section 91 contains a more general clause which assigns to the federal government responsibility for peace, order and good government. While this clause is generally interpreted to assign the federal government responsibility for all matters not specifically mentioned, there is considerable controversy with respect to the true extent of federal power under this clause. As a result of the rather complex division of legislative power and the proprietary rights of provincial governments, the general control of water resources is with the provincial legislatures, while the federal parliament has specific powers with respect to navigation and fisheries and concurrent interest with regard to agriculture.

A special situation exists in the case of interprovincial waters. The jurisdictional situation in relation to these waters has never been clearly defined and there has been little or no litigation on interprovincial waters. To compound the situation there are no clear answers to the basic questions of which body of law and which courts apply in the case of disputes over interprovincial waters.

In view of the complexity and uncertainty involved in the definition of government jurisdiction over water resources, it is not surprising that Canada is without a clearly stated national water policy. It is not possible to envisage a situation in which one or the other of the senior levels of government is able to undertake a comprehensive management scheme on a major waterway. Rather, all such undertakings must involve cooperative efforts on the part of both the federal and provincial governments. The Canada Water Act, passed by the federal parliament in 1970, provides a basis for agreements between the federal and provincial governments for joint planning and management of water resources on a drainage basin or regional basis where a significant national interest is involved. It must be pointed out that the federal treasury plays a major role in attracting provincial governments into such joint studies. On the other hand, there seem to be some valid questions with respect to such joint undertakings which involve research and planning without any prior commitment with regard to the implementation of findings and recommendations.

RECENT PROGRAMME EXPERIENCE

Table 4.3 has been prepared to summarize federal-provincial water management agreements for the period 1965-1975. The agreements referred to have been divided into four major classes: traditional, comprehensive, water quality and environmental impact. The following discussion centers upon programmes which are representative of each of the four classes identified in the table.

A. Traditional Water Management: The Floodplain

Positive values have long been associated with projects to put Canada's abundant water resources to work for the "self-evident" needs of a young and growing economy. Traditional management may be characterized by: 1. physical supply (as opposed to social demand)-oriented investigations directed by hydrologists and engineers, toward 2. reliance on structures like dams, dykes, locks and generating plants, to fix 3. specific problems or crises on a one-at-a-time basis. Our response to flooding continues to follow this pattern, although other instances of traditional water management are apparent also (Table 4.3).

Floods and flood threats are a recurring problem in Canada. Major disasters struck Vancouver in 1948, Winnipeg in 1950, and Toronto in 1954, but significant damages are experienced every year. The spring 1974 floods in the southern prairies, southwestern Ontario and western Quebec caused an estimated $175 M damage.

Site advantages of the floodplain for habitation and transportation are a matter of historical record. The Saint John, St. Lawrence, Lower Great Lakes, Red, Saskatchewan, Bow and Fraser lowlands support today's urban-industrial concentrations, as well as some of the most productive agricultural enterprises.

Canadian flood control policies and programmes[12] have consisted of two basic kinds of measures; providing, on the one hand, emergency relief, and on the other, reservoirs, dykes and floodways for the respective purposes of compensating and protecting people and their property. Both measures are expensive. Assistance to Winnipegers in 1950 approximated $24M; subsequent protective works included $63M for a floodway to carry the Red River around the city, and $29M for storing and diverting the Assiniboine upstream.

Government has overlooked some of the consequences of these programmes — that communities, below the dams, or behind the dykes, or otherwise compensated, would feel so safe as to rebuild and even itensify their use of the floodplain and, thereby, simply increase the damage potential of the next serious flood. The political pressure upon senior governments for financial assistance to those in distress was great, as was the pressure for control works to visibly reassure the community.

The net effect of this syndrome in the United States has been steadily rising damages from flooding, despite increasing expenditures by construction agencies for flood control.[13] There is little evidence, unless it is the slower pace of economic investment in Canada, to suggest that we are doing any better. Indeed, those programmes which were implemented under the Canada Water Conservation Assistance Act, from 1953 until its repeal in 1970, all focused on flood control works.

Only slowly is the lesson being learned that something must be done about regulating further floodplain occupance or at least forcing those who want to risk losses to bear most of the costs themselves. Under current federal-provincial agreements, dyke construction and reconstruction is underway along the lower Fraser River and on the north shore of Lake Erie, with little consideration being given for alternative measures, and with only minimal financial contribution from local governments (Table 4.3). The crisis atmosphere of each new flood makes it more expedient to promise dollars, dams and dykes.

TABLE 4.3

Federal-Provincial Basin Agreements*

1965-1975

Classi-fication	Location/Title	Period	Total Cost	Purpose	Remarks
	Northern Ontario Water Resources Studies	1965-75	(est.) $6 M	To *investigate water supply* possibilities and costs, including those of diversion elsewhere.	Joint letter of understanding instead of formal agreement; work-sharing
	Nelson River Power Dev't: Phase I (Manitoba)	1966-	(est.) $332 M	To *construct* facilities for developing power potential of Nelson River, including regulation of Lake Winnipeg and diversion of Churchill River.	Canada to build and lease back transmission lines, Manitoba to build storage, diversion and power projects; nearly complete.
	Saskatchewan-Nelson Basin Study (Alta., Sask., Man.)	1967-72	$5 M	To *investigate water supply* potential of basin, including what could be made available by storage and importation.	Costs 50% federal. No counter-part demand study is yet agreed upon.
T R A D I	Red River Valley Communities Dyking (Man.)	1967-72	$2.7 M	To *construct* ring dykes around several communities in floodplain above Winnipeg.	Costs 69% federal. Follows earlier agreements to construct Winnipeg Floodway and Portage Diversion.
T I O N	Fraser River Flood Control (B.C.)	1968-78	$63 M	To *construct* and reconstruct dykes mostly along the lower Fraser flood-plain, and to investigate upstream storage possibilities.	Federal costs will approximate 50%. Original agreement for $36M extended in 1973.
A L	Prairie Provinces Apportion-ment (Alta., Sask., Man.)	1969-	N.A.	To *apportion* eastward-flowing inter-provincial rivers among the three provinces, to reconstitute the Prairie Provs. Water Board as administrator.	50% of Board costs to be paid by federal government.

Southwestern Ontario Dyking	1972-77	$19 M	To *construct* and reconstruct dykes along north shore of Lake Erie for agricultural protection against storm-driven waves.	$2.7 M DREE agreement of 1972 supplemented in 1974 by $16.3 M agreement; costs 45% federal, 45% provincial, 10% local.
Great Lakes Shore Damage Survey (Ontario)	1973-75	$0.7 M	To *survey* high water and storm damage to the erosive shoreline.	Costs 50% federal. Follows high water levels on Lakes.
Okanagan Basin (B.C.)	1969-73	$2 M		Completed; costs 50% federal. Recommended projects accepted. Agreement to be signed in 1976.
Qu'Appelle Basin (Sask., Man.)	1970-73	$0.5 M		Completed; costs 50% federal. Recommended projects accepted. Agreement signed in 1975.
Saint John Basin (New Brunswick)	1970-74	$0.9 M	To *formulate plan(s)* for future management of basin, incorporating all legitimate uses and needs.	Completion date Dec. 1974; costs 90% federal. Emphasis on public participation.
Souris Basin (Sask., Man.)	1974-77	$1.1 M		U.S. Garrison Diversion Project is an external factor with significance for this Canadian study; costs amount to 60% federal
Shubenacadie Basin (Nova Scotia)	1975-77	$0.7M		Lesser of 50% of costs or $365,000 to be assumed federally.
Lower Great Lakes (Ontario)	1971-75	$256 M	To assist financially in construction of sewage *treatment works* ($250 M) and in research ($6 M).	CMHC to accelerate its federal loan arrangements to $167 M. This programme fulfills Canada's commitments to 1972 international agreement on Lakes.
St. Lawrence River (Quebec)	1972-77	$3.9 M	To *assess* water quality and indicate pollution sources.	1972 letter of intent was followed by formal agreement in 1973; costs 50% federal.

COMPREHENSIVE

WATER QUALITY

Lake Winnipeg, Churchill and Nelson Rivers (Man.)	1971-74	$2 M	To *assess* impact of Manitoba Hydro's storage and diversion projects, and recommended mitigation measures.	Followed 1966 agreement for construction (see above). Study too late for influencing major project design. Costs 50% federal.
Peace-Athabasca Delta (Alta., Sask.)	(1) 1971-72 (2) 1974-75	(1) $1.6 M (2) $2M	(1) To *assess* low water conditions and effects in Delta and (2) to *build* weir on Rivière des Rochers as corrective measure.	Followed construction and filling of reservoir behind Bennett Dam in B.C. First agreement was informal, work-sharing; costs 50%+ federal.
James Bay (Quebec)	1971-77	$10 M+	To *assess* environmental concerns and conduct biophysical inventory of region scheduled for hydro-electric and other developments.	Informal work-sharing arrangements in 1971 preceded $10 M agreement of 1972; federal share of latter is 60%.
Churchill River (Sask., Man.)	1973-75	$2.5 M	To *assess* the impacts of alternative proposals for hydroelectric and park developments.	Costs allocated 50% to Canada, 43% to Saskatchewan, 7% to Manitoba.

ENVIRONMENTAL

*Including both studies and implementation programmes after January 1, 1965, but excluding international investigations (IJC) and agreements with the United States; excluding also national financial assistance programmes which are not specific to a basin region, e.g. CMHC loans.

Some alternative possibilities for reducing losses and assigning local responsibility include improved forecasting and warning systems, land use regulation, flood proofing of buildings, and flood insurance. Mapping and reporting publicly upon the risk of occupying urban floodplains is being tested at several locations across Canada, and consideration is being given to withholding housing development approval or damage assistance to communities which fail to heed warnings in high-risk areas. The first visible commitments by government to these newer strategies is only now emerging in the 1975 negotiations toward federal-provincial accords and shared-cost programmes for flood damage reduction.

B. Comprehensive Management: The Exception or the Rule?

Until the later 1960's, most challenges for Canadian water managers were quickly reduced to their physical dimensions, calling for measurement of levels and flows, regulation, storage and diversion by all manner of control works. But water was proving neither an inexhaustible nor an indestructible resource. Values other than economic growth began to assume new importance and a wider range of means to satisfy them were advanced. Planning processes were faced with a need to restore water quality, preserve scenic and historic sites, respect established lifestyles, and generally anticipate tradeoffs among competing resource uses at the least economic, social and environmental cost. Existing legislation and programmes were inadequate to respond to these larger challenges.

About 1967 there began a series of new initiatives designed to make Canadian water management more comprehensive in scope. These included the enactment of new legislation, the reorganization of government agencies, and the enactment of comprehensive intergovernmental basin planning agreements intended to overcome the frustrations of divided jurisdiction and to test means of evaluating the demands of all legitimate interests.

Pilot comprehensive studies were undertaken in the Okanagan (B.C.), Qu'Appelle (Sask.-Manitoba), and Saint John (N.B.) basins immediately preceding, but fully consistent with, the provisions of the Canada Water Act of 1970. Disciplinary contributions to these studies extended beyond hydrology and engineering to tasks in economic forecasting, ecological interrelationships and public participation, directed toward the formulation of a future management plan which considered and mediated among all legitimate interests. By the end of 1974 comprehensive management plans were complete for these three basins. Similar joint planning is now underway on the Souris (Sask.-Manitoba) and is proposed for the Shubenacadie (N.S.) (Table 4.3).

Some of the benefits expected of a comprehensive approach to intergovernmental water planning have been realized. Such an approach is people — rather than water — oriented; it looks to future prospects not simply present problems; it is flexible in that implementation can be phased over time in a manner that allows for changing circumstances. On the negative side, however, it must be admitted that tremendous difficulties have been encountered thus far in mounting and coordinating such diverse investigations and in achieving consensus on management plans. Indeed, the relatively slow pace and supposedly unbiased nature of such planning may make it unattractive in a political milieu where single-issue crises (one year pollution, a second year energy needs, a third year floods) continue to overpower long range considerations.

Whatever the reason, the momentum of a comprehensive water management approach seems to have fallen off recently. Of the plans formulated to date, only the Qu'Appelle Basin plan has been accepted for implementation (1975). An implementation agreement is expected in 1976 for the Okanagan Basin.

C. Water Quality: The Great Lakes

Pollution levels in the air and water around major population centres generated such public alarm in the mid-1960's that they became major national issues around the world. In North America, the number one pollution problem appears to be the Great Lakes. The problem is magnified for Canadians by the much heavier input of wastes from the United States side of the Lakes.

In 1964, the governments of Canada and the United States instructed the International Joint Commission (IJC) to determine the extent and nature of transboundary pollution, and to recommend remedial actions where appropriate for Lakes Erie and Ontario and the international section of the St. Lawrence River. The Commission, in turn, established investigative boards with membership drawn from federal, provincial and state agencies to carry out its charge. Thus began the most intensive scientific investigations into water pollution ever conducted. Six years of study culminated in unanimous findings of serious transboundary pollution as well as recommendations for immediate corrective action on the part of the IJC.[14]

Phophorus in municipal and industrial effluent was identified as the chief culprit causing accelerated eutrophication of the Lower Lakes. The IJC recommended that the phosphorus content in detergents be markedly reduced and that treatment facilities be built, or upgraded, to remove phosphorus from municipal and industrial wastes. Other recommendations included: 1. the establishment of international water quality objectives; 2. contingency planning for oil spills; 3. strengthened surveillance; 4. extension of pollution investigations into the Upper Lakes and into land drainage problems (non-point discharges). Since most of the waste loading was identified as coming from the United States, it was estimated that the cost of the needed treatment facilities would be roughly $120M for Canada and $1,375M for the U.S.

Canada moved immediately to reduce phosphorus content in detergents through provisions (Part III) of the Canada Water Act of 1970. The United States government did not enact similar restrictions, although some states in the Great Lakes drainage basin have done so. Another Canadian initiative was an agreement struck between the federal and Ontario governments in anticipation of international action on the IJC recommendations. The Canada-Ontario Agreement of 1971 on Lower Lakes Water Quality makes $250M available for municipal sewage treatment plants ($167M of which represents an acceleration of federal CMHC loans to municipalities) and $6M for joint research into sewage treatment. This represents Canada's financial commitment to restoring the quality of the Lower Lakes.

A formal international agreement between the two countries followed in April 1972. Canada and the United States agreed on most of the recommendations of the IJC, and set a target date, December 31, 1975, for having construction programmes "completed or in the process of implementation." Progress has been generally satisfactory on the Canadian side. But the impoundment of funds by the U.S. Administration means that implementation of sewage plant construction for many cities, like Detroit, Niagara Falls and Buffalo, will be barely begun (technically meeting the terms of the agreement) by the end of 1975.[15]

Meanwhile, in progress reports on the condition of the affected waters, the IJC has concluded that continued deterioration has apparently been arrested, although there is as yet no valid statistical evidence to suggest that water quality is improving.

D. Environmental Impact:
Hydroelectric Developments on Northern Rivers

Recent examples of provincial hydroelectric development of northern rivers illustrate clearly the conflicting jurisdictional responsibilities and viewpoints of provincial and federal governments, and the increasing importance of environmental impact assessment considerations in planning major water developments. In the discussion which follows, reference is made to three major hydroelectric developments on northern rivers. Each case involves some degree of federal-provincial cooperation; each case has involved a considerable amount of controversy; and in each case, questions have been raised with regard to the true environmental, economic, and sociological consequences of the projects.

The three projects referred to are: the W.A.C. Bennet Dam, which was constructed in British Columbia; the Churchill-Nelson Developments under construction in northern Manitoba; and the recently initiated James Bay Project in northern Quebec.

The W.A.C. Bennett Dam on the Peace River in northwestern British Columbia, constructed by the British Columbia Hydro and Power Authority, was completed in 1967. In the early 1960's, at the time of the initiation of the construction, few doubts were expressed about the benefits of the project. However, recent studies have shown that downstream environmental, economic and sociological impacts have been of major proportions.

The major environmental and related socio-economic impacts of the Bennett Dam have occurred in the Peace-Athabasca Delta, located in northeastern Alberta, a distance of 730 miles downstream from the dam site (Figure 4.6). These impacts have been caused by the modified flow regime of the Peace River, which has resulted from both the reservoir filling activity and the subsequent operation of the dam for hydroelectric power generation.

The delta is characterized by large flat areas of accumulated sediments, active and inactive river channels, several large shallow lakes, and hundreds of shallow perched basins. This delta is one of the largest fresh water deltas and the largest boreal delta in the world. The area has existed in a relatively natural state and has regional, national and international significance. The existence of the delta depended on a rather unique natural hydrologic regime which was altered by the operation of the Bennett Dam. Under natural flow conditions, the late spring and early summer peak levels on the Peace River resulted in a reversal of flow, with water from the Peace River flooding overland in a southerly direction through the delta. This southerly flow from the Peace River, in combination with the flow from the Athabasca River, was of particular importance in providing annual flooding of the delta which replenished water supplies in the perched basins and maintained the levels of the delta lakes, including Lake Athabasca. This natural hydrologic regime was the primary factor accounting for the ecology of the delta. The extreme seasonal and annual fluctuations in water levels were important in maintaining large areas of the delta in early successional stages with respect to plant communities, a most productive situation for wildlife. In recent years, lower than normal water levels have been observed in the Peace-Athabasca Delta and Lake Athabasca as a result of alteration of the natural regime of the Peace River for the purpose of hydroelectric power generation.

In January 1971, in response to growing public concern over the delta situation, the governments of Canada, Alberta, and Saskatchewan established the Peace-Athabasca Delta Project Group to undertake "a

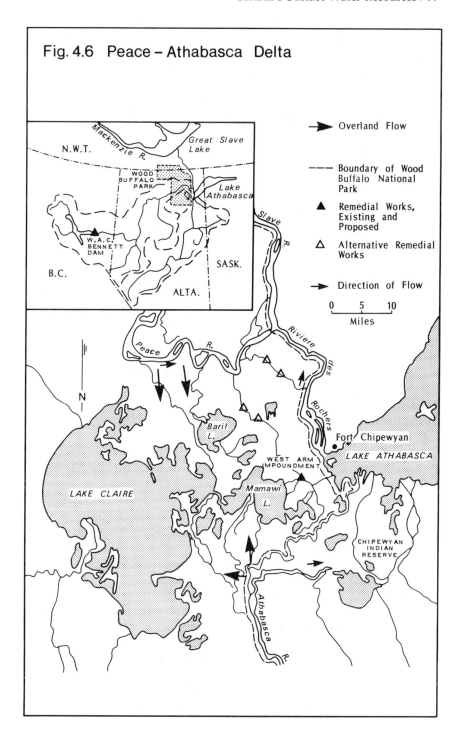

Fig. 4.6 Peace – Athabasca Delta

detailed investigation of the problem of low water levels in Lake Athabasca: their cause and their effect on the delta and upon the local people." During 1971, the Project Group studied means of restoring water levels in order to limit the ecological changes which were taking place. As a result of these initial studies a temporary rockfill dam was constructed on the West Arm of the Chenel des Quartres Fourches. More recently, the Peace-Athabasca Delta Project Group has completed its studies and published two reports.[16] The Project Group concluded that the Bennett Dam has been responsible for hydrologic and ecologic changes in the Peace-Athabasca Delta, and that these changes had adversely affected the fishing and trapping based economy of the native peoples of the area. The Project Group also examined several alternative types and locations of permanent remedial works and recommended that a permanent submerged weir control structure be established at the Little Rapids Site on the Riviere des Rochers to restore water levels in Lake Athabasca and the rest of the delta. The construction of this remedial weir was initiated during the winter of 1974-75.

The construction of the W.A.C. Bennett Dam, and the ensuing problems with respect to environmental, economic and sociological impacts, is a classic case demonstrating the need for a complete project assessment prior to construction. Recognizing the interprovincial nature of the Peace River and the legislative interests of the three provinces and the federal government, the need for close cooperation among the various governments is obvious. There are many lessons to be learned from the Bennett Dam and its wide-ranging impacts. It is reasonable to expect that the experience associated with the unexpected impacts of the Bennett Dam should be applied elsewhere to ensure more complete impact evaluations for future developments.

A second case in which a provincial government agency (Manitoba Hydro) has embarked upon the major development of northern rivers is provided by the hydroelectric projects involving Lake Winnipeg, the Churchill and the Nelson Rivers (Figure 4.7). Public controversy over the proposals was sparked in the late 1960's when Manitoba Hydro applied for a licence to allow the flooding of Southern Indian Lake and Granville Lake to approximately 35 feet above their existing levels, and the diversion of up to 55,000 c.f.s. of Churchill River water, via the Rat and Burntwood Rivers to the Nelson.[17] Public hearings were held and a great deal of concern was voiced about possible environmental damage and the detrimental effects of the project on the natural resources upon which depended the livelihood of the 2,000 native people of the region. Particular concern surrounded the relocation of two Indian communities slated for flooding.[18] In 1970, new plans were announced which involved the regulation of Lake Winnipeg and the diversion of 30,000 c.f.s. from the Churchill to the Nelson Rivers. The regulation of Lake Win-

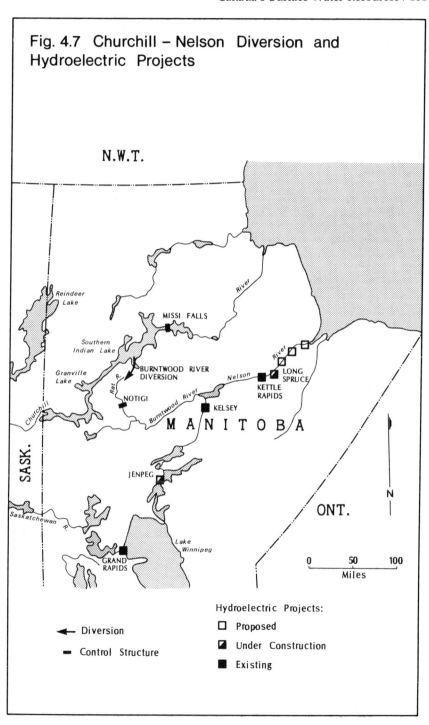

Fig. 4.7 Churchill – Nelson Diversion and Hydroelectric Projects

nipeg for the combined purposes of flood control and hydro production was approved following public hearings, and the JENPEG project was initiated with a projected completion date for the winter of 1974-75. The new proposal for a lower level diversion of the Churchill River into the Nelson had two major advantages; the level of Granville Lake would not be affected, and no communities would be flooded.

In August of 1971, the federal and provincial governments entered into a joint agreement for a study of Lake Winnipeg, the Churchill and the Nelson Rivers. The objective of the study, as stated in the agreement, was to:

> determine the effects that regulation of Lake Winnipeg, diversion from the Churchill River and development of hydroelectric potential of the Churchill River diversion route are likely to have on other water and related resources use and to make recommendations for enhancing the overall benefits with due consideration for the protection of the environment.

The terms of reference for the study include reference to the effects on the water regime, effects on the uses of water and related resources, and social implications. The agreement had a four-year term to 1974, and involved joint federal-provincial financing totalling $2M. The major problem associated with the agreement was that there was no guarantee that Manitoba Hydro would consider the recommendations. The study was intended only as a basis for investigation of possible impacts and not as an input to the basic construction decisions. In May 1973, more than a year before the scheduled completion of the federal-provincial study, the Manitoba government granted an interim licence to Manitoba Hydro permitting the diversion of water from the Churchill to the Nelson River and the impoundment of water on the Rat River and Southern Indian Lake. The major impact questions which had not been answered fully included the probable effects of increasing the flows of the Rat and Burntwood Rivers by as much as 500 percent, the probable effects of flooding on the shoreline and water quality of Southern Indian Lake, the impacts of drastically reduced flows in the downstream portion of the Churchill River, and the resulting economic and social impacts.

From Manitoba Hydro's point of view, the regulation of Lake Winnipeg and the diversion of the Churchill River represent the least cost solution to the problem of supplying the future energy requirements of Manitoba. While the Nelson River was already partially developed for power at the time of the controversy, the Churchill was one of the last free flowing rivers in Manitoba. In a paper entitled "The Destruction of Manitoba's Last Great River" Newbury and Malaher[19] advocate delaying a decision on the Churchill Diversion for several years. These authors calculate that the development of the Nelson River power resources without the Churchill Diversion would result in the production of over 5,000 megawatts of power with costs increased by five to ten percent. This level of power output is sufficient to meet the projected power demands of Manitoba through 1990. Even if the decision were then taken to divert the Churchill, only an additional four to six years of projected growth demands could be satisfied.

In the case of the hydroelectric developments in norther Manitoba, many of the studies necessary to provide a full impact assessment were underway. However, provincial government decisions were such that many of these studies will not be available until construction is well advanced. If adverse impacts are identified some modifications may be undertaken to mitigate damage, but the decisions to go ahead have already been taken.

In 1971, Premier Robert Bourassa of Quebec announced his government's plans for a massive hydroelectric project, involving several major rivers flowing into James Bay in northern Quebec, and the Provincial Legislature of Quebec passed the James Bay Region Development Act (Statutes of Quebec 1971, Chapter 34) establishing the James Bay Development Corporation. The James Bay Development Corporation Territory is an area in excess of 140,000 square miles, including more than 20 percent of the surface area of the Province of Quebec. The hydroelectric development of this region is the responsibility of the James Bay Energy Corporation, which is a subsidiary of the James Bay Development Corporation, and of Hydro Quebec. The initial proposals for hydroelectric power development involved portions of seven major river basins in two separate schemes (Figure 4.8). The southern scheme, The Nottaway-Broadback-Rupert (NBR) scheme, involved the damming and diversion of water from the Nottaway and Broadback Rivers and its transfer into the Rupert River along which seven power plants, with a total generating capacity of over 5,000 megawatts, were to be constructed. The second scheme, the northern or La Grande scheme, involved the damming and diversion of waters from portions of the basins of the Eastmain, the Great Whale (La Grande Baleine), and Caniapiscau Rivers into the La Grande River along which four major power plants with a total generating capacity of over 8,000 megawatts were to be constructed.[20] On the basis of more detailed study of the two schemes, the James Bay Energy Corporation reached the conclusion that the northern, La Grande, scheme was the most attractive, and initial development plans are concentrating on this scheme.

Although the initial political decision to proceed with the James Bay Project was taken by the provincial government without the completion of impact studies, the federal and provincial governments did become involved in joint studies immediately after the passage of the James Bay Region Development Act in July of 1971. In August 1971, an exchange of letters between the Federal Minister of Environment and the Quebec

Minister of Natural Resources established terms of reference for a Joint Federal-Provincial Task Force to make a preliminary evaluation of the potential environmental impacts of the proposed developments. The task force presented its report after only five months of study. This report did not address the question as to whether or not the potential impacts are of great enough significance to require a re-evaluation of the project. In fact, it is stated in the report that:

> It is understood that the decision to proceed has been taken. This report therefore does not reflect any personal or collective reservations held by Task Force Members as to whether society really needs the project, whether there are more economical and less environmentally disturbing ways of harnessing energy resources to meet Quebec's future electric power requirements, or whether society should strive to restrain its electric demands rather than increase its supply. It was assumed that these fundamental questions had been adequately considered by the authorities prior to making their decision to proceed.

There is little evidence available to support this assumption. Much has been written to suggest that few, if any, of these questions have ever been studied in detail. However, taking into account the division of jurisdiction between federal and provincial governments, it is understandable why such an assumption was probably necessary in order to have a Task Force established at all.

The Task Force Report strongly recommended that intensive studies be undertaken of the potentially serious impacts of the project on the native population of the area, and that the James Bay Project be used as a large scale natural laboratory for multi-disciplinary studies of environmental problems. The recommendations of the Task Force were followed in November 1972 by the signing of a formal agreement between the federal government and the James Bay Development Corporation to provide for a four-year biophysical inventory and environmental impact programme in the James Bay Region (Table 4.3). While the scope of the agreement seems to be commendable, a major question remains as to what use will be made of the data collected and studies completed. There is no stipulation in the agreement requiring that comprehensive environmental impact statements be compiled, or that such statements be employed in planning the developments. In view of the divided jurisdiction, it seems to be assumed that such documents will be compiled and considered by the James Bay Development Corporation.

The present situation with regard to the James Bay Project is that a large number of environmental studies are underway concurrently with the first phase of construction. Recent government reports list over 40 separate projects of national, mutual, or provincial interest which are either under consideration, in progress, or completed.[21] It is the hope of the government agencies involved that beyond the initial stages of con-

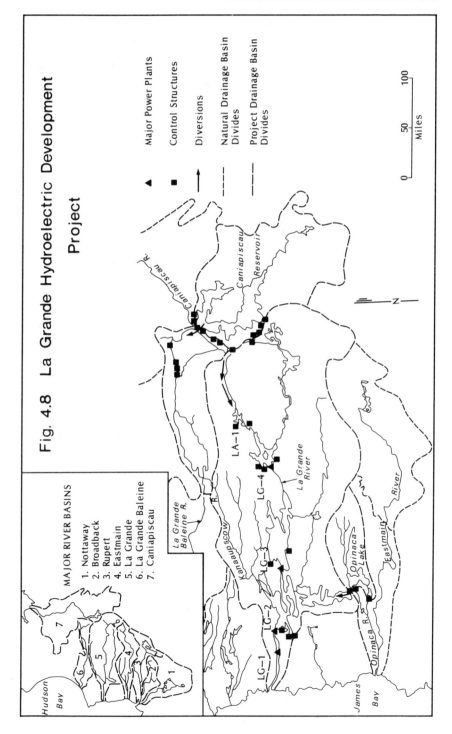

Fig. 4.8 La Grande Hydroelectric Development Project

Major Power Plants
Control Structures
Diversions
Natural Drainage Basin Divides
Project Drainage Basin Divides

0   50   100
Miles

MAJOR RIVER BASINS

1. Nottaway
2. Broadback
3. Rupert
4. Eastmain
5. La Grande
6. La Grande Baleine
7. Caniapiscau

struction which are now underway, the environmental studies will be completed in time to be considered by the James Bay Energy Corporation when decisions are taken on later phases of the project.

While it is beyond the scope of this chapter to detail either the engineering or environmental studies now under way, it is important to recognize the potential implications of these studies. Environmental impact assessments could be compiled, based on the current federal and provincial studies, and these assessments could be available in time to be taken into account at the time of the decisions on the second and third phases of the project. While there are no guarantees that environmental assessments will be completed, at least the necessary data will be available.

The three hydroelectric developments on northern rivers referred to in the preceding discussion illustrate the growing importance of environmental impact assessment. In the case of the Bennett Dam, the impact assessment was carried out after the fact, and remedial measures have been initiated. In the case of the Churchill-Nelson Developments, the impact assessment was initiated prior to construction. However, provincial government policy was such that the decision to proceed was taken prior to the completion of the environmental impact assessment work. In the final case considered, the James Bay Project, the impact assessment programme, while proceeding concurrently with the initial phase of construction, is intended to provide data inputs to the decision making for the subsequent phases of the project.

The importance of environmental impact assessment considerations is obviously increasing, but the problems associated with the division of jurisdiction and lack of uniform policies still place in question the use that will be made of future impact assessments.

NOTES

1. Canada. (1975). *Canada Water Yearbook*. Ottawa: Information Canada.
2. Canada. (1969). *Water* by W.V. Morris, Department of Energy Mines and Resources. Ottawa: Queen's Printer.
3. Bocking, Richard C. (1972). *Canada's Water: For Sale?* Toronto: James, Lewis and Samuel.
4. Canada. (1972a). "Estimates of Current Water Use in Canada." Montreal Engineering Company Limited report for Environment Canada. Ottawa.
   Canada. (1972c). "Water Use in the Canadian Primary Manufacturing Industries," by D.M. Tate, Environment Canada. Ottawa.
   Canada. (1972c). "Water Use in the Canada Primary Manufacturing Industries", by D.M. Tate, Environment Canada. Ottawa.
5. *Ibid.*

6. International Commission on Large Dams, Canadian National Committee. (no date) "1970 Register of Dams in Canada," edited by H.K. Pratt.

7. Canada. (1971a). "Municipal Sewage Disposal — Trends, Problems, Solutions". Unpublished report by G. Seaden, Central Mortgage and Housing Corporation. Ottawa.

8. International Lake Erie and Lake Ontario-St. Lawrence River Water Pollution Boards. (1969). *Report to the International Joint Commission on Pollution of Lake Erie, Lake Ontario and International Section of the St. Lawrence River*. Volume 1. Ottawa and Washington.

9. Canada. (1971b). "Subsurface Disposal of Waste in Canada." *Inland Waters Branch Technical Bulletin No. 49* by R.O. Van Everdingen and R.A. Freeze. Environment Canada. Ottawa.

10. Gibson, D. (1969). "The Constitutional Context of Canadian Water Planning." *Alberta Law Review*, 7(1), 71-92.

11. Hunter, H.D.G. (1971). "Whose Jurisdictions." In *Management of Canada's Water Resources*, Proceedings of a Conference Sponsored by the Association of Consulting Engineers of Canada, the Engineering Institute of Canada and the Canadian Water Resources Association, 48-58.

12. Canada. (1975). *op. cit.*

13. National Academy of Sciences-National Research Council. (1966). *Alternatives in Water Management*. Publication 1408. Washington, D.C.

14. International Lake Erie and Lake Ontario-St. Lawrence River Water Pollution Boards. (1969). *op. cit.*

15. International Joint Commission. (1974). *Second Annual Report on Great Lakes Water Quality*. Ottawa and Washington.

16. Peace-Athabasca Delta Project Group. (1972). *The Peace-Athabasca – A Canadian Resource: Summary Report on Low Water Levels in Lake Athabasca and their Effects on the Peace-Athabasca Delta*.
Peace-Athabasca Delta Project Group. (1973). *The Peace-Athabasca Delta Project: Technical Report on Low Water Levels in Lake Athabasca and their Effects on the Peace-Athabasca Delta*.

17. Manitoba Hydro Task Force. (1970). *Report on Expansion of Generating Capacity in Manitoba*. Winnipeg.

18. Mudry, N. (1973). "Changing Attitudes in Water Resources Development in the Province of Manitoba." *Water Resources Bulletin*, 9(3), 607-12.

19. Newbury, R. and Malaher, G.W. (1973). *The Destruction of Manitoba's Last Great River*, Canadian Nature Federation Special Publication No. 2.

20. James Bay Development Corporation. (1972). *Development of the James Bay Region*. Montreal.

21. James Bay Development Corporation-Environment Canada. (1974). *Environmental Studies (1973). James Bay Territory and Surrounding Area*.

5

Hydrogeology and Groundwater Resource Evaluation and Conservation in Canada

M.L. Parsons, Engineering Division, Canadian International Development Agency, Ottawa

"Subsurface space" consists of the voids between rock particles, fissures and solution cavities which are found in the earth's crust. Because the fluids that normally occupy such space are compressible, man is able to exploit subsurface space for a variety of purposes, including the recovery of groundwater as well as the artificial storage of water and other fluids.

Subsurface space can therefore be viewed as a resource, requiring for its proper management and adequate conservation a knowledge of the geological framework, the physical properties of the permeable medium through which fluid, mass and heat transfer occur and the dynamic processes involved in such transfer. Within the broad context of subsurface space hydrogeology deals specifically with the character, source and mode of occurrence of water, the lower limit of which is taken at the depth where the combined effect of temperature and pressure no longer permits the existence of water in the liquid phase. This depth consistently exceeds 30,000 feet.

Some appreciation of the volumetric significance of subsurface space, particularly that component of it which stores fresh groundwater resources, can be gained by considering the distribution in the hydrological cycle of the world's fresh water, estimated to be 2.5 percent or about eight million cubic miles of the total 326 million cubic miles of water. Of the eight million cubic miles nearly seven million are stored in the polar ice caps and glaciers, leaving something over one million cubic miles of fresh water for man's use and conservation. This amount may be further subdivided, according to Prince,[1] as follows:

fresh recoverable groundwater	1,000,000 cubic miles
fresh water lakes	30,000 cubic miles
atmospheric water	3,300 cubic miles
river water	300 cubic miles

These data indicate that subsurface space is indeed vast, and that groundwater, on a volumetric basis, constitutes the bulk of man's fresh water resources. Fortunately, groundwater is widely available to man almost everywhere at relatively low cost with the application of fairly simple digging or drilling technology. The subsurface provides an immense storage reservoir which, as a source of water supply, is generally less susceptible than surface storage to the effects of drought and pollution, provided that development is based on adequate hydrogeological information and appropriate well construction techniques. Thus, properly developed groundwater supplies are not only able to withstand fairly prolonged periods of little or no recharge, but are also able to meet extreme production demands over relatively prolonged periods of some months, if such a contingency is allowed for in well field and water system design.

Canada's groundwater resources, at least those that are currently exploited, lie chiefly within 1,000 feet of the earth's surface and it is in relation to this zone that this chapter will attempt to:

1. outline the hydrogeological framework of groundwater, its quality and the extent to which exploratory and evaluation work has progressed in Canada;
2. discuss briefly the approach toward groundwater evaluation and development, illustrating the diversity of hydrogeological, managerial and environmental aspects; and
3. discuss the environmental implications of waste disposal and other of man's activities in relation to groundwater conservation.

GROUNDWATER OCCURRENCE

The Groundwater Flow System

Hydrology has as one of its fundamental hypotheses the continuity of the hydrologic cycle, the subsurface component of which is a flow system involving both soil moisture and groundwater movement. Soil moisture occurs in the near-surface unsaturated zone where the pore space is filled partly by liquid and partly by vapour. Groundwater, by definition, occurs in the saturated zone, the top of which is taken as the phreatic surface (or water table) where the hydrostatic pressure of the groundwater is equivalent to atmospheric pressure. The groundwater flow system is taken normally to include the movement below the phreatic surface, where water moves through the geological materials from regions in the system having high potential energy to regions of relatively low potential energy. Movement occurs through the interstices between rock particles (sand grains, for example), along rock con-

duits or fissures, commonly developed along planes of structural weak-
ness such as joints, and through caverns or channels developed by
dissolution processes in carbonate rocks. The theory of groundwater
flow, being physically analogous to heat flow and to flow of electricity, is
rather well known, and is fundamentally based on Darcy's Law and the
law of conservation of mass. Hubbert[2] is widely credited with having
developed the theory of regional groundwater movement, in which he
visualized recharge of meteoric water to the groundwater flow system as
occurring in topographically high areas and discharge toward the earth's
surface in topographically low areas (Figure 5.1).

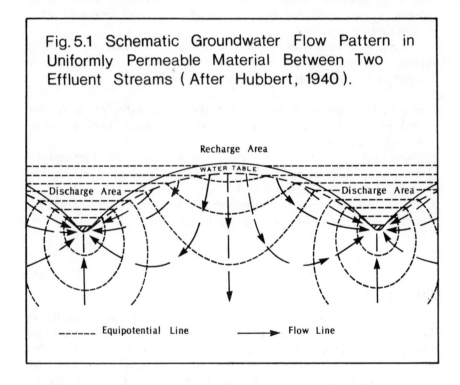

Fig. 5.1 Schematic Groundwater Flow Pattern in
Uniformly Permeable Material Between Two
Effluent Streams (After Hubbert, 1940).

The nature of the groundwater flow system is dependent on a combination of climatic, geomorphological and geological factors: rates and
amounts of precipitation and evapotranspiration, which effect soil moisture and therefore recharge to and discharge from the flow system;
topographic configuration, which, under certain climatic conditions, influences the shape of the phreatic surface and thus the distribution of
potential energy in the system; the overall composition and geometry of

geological materials and the kind and distribution of porous and permeable rocks such as sand and gravel, fissured rock and cavernous carbonate strata, which govern the occurrence of groundwater and its ultimate recoverability.

Surface manifestations of groundwater flow systems and particularly of discharge take on a variety of forms: seepage to the surface in the form of springs, some of which are associated with mineral deposition and quicksand; formation of saline soils, particularly in the Interior Plains; stream baseflow, which is often more highly mineralized than flow during the higher runoff seasons; saline lakes and differences in salinities of lakes in recharge and discharge areas; growth of phreatophytic (water-seeking) and halophytic (salt-tolerant) vegetation; growth of certain brackish water-loving shellfish in discharge areas along coastal regions in the Maritime Provinces; and peculiar features in the Arctic, such as pingos, together with unusual winter river phenomena, such as icings and open stretches of water. Thus, hydrologic continuity exists between man's surface environment and subsurface space. Awareness and understanding of this continuity is fundamental to groundwater conservation and protection.

Bedrock Aquifers — An Unknown Quantity

Most of the bedrock of Canada remains virtually unexplored in terms of its potential for groundwater resources, although certain strata constitute aquifers which provide municipal and industrial water supplies, while others are not prospective for groundwater purposes. For example, the Canadian Shield bedrock consists of fissured igneous (largely granite), metamorphic and some sedimentary rock, all of which generally lack favourable properties of porosity and permeability normally associated with large groundwater resource development. However, the fissure permeability of Shield bedrock is adequate nearly everywhere for domestic water supply. Similar prospects apply to the folded and faulted bedrock of the Appalachian and Cordilleran belts. On the other hand, the undisturbed portions of sedimentary basins, including the Carboniferous basin underlying a large part of the Maritime Provinces, the Palaeozoic basin of the St. Lawrence Lowlands and the sedimentary basin underlying the Interior Plains contain productive aquifers, but remain largely unexplored in terms of their overall groundwater potential. In most regions of Canada the bedrock is mantled by glacial drift containing aquifer materials. Thus, the lack of hydrogeological exploration of the bedrock is due to some extent to the presence of more accessible and generally more productive drift aquifers.

The best known bedrock aquifers of the maritimes occur in the flat-lying Permian-Pennsylvanian strata which underlie Prince Edward

Island, much of New Brunswick and part of Nova Scotia, and in the Triassic Wolfville Formation underlying the Annapolis-Cornwallis Valley of Nova Scotia. Fissured sandstones in New Brunswick and Prince Edward Island provide large municipal water supplies for communities such as Summerside and Charlottetown, Prince Edward Island and Shippegan and Chatham, New Brunswick. However, little is known of the groundwater potential of the Carboniferous basin as a whole which, for example, includes the Boss Point Formation known to be the source of spring and well discharges of the order of a million imperial gallons per day (igpd). Good water-bearing strata may be penetrated almost anywhere within the boundaries of the Wolfville Formation, which in contrast to other bedrock aquifers in the Appalachian region, owes its permeability largely to intergranular pore space and only secondarily to fissures. Wells 200 to 400 feet deep in the formation commonly produce 100 thousand and as much as one million igpd.

Elsewhere in the Appalachian region, hydrogeological exploration and evaluation, to date lacking for example in all of Newfoundland, could lead to the discovery of carbonate aquifers in the Great Northern Peninsula of Newfoundland where karst features have been observed, and in the Gaspé where reports of appreciable porosity and permeability in lower Palaeozoic sedimentary rocks[3] would indicate the presence of substantial groundwater resources.

The plains-like St. Lawrence Lowlands, for the most part, are underlain by unfolded Palaeozoic sedimentary strata, in places containing abundant groundwater resources. Cambrian sandstone and Ordovician, Silurian and Devonian carbonate strata have permeability due largely to the presence of fissures along joints and bedding planes. Certain of the carbonate rocks also contain organic reef structures and solution caverns, and where these are combined with good fissure development, the strata create highly permeable and productive aquifers. For example, wells penetrating Ordovician-Silurian strata in southwestern Ontario yield on the order of one million igpd[4], while in the Montreal area wells producing from Cambrian strata yield 100 to 700 thousand igpd[5] and from Ordovician strata as much as 1.5 million igpd. Such high yields are exceptional in that average well yields from most bedrock strata are less than 30 thousand igpd.[6] It should be noted, of course, that reported well yields, rather than reflecting groundwater potential, represent to a large degree water demands by the consumer. The exploration for and discovery of groundwater supplies to meet these demands has generally been a trial-and-error process rather than one of systematic hydrogeological analysis seeking bedrock conditions favourable to groundwater development.

The Interior Plains are underlain by a thick sequence of undeformed low-dipping strata of lower Palaeozoic to Tertiary age. Groundwater in

Lower Cretaceous and older strata is normally too saline, ranging as high as 300,000 parts per million (ppm) of total dissolved solids (tds), to be of significance as a water resource. However, a tds of less than 5,000 ppm may occur in these strata where they are sufficiently close to the earth's surface to be influenced by recharge of fresh water. Such favourable areas occur along the subcrop belts of the Rocky Mountain Foothills and adjacent to the Precambrian Shield. In the latter belt, for example, Render[7] noted that groundwater has been obtained from an Ordovician carbonate aquifer underlying the Winnipeg area for more than 130 years and currently yields 3 billion gallons of water annually, largely for the purposes of commercial cooling. On a broader scale, vast subcrop areas of Palaeozoic and Lower Cretaceous strata adjacent to the Shield and extending through central Manitoba and north central Saskatchewan have only recently been recognized for their groundwater resources potential,[8] the evaluation of which awaits hydrogeological investigation.

Upper Cretaceous and Tertiary strata, chiefly interbedded shale and poorly consolidated sandstone formations, comprise most of the bedrock subcrop in the region. The best bedrock aquifer potential of the Interior Plains is in Alberta where the extensive sandstone sequences (Milk River sandstone; Belly River, Upper Bearpaw, Paskapoo and Edmonton Formations) are thickest and most permeable. The thickness and permeability of these strata diminish eastward into Saskatchewan and accordingly become relatively poorer as aquifers. Nevertheless, these aquifers are sufficiently productive over a broad expanse of the prairies to meet most domestic water requirements, whereas wells in the Paskapoo and parts of other formations in Alberta may yield on the order of 100 thousand igpd, which is adequate for many municipal requirements.

Little or no groundwater is produced from the bedrock of the Cordilleran region, although evidence of groundwater movement in the bedrock and of aquifer occurrence exists in the form of the well known springs in the southern Rocky Mountains and discharge into mine workings. In addition, the plateau volcanic rocks in British Columbia's interior are potential aquifers, being recharged by snow melt and discharged by springs occurring at the base of ancient lava flows. This spring discharge maintains the flow of many streams during the drier seasons. Perhaps the best potential for groundwater development is in western Alberta where two high-yield aquifers in Palaeozoic carbonate strata have been reported.[9]

Drift Aquifers — The Focus of Development

Nearly all of Canada was glaciated during Pleistocene time resulting in scouring and erosion of the pre-glacial erosional surface, and the subsequent deposition, chiefly during the deglaciation phase, of drift comprised of unconsolidated deposits of till, boulders, sand, gravel and lacustrine clay. The preponderance of till, a relatively impermeable material, in the unconsolidated deposits is often cited as an indication of low groundwater resource potential, while, on the other hand, outwash materials in the form of numerous and often sizeable deposits of sand and gravel provide excellent water-bearing strata. In the Prairie Provinces where the hydrogeology of surficial deposits is well known, alluvial fans at the mouths of meltwater channels and beach deposits of former glacial lakes comprise some of the better aquifers. In general, high-yielding aquifers occur as inter-till sand and gravel beds or as blanket sands, the former preserved discontinuously at the interface between tills representing successive glaciations, and the latter as laterally extensive and continuous strata reaching a thickness of as much as 100 feet.

Outwash sands and gravels in the form of kames, eskers and deltas provide significant aquifers in Ontario, notably north of Lake Ontario where the confluence of two main glacial lobes is marked by an extensive elongate kame moraine. Similar deposits near London form an aquifer which, during the period of 1959 to 1967, provided the water supply averaging 2.6 million igpd to that city[10].

In the St. Lawrence Lowlands of Quebec, aquifer occurrence is related primarily to deposits associated with the marine advance and eventual drainage of the Champlain Sea which existed in post-glacial time. Sand, gravel and boulders deposited as beaches during the advance of the sea are preserved largely in bedrock depressions and are underlain by extensive marine clay strata which accumulated on the sea bed. The ancient beach deposits yield as much as 150 thousand igpd to wells. The process of drainage of the Champlain Sea resulted in terrace and alluvial sand deposition and these sands constitute some of the best aquifers in the St. Lawrence Lowlands, supplying up to 1.5 million igpd for municipal water supply purposes.

The valleys of the Appalachian and Cordilleran regions, during the deglaciation, served as "sinks" of sand and gravel deposition which resulted in the build-up of vast thicknesses of permeable materials, in places interbedded with tills as a result of successive glacial retreats and advances. These deposits, some only local in extent, others very extensive, have very large groundwater development potential, particularly where coincident geographically with high precipitation. Production from such aquifers in the Annapolis-Cornwallis Valley for example may amount to millions of gallons per day.[11]

One of the most critical areas of groundwater development requiring careful conservation and management, in view of the heavy demands for agricultural, municipal and industrial purposes, is the Fraser River's humid coastal lowland extending 100 miles from Hope to Vancouver. The lowland is made up of relatively flat-topped uplands and flat-bottomed valleys, and is underlain by unconsolidated deposits commonly more than 600 and as much as 1,800 feet in thickness. These deposits constitute a layered aquifer system with the permeable strata including, in addition to surficial sand and gravel, an outwash sand and gravel unit confined between clay units and a fluvial sand and gravel unit confined beneath till. Flowing artesian conditions exist in the confined aquifers from which wells produce as much as 300 thousand igpd; the unconfined surficial aquifers provide municipal, industrial and irrigation water supplies at rates as high as 1.5 million igpd from depths of only 50 to 125 feet.

Valley-centred, highly permeable aquifers, such as the foregoing, have a strong influence on stream flow, and indeed a large percentage of stream flow is derived directly from groundwater discharge. In an opposite sense, when heavily exploited such aquifers may simply serve as conduits through which river water is induced to flow toward the well intake. Clearly, in such cases it is particularly important for water management purposes to understand the total aquifer system, including not only the hydraulic relationships amongst the various hydrogeological units, but also the hydrologic relationship between the groundwater and the surface water.

Permafrost — A New Challenge

A unique hydrogeological feature of Canada's northern region is the presence of permanently frozen ground — or permafrost, which occurs discontinuously in the southerly sub-arctic and more or less continuously in the more northerly colder environment. Although there has been little need for development of groundwater resources in this sparsely populated region, recent proposals for highway and pipeline construction have prompted considerable study of permafrost conditions and the groundwater regime. These studies, coupled with petroleum exploration drilling, have indicated significant occurrences of groundwater in some of the carbonate strata of the Interior Plains and in the unconsolidated outwash deposits and deltaic sands in the Mackenzie Lowlands.

Visible evidence of groundwater flow in permafrost regions includes springs, open-water reaches in otherwise frozen rivers and halophytic vegetation. Conical iceforms, known as pingos, numbering in the hundreds in the central Yukon Plateau, are thought to originate at points of perennial groundwater discharge. Large springs discharging into certain rivers in the Yukon and Alaska maintain open water during the winter and are important as spawning grounds for certain species of anadromous fish.

Frozen ground has a relatively small but finite permeability and thus acts as a confining layer which tends to retard groundwater movement. Thus, its distribution has a dominating influence on flow patterns and rates of groundwater movement. For descriptive purposes, groundwater is classified as suprapermafrost, intrapermafrost and subpermafrost[12]. Suprapermafrost water is seasonal in occurrence due to thawing within a few feet of the earth's surface, and is exploited by shallow dug wells during the summer. Intrapermafrost groundwater occurs in thawed zones in the permafrost, perhaps due to high salinity or high flow rates which prevent freezing. Such zones commonly occur in alluvium near rivers, in abandoned river channels, or in association with surface water bodies, and are important as sources of water supply for communities such as Mayo in the Yukon and Hay River in the Northwest Territories. Subpermafrost groundwater occurs beneath the confining permanently frozen layer and is often under high pressure which may result in flowing artesian conditions when wells penetrate through the permafrost.

Thus, the challenge of northern development has brought with it a new challenge in Canadian hydrogeology — one which calls for a full understanding of the groundwater-permafrost regime and its relationship with surface phenomena and the environment.

GROUNDWATER QUALITY

Groundwater begins to acquire its particular chemical character at the recharge end of the flow system when meteoric water first infiltrates the soil and dissolution of the soluble soil components (mainly carbonate and sulphate minerals) occurs. As water moves along its flow path through the solid medium, chemical processes taking place tend to alter the constituents in type and amount depending on a variety of factors such as the compositional changes of the solid medium, the rate of flow and the length of path traversed by the groundwater.

Chebotarev[13] determined, for example, that between the "water divide" (recharge area) and the "erosion basis" (discharge area) the following chemical sequence along the path of flow can be distinguished; bicarbonate water (HCO_3-), sulphate water (SO_4=) and chloride water (c_2-). Chebotarev explained that while the least soluble salts are precipitated first and the most soluble salts last, at any given time and distance from the recharge area the chemical components of higher solubility will be found in water in greater relative abundance.

Chebotarev's rule, coupled with concepts of regional groundwater flow systems, has provided a theoretical framework within which groundwater has been intensively examined in the Interior Plains, where quality is often critical in development of water supplies. Perhaps the most intensive quality study of any province was done in Saskatchewan by Rutherford[14], who defined the major chemical types of groundwater throughout the province's sedimentary basin. He attributed the ionic composition to processes of dissolution of carbonate minerals and gypsum in the soil and sodium chloride in sedimentary rocks. Cation exchange, in which sodium ions in clay minerals are replaced by calcium and/or magnesium ions, results in "softening" of the groundwater, while sulphate reduction in coal deposits results in further chemical modification. Rutherford was thus able to map, on a broad scale, groundwater quality zones characterized by various vertical water quality sequences, and to relate the zones more to specific geological environments rather than to flow systems. Although similar hydrochemical characteristics exist in Alberta and Manitoba, it is noteworthy that high-yield aquifers[15] in Alberta and Manitoba generally contain less than 2,000 ppm, whereas aquifers in Saskatchewan tend to have higher ionic concentrations ranging up to, and in some cases exceeding, 3,000 ppm.

Such large scale regional variations may reflect climatic contrasts, in that the quantity of groundwater recharge under arid climatic conditions, as a general rule, is small in comparison to recharge under humid conditions. Consequently residence times of groundwater in arid zones tend to be longer, leading to greater dissolution. For example Meyboom[16] observed that while Interior Plains areas, with a total annual precipitation of more than 18 inches, have moderately mineralized (less than 1,000 ppm) groundwater of a bicarbonate type, areas with less than 16 inches precipitation have poorer quality groundwater (1,000 to 2,500 ppm) of a sulphate type.

The more humid hydrogeological regions of Canada with few exceptions have significantly better quality groundwater than the arid Interior Plains. The total dissolved solids of Appalachian groundwater normally amount to a few tens to a few hundreds of ppm's, although there are often local quality problems such as excessive concentrations of iron, manganese and sulphate thought to be derived from rocks of pre-Carboniferous age, and high concentrations of calcium sulphate and sodium chloride derived from evaporite rocks of Mississippian age. In addition, development of groundwater supplies in the coastal zone must take cognizance of saline groundwater, which normally occurs beneath and adjacent to the seabed, and which can be induced to move inland into freshwater aquifers in response to excessive pumping of water wells.

Groundwater throughout the St. Lawrence Lowlands is generally of good quality, containing a few hundred ppm of total dissolved solids with the chemical composition strongly reflecting the bedrock chemistry. Hence calcium and magnesium bicarbonate water is found in limestone and dolomite aquifers, sulphate water in association with the gypsiferous strata of Upper Silurian age and sodium bicarbonate water with hydrogen sulphide in black shale. Groundwater associated with Champlain Sea sedimentation often contains high concentrations of sodium chloride which is leached from the marine clay.

In the Cordilleran region the relatively high permeability of hydrogeological materials coupled with the high precipitation and therefore available recharge results in low concentrations of dissolved mineral constituents in the groundwater. For example, groundwater of the Fraser River lowland commonly has less than 100 ppm of total dissolved solids whereas the high-yield aquifers of western Alberta have generally less than 400 ppm.

Thus, groundwater in Canada is of relatively good quality in most areas and suitable for a variety of domestic, agricultural, municipal and industrial purposes. A base of hydrochemical information is being established to guide the development of the good quality water while avoiding sources of poorer water. Poorer quality groundwater such as the brackish water found in many of the Cretaceous strata underlying the Interior Plains may become useful in the future when the costs of treatment processes, including desalinization, become more economical.

GROUNDWATER EVALUATION AND DEVELOPMENT

Although it would be difficult if not impossible to put forward a single universally acceptable approach toward evaluating and developing groundwater resources, there are a number of major activities which are prerequisite to providing the basic information for good groundwater management. Let us attempt to outline these activities briefly and in the order in which they would, in general, apply in many practical cases.

1. Determination of the hydrogeological framework on a regional scale and evaluation of the groundwater flow system;
2. Assessment of the hydrometeorological characteristics, including precipitation, runoff and evaporation, influencing recharge to and discharge form the groundwater flow system;
3. Determination of water quality and the hydrologic properties of the geological units comprising the system, and identification of favourable aquifer materials;
4. Prediction, by means of modelling or other suitable methods, of the response of the hydrogeological system to water withdrawal over the long term;
5. Assessment of the sustainable yield of the system. (The sustainable yield (safe yield) of a hydrogeological system, although not precisely defined in the scientific literature, generally refers to the maximum

groundwater withdrawal rate that can be achieved without either significantly depleting the groundwater resource or deteriorating its quality over time and without leading to alteration of the system's hydrologic properties such that the potential for water production would be significantly diminished. Evidently, over the long term, the sustainable yield would be a rate of production not exceeding the rate of recharge to the system. Evaluation of the sustainable yield is an ultimate objective of the investigation of groundwater resources and is fundamental to their management and conservation. Nevertheless, the sustainable yield has been estimated for only a few areas in Canada, for there are only a few where adequate data are available for this purpose.)

6. Identification of environmental, economic and managerial factors relevant to groundwater development;
7. Design and implementation of a production well programme based on appropriate aquifer testing and a knowledge of water demand;
8. Provision for long term observation of the response of the hydrogeological system as reflected in piezometric (water-pressure) measurements and water quality analyses to insure that groundwater withdrawal rates are within the limits of the sustainable yield and in harmony with environmental and management factors.

Of the foregoing, the first five points would comprise the evaluation phase of groundwater resource management, whereas, the last three points would pertain to the development phase.

For illustrative purposes let us briefly examine the application of these activities in practice by comparing two distinctly different cases of groundwater evaluation and development, namely those of Shippegan, a community situated on Taylor Island, New Brunswick[17] and Regina, Saskatchewan.[18]

A Comparative Study

Groundwater usage by both Shippegan and Regina preceeded by many years the comprehensive groundwater studies noted above, the undertaking of which was motivated by the emergence of a water quality problem in the case of Shippegan and a water shortage problem in the case of Regina. Shippegan's proximity to the sea, coupled with heavy well pumping, resulted in the intrusion of saline water into the fresh water aquifer underlying the community. Regina, on the other hand, required additional water to meet peak demands on its system and groundwater proved to be the most economical source of supply.

The two cases differ substantively in most respects. Table 5.1 summarizes the major features of each case for the purpose of comparison.

TABLE 5.1

Comparison of Hydrogeological Systems and Groundwater Development of Taylor Island, New Brunswick and Regina, Saskatchewan

FACTOR	TAYLOR ISLAND (Community of Shippegan)	REGINA AREA
Physiography	— Small peninsula with topographic relief of only 14 feet.	— Broad plain of glacio-lacustrine origin with relief of 330 feet.
Hydrogeology	— Interbedded sandstone and mudstone with thin mantle of glacial drift.	— Glacial complex of till, clay, sand and gravel underlain by bedrock at depth of 100-400 feet
	— Fissure permeability.	— Intergranular permeability.
Hydrometeor-ology	— Humid climate with 39.8 inches mean annual precipitation and 39.2°F mean annual temperature.	— Semi-arid climate with 14.8 inches mean annual precipitation and 35°F mean annual temperature.
	— 9 frost-free months.	— 5 frost-free months.
	— Surface runoff negligible due to high rates of infiltration and evaporation.	— Surface runoff mainly during snow-melt period; otherwise minimal due to evaporation.
Groundwater flow system	— Confined essentially to peninsula; recharge throughout most of the year with maximum rates in spring and fall and totalling about 50 percent of annual precipitation; natural discharge to the sea.	— Regional in extent covering as much as 1,400 square miles; periodic recharge amounting on average to less than one percent of precipitation; natural discharge to topographic lows, mainly to stream valleys.

Water quality	— Fresh groundwater normally 200 ppm total dissolved solids with less than 30 ppm chloride; saline groundwater varying to greater than 10 thousand ppm. — Acidic peat bog water.	— Normal range in total dissolved solids is 800 to 2,000 ppm, being low in chloride content and high in sulphate and bicarbonate and therefore "hard".
Sustainable yield	— Fresh water: 750,000+ igpd. — Saline water: 3+ million igpd.	— 27 million igpd from total hydro-geological system which includes 4 major aquifers.
Water use	— Fresh water for municipal purposes; fresh and saline water for industrial purposes. — 1980 demand for fresh groundwater projected at 272 million gallons; current production capacity for saline water 3 million igpd.	— Fresh groundwater supplements surface water supply for municipal and industrial purposes. — Current groundwater use is 8 million igpd.
Environmental Aspects	— Saline water intrusion from the sea due to local over-production. — Presence of acidic peat bogs which contribute poor quality water to groundwater regimen. — Local nitrate contamination from industrial effluent and domestic septic tanks. — Lack of adequate solid waste management may lead to contamination of unconfined aquifers.	— Groundwater withdrawal modifies stream regimes in the Regina area, creating an influent condition in Boggy Creek and interfering with natural discharge to Waskana Creek. — Possibility of nitrate contamination from agricultural sources. — Sand and gravel exploitation and aquifer preservation may require rationalization.

Management Aspects	— High cost of pipeline construction to well field distant from users. — Need for centralized control of groundwater development, particularly by individual consumers. — Requirement for surface reservoir (supplied by fresh groundwater) to meet peak demands and to permit fresh groundwater withdrawal at constant rate.	— Economical (within limits) to use groundwater to maximum possible extent because both initial capital expenditure and operating costs are lower for groundwater than for surface water. — Need for centralized control of development. — Use of groundwater to augment base load and to meet peak loads because of immense storage capacity of aquifers. — Existing well fields in each of four major aquifers and within 15 mile radius of city.
Well field development	— Newly developed well field with coordinated pumping of both fresh and saline groundwater to stabilize fresh-saline interface in the subsurface.	— Same.
Monitoring	— Observation of piezometric fluctuations to monitor recharge, seasonal decline and effects of pumping. — Water quality analysis to detect any increase in chloride content and other constituents that may derive from sources of pollution.	

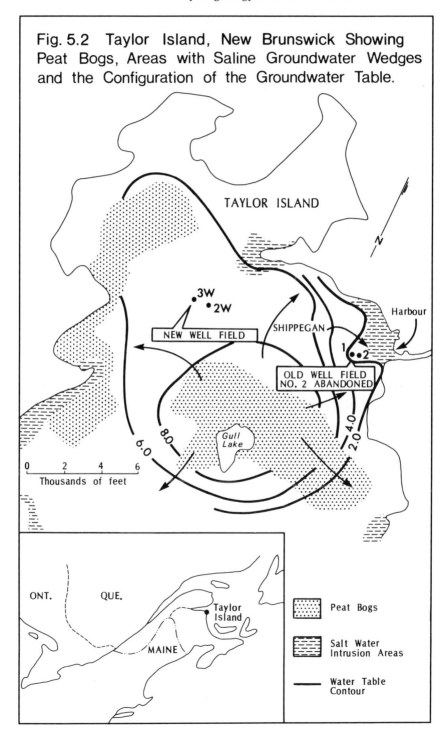

Fig. 5.2 Taylor Island, New Brunswick Showing Peat Bogs, Areas with Saline Groundwater Wedges and the Configuration of the Groundwater Table.

The hydrogeological system of Taylor Island (Figure 5.2) is bounded at depth by a fresh-saline groundwater interface, and of course laterally by the sea. The major hydrogeological constraint, aside from the presence of saline water, derives from the small area and topographic relief of the island, and thus limited groundwater storage of the system.

As a result of this problem, comprehensive studies summarized by Andrew and Rigney[19] indicated that groundwater development on Taylor Island, notwithstanding critical hydrogeological constraints, was the only economical means of providing water, and that the Island's resources were adequate to meet Shippegan's 1980 fresh water demands estimated to be 272 million gallons annually. The annual production was to be distributed monthly (Figure 5.3) to account for variations in seasonal recharge to the groundwater regime. It is noteworthy that the study also recommended that certain industrial demands and in so doing contributed to stabilizing the further intrusion of saline water into the fresh groundwater.

Factors which influenced the siting of the new well field for fresh groundwater (Figure 5.2) included the superior hydrologic properties of the unconfined aquifer underlying the locale, and the need to locate as

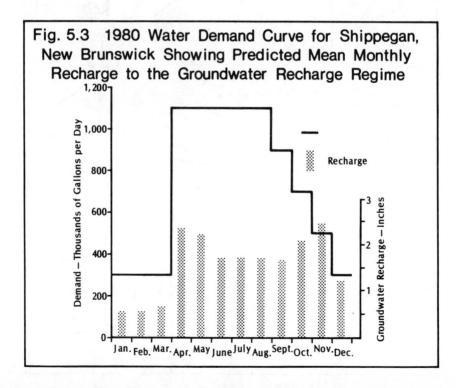

Fig. 5.3 1980 Water Demand Curve for Shippegan, New Brunswick Showing Predicted Mean Monthly Recharge to the Groundwater Recharge Regime

far as possible from the sea to prevent saline water intrusion and from the peat bogs, which are sources of poor quality acidic water. Counter-balancing these hydrogeological factors were pipeline construction costs which increase in proportion to the distance between wells and consumers.

The areas of new well installation are equipped with a network of observation wells for long term monitoring of piezometric levels as well as water quality. Water quality is obviously of prime concern with respect to sea water intrusion, but also with respect to contamination from surface sources, particularly in view of the unconfined nature of the aquifer in the area of the new well field. The significance of this aspect was clearly underlined in April, 1970, a few months after the first new well was placed into production, by an accidental spillage of 600 to 1,200 gallons of fuel a mere 1,500 feet from the well. Emergency measures to clean up the spill and to prevent phenols from infiltrating the aquifer, including a year-long cessation of pumping, are credited with preventing serious and possibly irreparable contamination of the groundwater supply.

In contrast to Shippegan, the siting of Regina, despite the aridity of the climate, was indeed fortuitous with respect to groundwater resources. The hydrogeological system is vast in extent being centered on the Condie moraine (Figure 5.4a) which marks a stable ice-frontal position of the wasting continental glacier. The overall system is bounded on the north by the Qu'Appelle Valley and on the south and east by the terminus of permeable glacio-fluvial deposits. Within the drift complex are four major sand and gravel units constituting aquifers capable of yielding large quantities of water for municipal and industrial purposes.

The principal hydrogeological constraint in developing the groundwater is the limited recharge potential in view of the low precipitation, high evaporation potential, short frost-free season and presence of lacustrine clay overlying most of the aquifer materials. Nevertheless, in contrast to Taylor Island, the areal extent of the system is large and recharge is known to occur in the topographically high portions of the Condie moraine, with lateral transmission through the glacio-fluvial material underlying the clay and discharge along the major topographic lows. Locally, glacial landforms such as kames create highly permeable gaps in the confining clay layer thereby providing favourable recharge conditions.

The effect of heavy pumping in one specific aquifer, namely the Regina aquifer (Figure 5.4b), was reported by Lissey[20]. A large cone of depression in the piezometric surface had formed in the eastern portion, leading to induced recharge of the aquifer from Boggy Creek. Lissey also noted that induced leakage from the overlying confining layer also contributed recharge, while natural discharge occurred along Waskana

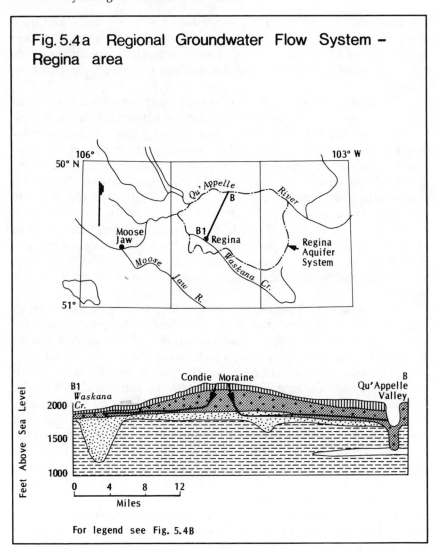

Fig. 5.4a Regional Groundwater Flow System – Regina area

For legend see Fig. 5.4B

Creek. It is interesting to note that beyond the cone of depression a comparison of the groundwater levels in 1960-61 to those of the 1930-40 period indicates that no regional decline had occurred. Recently it has been shown that more generally in Saskatchewan, water levels have not declined over the long term.[21]

From the management point of view, Regina's water supply is a good example of the integrated use of both surface water and groundwater resources, with the latter component (about 40 percent) being used

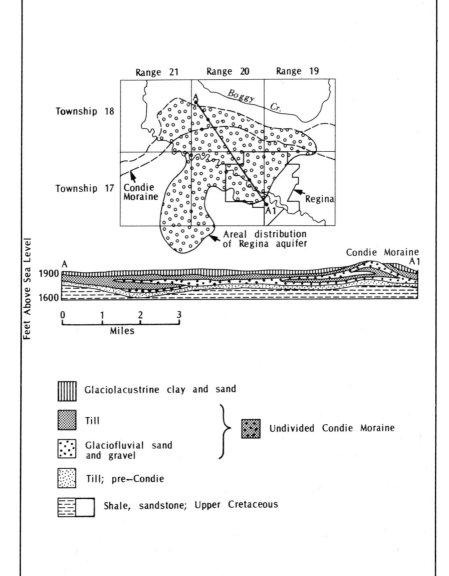

Fig. 5.4b Areal Distribution and Stratigraphy of the Regina Aquifer

to augment the surface water supply, derived from Buffalo Pound Lake in the Qu'Appelle Valley. Because both initial capital costs and operating costs for the same production volume were lower for groundwater than for surface water use, groundwater was to be used to the maximum possible extent as well as to meet peaking demands. In this respect the peaking capacity of the Regina aquifer, for example, has been estimated at 40 million igpd over a six month period.

Usage of Groundwater

The foregoing examples demonstrate in a limited way the rather large scale municipal-industrial use of groundwater. More generally groundwater is used in virtually every region of Canada for domestic and small scale municipal purposes as well. Cherry[22] estimated that total groundwater usage in Canada, excluding private industrial supplies, is about 500 million igpd or 20 percent of the entire municipal and rural water consumption. More than half the farms of the Interior Plains region and about 65 of the approximately 140 municipal water supply systems serving communities having populations greater than 1,000 are dependent either partly or entirely on groundwater.

Groundwater usage by communities of similar size in the heavily populated St. Lawrence Lowlands region is also large, amounting to greater than 70 percent of the total groundwater consumption by such communities across Canada.[23]

GROUNDWATER DEVELOPMENT AND THE ENVIRONMENT

Groundwater resource management and conservation is concerned not only with water quantity and its natural quality, but also with the effects of man's activities on the subsurface environment.

Solid Waste Disposal

Sites for solid waste land fill, the most common method of disposing of society's garbage, must be selected with careful consideration, not only of surface drainage and other aesthetic factors, but also for the hydrogeological characteristics of the underlying material in order to prevent or at least minimize contamination of subsurface space.

Basically, the potential for contamination arises from the leaching of the soluble component of the refuse by infiltrating precipitation or by groundwater which may eventually accumulate in the landfill itself. The danger of contamination varies depending not only on the hydrogeology of the site but on the climate. In arid areas, for example, low precipitation and therefore low rates of infiltration may not be adequate to produce a leachate from buried refuse, and if the waste disposal site is located where the water table is deep, attenuation of any leachate that might be produced in a wet season may occur in the unsaturated zone before reaching the phreatic surface. Under humid conditions the hydrogeological conditions of solid waste disposal sites are more critical, and the lack of such favourable conditions may result in leachate, high in dissolved solids and of an acidic and perhaps even toxic nature, infiltrating into the groundwater flow system.

Attentuation of the leachate is affected by processes of ion exchange, dilution and dispersion as the leachate moves along the path of flow. The significance of these processes is dependent on a diversity of factors including the nature of the rock materials, the type and magnitude of their porosity and permeability and the direction of groundwater movement in the vicinity of the landfill. Clearly, thorough hydrogeological evaluation is essential to the siting of solid waste disposal operations. Sites lacking the favourable natural conditions require artificial protective measures such as clay liners to prevent contamination. In all cases monitoring of the groundwater regime in the vicinity of landfills before and after site establishment is desirable as part of the landfill management which ought to be concerned with prevention of subsurface as well as surface environmental degradation.

Liquid Waste Disposal

The disposal of liquid mixtures involves a variety of technologies including septic systems, subsurface injection and effluent irrigation on land. The successful application of these methods depends on certain properties of the subsurface, whether it be the soil zone or a zone thousands of feet deep in the crust, to assimilate or store the waste material. On the contrary, lagoon disposal is dependent on the ability of the soil to prevent infiltration. Lagoons are used widely in Canada for municipal sewage disposal, and also have come into use for storage of brines, a by-product of the Saskatchewan potash industry[24]. A geophysical survey of one such lagoon (or brine pond) has provided a basis for inferring that brine leakage from the pond into the subsurface is occurring[25]. Although such leakage may not be harmful in every case, clearly brine ponds need to be situated carefully with respect to groundwater regime to insure that contamination of existing or even future water supplies does not degrade their quality.

In constrast to lagoon technology, effluent irrigation utilizes the naturally occurring processes such as biological activity, the screening action of soil particles and the absorption of chemical nutrients by plant roots as a purifying treatment. Parizek,[26] who described these processes collectively as a "living filter" (Figure 5.5), concluded that with adequate information about the soil and underlying bedrock and with proper

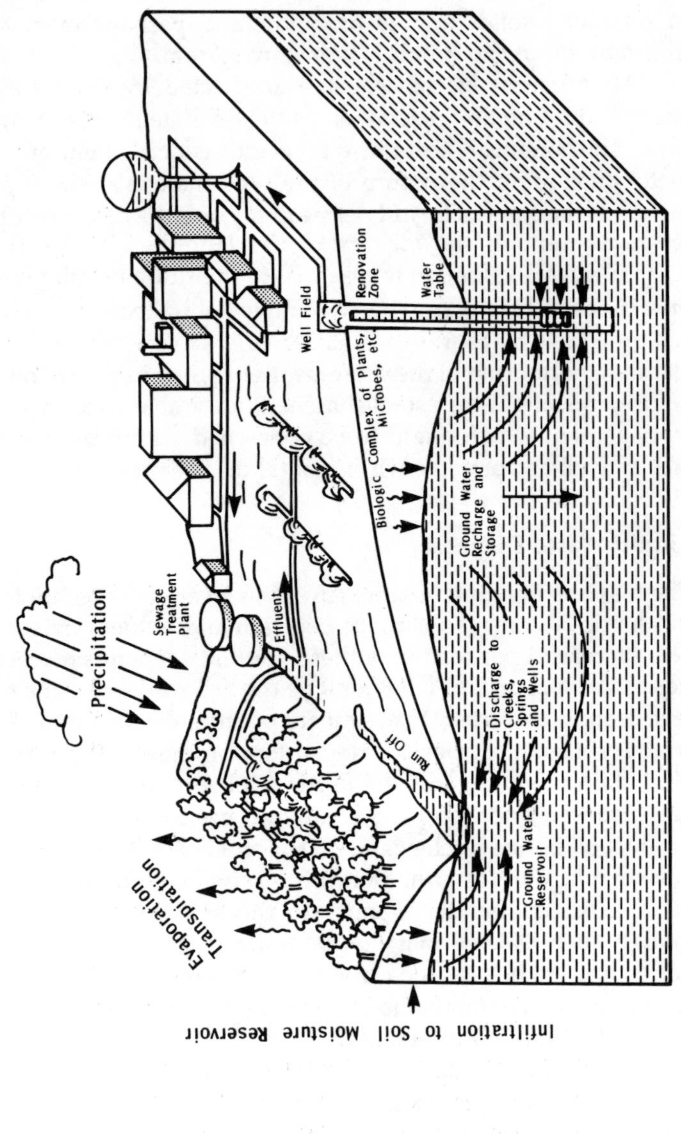

Fig. 5.5   The Waste Water Renovation and Conservation Cycle

management, the safe disposal of effluent on land can be carried out under a wide variety of field conditions. Renovation of effluent utilizing the living filter, according to Parizek, not only leads to recharge of clean water to the groundwater reservoir, but also to direct economic benefits including increased crop yields ranging from 17 to 300 percent and increased growth rates of certain tree species.

Gibb and Jones[27] have recently outlined the pollution hazard to groundwater stemming from septic tank usage. Soil permeability is a particularly sensitive parameter in the operation of septic systems. Where water is not readily absorbed into the ground, septic tank effluent may accumulate at the surface and eventually drain into streams. On the other hand, too large a permeability may lead to rapid infiltration of the effluent and poor attenuation of the contaminants with the result that groundwater may be polluted. Gibb and Jones speculated on the possible widespread occurrence of such pollution, noting that in Nova Scotia alone during 1972, some 1,800 private water wells, each often accompanied by septic tank installation, were constructed.

Deeper subsurface space is now being exploited for the purpose of disposal of industrial and other liquid wastes — a technology which is both technically feasible and economically attractive. However, this practice, which is expanding at an increasing rate (Figure 5.6) in Canada, will result in irreversible pollution of certain subsurface formations as the waste will be subject to disposal by diffusion and convection in natural groundwater flow systems for years to come — with the possibility of eventual discharge to the earth's surface. Although there are still a relatively small number of injection wells in Canada, the disturbing aspect is that many of the wells are too shallow (less than 2,000 feet deep) for safe disposal, some are located in geologically unsuitable environments, and adequate records pertaining to injection rates, pressures and other aspects are either not kept or not available.

Notwithstanding the foregoing, there are favourable geological and hydrological criteria which could provide for this negative use of subsurface space. For example, Van Everdingen and Freeze[28] indicated that regions with potential for safe subsurface disposal should be underlain by an extensive, thick sedimentary sequence, be free from major faulting and seismic activity and have low hydrodynamic gradients prevailing over a large portion. Such conditions provide relatively large amounts of confined storage space, relatively low rates of groundwater movement and long travel paths. Injection must be undertaken in such a manner as to prevent build-up of excessive formation pressures during disposal and injected fluids must be chemically compatible with the recipient formation. Obviously fresh water formations or those containing economic mineral resources must not be selected as recipient formations. Clearly, a thorough knowledge of subsurface space, its resources,

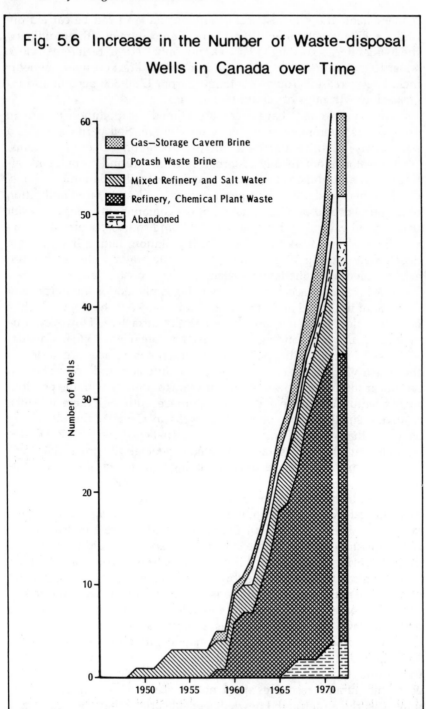

Fig. 5.6 Increase in the Number of Waste-disposal Wells in Canada over Time

and its relationship with the surface are prerequisite to the implementation of subsurface waste disposal and more generally to the conservation and sound management of groundwater resources.

Other Forms of Subsurface Contamination

In addition to the effects of waste disposal the quality of groundwater may be threatened or is frequently degraded by other forms of contamination.

The accidental spillage of gasoline in the vicinity of the Shippegan aquifer has previously been referred to, although fortunately no apparent damage resulted. Other gasoline spills in Canada and elsewhere have caused extensive and probably irreparable damage to groundwater supplies. One of the better documented cases involves a carbonate terrain in Pennsylvania where gasoline removal operations during a period of approximately 30 months recovered 216,000 gallons of gasoline from the shallow groundwater reservoir in a one-third square mile area. Adjacent to the area at the time were three petroleum product storage tank farms and two product transmission pipelines.[29]

Contamination of groundwater arising from the use of agricultural fertilizers and deriving from agricultural wastes, after years of accummulation, is now being investigated with some rather alarming results. For example, in the Fraser River lowland, with its rich endowment of groundwater resources, as well as agricultural soils, groundwater quality is deteriorating where excess fertilizing of berry crops has resulted in nitrate contaminations. Nitrate concentrations as high as 263 ppm in some aquifers have been reported, compared to a drinking water standard of a maximum nitrate concentration of 10 ppm.

Phenols and nitrates are only two of a possibly large number of potentially dangerous contaminants in subsurface space. In their extensive review of groundwater pollutants, Gibb and Jones[30] noted that little is known of the travel of viruses and bacteria in soils, and although indications are that they are filtered or absorbed by the soil, one case of virus isolation from well water has been reported. Other contaminants may include such materials as pesticides and solvents which may be indiscriminately poured down the drain and eventually infiltrate into the groundwater flow system. Pollution of these types (gasoline, agricultural and others) is not readily abated, particularly as a considerable time span often lapses before its effects become noticeable. Consequently emphasis must be placed on prevention of such subsurface environmental degradation through a greater awareness of the vulnerability of the groundwater regime and through appropriate application of hydrogeological principles in relation to waste disposal practice.

CONCLUSION

Groundwater resources, potable and otherwise, may be found in abundance in all physiographic regions of Canada despite the occurrence of broad expanses of glacial till, low permeability bedrock and permafrost. Although these factors tend to detract from the groundwater resource potential they do not negate it. Their very existence in conjunction with many other complex hydrogeological features makes thorough and systematic exploration and evaluation mandatory as a prerequisite to the development and proper management of groundwater resources as well as the general utilization of subsurface space. Such exploration and evaluation work in Canada is only in a formative stage and will likely continue to grown as the resource value of groundwater is being recognized and its management in conjunction with surface water resources is being practised.

There is a broad spectrum of environmental problems associated with groundwater development and more generally with subsurface space utilization. In particular in Canada attention is being focussed on subsurface environmental degradation deriving from waste disposal, for certain areas have already experienced such problems. The solution to these problems appears to rest mainly in adequate hydrogeological evaluation of waste disposal sites and proper design, construction and operation of disposal installations. Ultimately, of course, the optimal utilization of subsurface space ought to be taken into full account in land use planning. Only through such planning will subsurface space be used to its greatest advantage, and will spoilage of valuable groundwater resources and other environmental damage be prevented.

NOTES

* The author wishes to acknowledge the contribution of Mr. Don Lennox and his group in the Hydrology Research Division, Environment Canada, for commenting on the above chapter. E.C. Halstead is also thanked for providing information on the Fraser River Delta.

1. Prince, A.T. (1971). "The Water Environment." *CIM Bulletin*, LXXIV, (August).

2. Hubbert, M.K. (1940). "The Theory of Groundwater Motion." *Journal of Geology*, 48, (8), 785-944.

3. Carr, P.A. (1967). "Appalachian Hydrogeological Region." *Groundwater in Canada*. Geological Survey of Canada, Economic Report No. 24, Chapter III.

4. Scott, J.S. (1967). "St. Lawrence Lowlands Hydrogeological Region." *Groundwater in Canada*. Geological Survey of Canada, Economic Report No. 24, Chapter IV.

5. Prévôt, J.M. (1972). *Hydrogeological Map of the St. Lawrence Lowlands*. Hydrogeology Service, Waters Branch, Department of Natural Resources of Quebec.

6. Scott, J.S. (1967). *op. cit.*

7. Render, F.W. (1970). "Geohydrology of the Metropolitan Winnipeg Area as Related to Groundwater Supply and Construction." *Canadian Geotechnical Journal*, 7 (3), 243-74.

8. Saskatchewan-Nelson Basin Board. (1972). *Water Supply for the Saskatchewan-Nelson Basin*. Canada, Alberta, Saskatchewan, Manitoba. Appendix 7; "Environmental Considerations." Section F; "Groundwater."

9. *Ibid*.

10. Jeffs, D.N. and A.A. Mellary. (1972). "Drawdown and Recovery of an Artesian Sand and Gravel Aquifer, London, Ontario Canada." *Proceedings, 24th International Geological Congress*. Montreal. Section 11, 5-15.

11. Trescott, P.C. (1968). *Groundwater Resources and Hydrogeology of the Annapolis-Cornwallis Valley, Nova Scotia*. Halifax, Nova Scotia. Nova Scotia Department of Mines, Memoir 6.

12. Owen, E.B. (1967). "Northern Hydrogeological Region." *Groundwater in Canada*. Geological Survey of Canada, Economic Report No. 24, Chapter VIII.

13. Chebotarev, I.I. (1955). "Metamorphism of Natural Waters in the Crust Weathering." *Geochimica and Cosmochimica Acta*, 8, 22-48, 137-170 and 198-212.

14. Rutherford, A.A. (1967). *Water Quality Survey of Saskatchewan Groundwaters*. Saskatchewan Research Council, C-67-1.

15. Saskatchewan-Nelson Basin Board. (1972). *op. cit.*

16. Meyboom, P. (1967). "Groundwater Studies in the Assiniboine River Drainage Basin: Part II: Hydrologic Characteristics of Phreatophytic Vegetation in South-Central Saskatchewan." *Geological Survey of Canada Bulletin*, 139.

17. Brown, D.D. (1971). *Hydrogeology of Taylor Island, New Brunswick*. Ph.D. Thesis, University of Western Ontario.

18. Saskatchewan-Nelson Basin Board. (1972). *op. cit.*

19. Andrew, J.T. G. and J.M. Rigney. (1971). "Aquifer Contamination at Shippegan, New Brunswick." Paper Presented at the Annual Meeting of the American Water Works Association. Halifax: Nova Scotia.

20. Lissey, A. (1962). "Hydrogeology of the Regina Aquifer, Saskatchewan." *Proceedings of Hydrology Symposium No. 3 Groundwater*. NRC Association Committee on Geodesy and Geophysics, Subcommittee on Hydrology, 303-29.

21. Saskatchewan-Nelson Basin Board. (1972). *op. cit.*

22. Cherry, J.A. (1973). "Groundwater in the Interior Plains Region of Canada." Chapter Prepared for *An Overview of Water Resources*, to be published by Agassiz Centre for Water Studies, University of Manitoba.

23. Scott, J.S. (1967). *op. cit.*

24. Vonhof, J.A. (1971). "Waste Disposal Problems Near Potash Mines in Saskatchewan." Paper Presented to Meeting of the International Union of Geodesy and Geophysics, Moscow.

25. Lazreg, H. (1974). *Reconnaissance Resistivity Survey Around a Brine Pond, Esterhazy, Saskatchewan*. Inland Waters Directorate, Department of the Environment, Scientific Series No. 42, 8.

26. Parizek, R.R., L.T. Kardos, W.E. Sopper, E.A. Myers, D.E. Davis, M.A. Farrell and J.B. Nesbitt. (1967). *Waste Water Renovation and Conservation*. University Park, Pennsylvania: The Pennsylvania State University Studies, No. 23.

27. Gibb, J.E. and J.F. Jones (1974). *Pollution Hazard to Groundwater in Nova Scotia*. Water Planning and Management Division, Nova Scotia Department of the Environment, Bulletin 1.

28. Van Everdingen, R.O. and R.A. Freeze. (1971). *Subsurface Disposal of Waste in Canada*. Inland Waters Branch, Department of the Environment, Technical Bulletin No. 49.

29. Rhindress, R.C. (1971). "Gasoline Pollution of a Karst Aquifer." In *Hydrogeology and Geochemistry of Folded and Faulted Carbonate Rocks of the Central Appalachian Type and Related Land Use Problems*. Washington, D.C.: Geological Society of America and Associated Societies, 171-75.

30. Gibb, J.E. and J.F. Jones. (1974). *op. cit.*

PART 4
SOIL AND THE MANAGEMENT OF LAND IN CANADA

Introduction

There used to be a character in an old-time radio show who, when asked a question, always replied, "The answer lies in the soil." The basic message of the two articles included in this section of the book is that the answers to many crucial land use questions in Canada today do lie in the soil.

Answers, of course, will vary with the purposes of the questioner. For instance, a farmer contemplating a decision about which crops to plant in which of his fields will be primarily interested in any variation in the life support capacity of the topmost A horizon of the soil. A civil engineer, on the other hand, has no use for topsoil, except for landscaping purposes. Indeed, what is a resource for the farmer is a hazard for the engineer. The comparatively high organic content of the A horizon of most soils makes it a poor load bearer. And so, while it is the chemical nutrient value of the A horizon that counts for the farmer, it is the physical load bearing capacity of the B and C horizons which are important to the engineer.

But, of greater significance for our purposes is the fact that reliable answers to questions about soil capability are rarely self-evident. Perhaps in simpler times, experience was sufficient. In today's world, however, it is not enough. On the one hand, as the benefits of correct decisions have escalated, so too have the costs of wrong ones. On the other hand, the decision-making environment itself has grown immensely more complex. Increasingly, the question is not which crops or which type of building an individual should choose, but rather whether people should select crops *or* buildings. At the same time, the persons (planners, politicians) called upon to make decisions and recommendations in conflict situations such as these are generalists, not specialists. They are unlikely to know much, if anything, about soil and its varied capabilities to support diverse human activities — be they corn patches in Perth County or Commerce Courts in Toronto. They need help to assess soil resources. The bulk of this section of the book is devoted to the description of a wide array of technical means of providing such assessments of the suitability of soil resources for various purposes.

Hoffman's article presents us with information on a family of soil assessment procedures, each of which was initially developed for use in

138

a different field: agriculture; forestry; outdoor recreation; wildlife management; sanitary engineering; urban development. Perhaps the most important section of the article is his demonstration of how, when used in combination, these techniques enable us to make better-informed choices from amongst these various alternative purposes.

White, on the other hand, assumes that the choice of alternative uses has already been made. He is concerned solely with assessment of the capacity of soils to support engineering structures of various kinds: that is, land occupancy decisions at the micro-level of the building site. This contrasts with, yet complements, Hoffman's presentation of techniques useful for macro-level land use decisions.

Both papers in this section demonstrate a point that is worth underlining in this introduction — the complementary nature of pure and applied research. Too often these "ideal types" are thought of as two distinct species. In fact, they are points on a continuum distinguished only by their purpose. Further, each is dependent upon the other. More often than not, pure research into the general nature of a phenomenon is stimulated by some practical difficulty. Conversely, the solution of that difficulty will depend upon the prior availability of basic information on the nature and behaviour of the phenomenon.

Hoffman makes this point, early in his paper, when he stresses the importance of the basic soil survey to the development of soil assessment techniques. In essence, the various soil capability classification systems described in Hoffman's article are interpretations of the general information gathered for soil science purposes. They do not materialize out of the sky. Similarly, White demonstrates the importance of fundamental knowledge about the physical properties of soils in his discussion of the various testing procedures used by engineers to determine the design and placement of structures.

There is, however, one major point of difference between the two articles in this section that should be noted in conclusion. White's techniques determine land occupancy decisions. Hoffman's, on the other hand, merely condition such decisions. As noted earlier, White is concerned with post-planning, site level engineering decisions. Hoffman, in contrast, is concerned with pre-planning choices among various alternatives. At this stage in the decision-making process many other factors besides the limitations and potentials of soil resources must be taken into consideration. The techniques described by Hoffman are not panaceas. They can only provide useful advice on one important dimension of land use problems. White, in offering advice to engineers, must be a determinist. Hoffman, in offering advice to planners, cannot afford to be one.

6

Soil Capability Analysis and Land Resource Development in Canada

Douglas W. Hoffman, Centre for Resources Development,
University of Guelph

SOIL AND CANADIAN SOCIETY

Most of the things we do are based on the land. Buildings and roads, crops and trees, baseball fields, hiking trails and swimming beaches are all supported by the land in one way or another. However, some types of land are better than other types for a given use. In other words, some lands have a high "capability" for a specific use while others have a low "capability" for that use. The soil scientist, among other things, attempts to evaluate soils and land for various uses in terms of both their limitations and their potential. Such information can then be used in deciding where and when a change of land use should occur.

Soil Problems and Potentials

In general, it may be said that a good soil for agriculture is a good soil for any other use. The only major exception is recreation which often seeks the wilder, rougher landscapes. We might, therefore, speak of the availability of land in Canada on the basis of the amount of land that can be used for agricultural production.

According to the Census of Canada less than 10 percent of our 2,272 million acres is in farmland and slightly over half of that is cultivated. Such a small amount of the total land area is used for farming because only one-third of the country is climatically suited for agriculture. Rough terrain, bogs and other unsuitable soils further reduce the land available. Unfortunately, the land that is available for agricultural pursuits is also the most desirable for other uses. Most people wish to avoid the rigorous climate of the north, its muskegs and bare rocks, and as a result most of the occupied land is concentrated in southern Canada.

Despite the large amount of land in Canada the proportion of land devoted to various uses is not likely to change greatly from that shown for today (Figure 6.1). What is likely to happen is a great increase in the competition for the high quality land, with most of it going to the competitor providing the largest short term profits. Under present social and

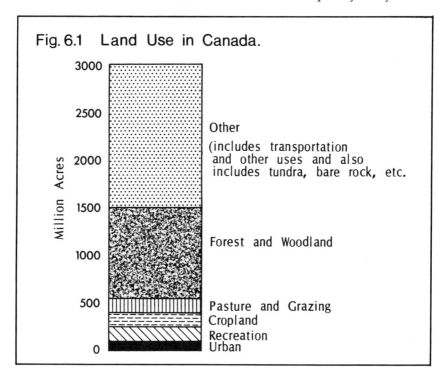

Fig. 6.1   Land Use in Canada.

economic conditions this could mean a loss of farmland to recreation and urbanization. Such land use change would not significantly alter the appearance of Figure 6.1 but it would seriously affect agriculture.

Arable land is that which can be safely cultivated year after year provided normal conservation practices are followed. It is the land of greatest value to the farmer. The amounts of arable land presently developed and estimates of the undeveloped arable land in each province are given in Table 6.1. These may seem large, especially in the west, but in the heavily populated parts of the country in British Columbia, Ontario, Quebec and the Maritime provinces arable land is clearly in short supply.

What is needed, among other things, is a system for evaluating land that can be used to distribute land according to the needs and desires of the people. One such system has been evolved and is used to measure Canada's land resources. It is called a land capability classification. Such a classification can be developed for every use. In Canada, land capability classifications have been developed to evaluate the suitability of the land for agriculture, forestry, wildlife and recreation.

TABLE 6.1

Developed and Undeveloped Arable Land in Canada

Territory or Province	Total area of census-farms	Estimated Undeveloped Arable Land (in acres)*
Yukon and N.W. Territories	4,268	354,000
British Columbia	5,292,310	2,010,000
Alberta	48,982,875	10,328,000
Saskatchewan	65,409,363	1,000,000
Manitoba	19,083,817	3,750,000
Ontario	17,826,045	8,000,000
Quebec	12,886,069	1,003,000
New Brunswick	1,811,695	Not Available (N/A)
Nova Scotia	1,851,895	N/A
Prince Edward Island	926,978	N/A
Newfoundland	49,513	N/A
CANADA	174,124,846	26,445,000

Source: Census of Canada, 1966
*Extrapolated by the author.

Soil Classification

The first step in evaluating soils is to establish a general classification. Barnes has said that:

> . . . interpretive soil classification must be preceded by the basic soil classification. . . . The basic soil classification must delimit kinds of soils sufficiently uniform in their characteristics that we can reasonably expect about the same results from a given use or treatment throughout the extent of any kind.[1]

Only after the soils of an area are classified and mapped may we proceed to interpret their value for specific uses.

In Canada the establishment of basic soil surveys took place over a period of 35 years, beginning in Ontario in 1914 and following in Saskatchewan and Alberta in 1921, Manitoba in 1922, British Columbia in 1931, Quebec and Nova Scotia in 1934, New Brunswick in 1938, Prince Edward Island in 1943, Northwest Territories in 1944 and Newfoundland in 1949. A look at the first soil map and report published in Ontario gives an indication of early soil survey methods and the soil classification system of the day.[2] In this preliminary survey the soils men drove

TABLE 6.2

Classification of the Soils of Southwestern and Central Ontario — 1923

Province	Group	Series	Type
Glacial and Loessal Province	Glacial Limestone Group	Guelph Series	Guelph stony loam Guelph sandy loam Guelph loam
		London Series	London loam London silt loam London clay loam London silty clay loam
	Glacial Sand and Shale Group	Milton Series	Milton loam Milton clay loam Milton clay
		Lockport Series	Lockport clay
Glacial Lake and River Terrace Province	Glacial Lake Group	Dunkirk Series	Dunkirk sand Dunkirk sandy loam Dunkirk loam
		Haldimand Series	Haldimand clay loam Haldimand clay
		Clyde Series	Clyde sandy loam Clyde loam Clyde clay loam Clyde clay
		Warners Series	Warners loam
		Hastings Series	Hastings stony clay loam
Organic Soils			Muck and peat

up and down every other concession road or side road to find out what series of soils existed and to chart out their areas. The travelling was done by car with frequent stops to make borings where a change of soil was indicated. The soils were grouped into four categories on the basis of the composition of materials from which the soils were formed, the mode of deposition of the materials and soil texture. Table 6.2 shows this classification system.

Since 1923, soil classification systems have undergone considerable change and today they are very sophisticated. The most recent general classification of soils is described in *The System of Soil Classification of Canada*[3]. This general classification provides the basis for evaluating soils for various uses.

The soils of most of the settled portions of Canada have been mapped and classified and soil maps and reports are available from Ministries of Agriculture in all provinces. Information from these maps and reports and others similar to them is used to determine soil capability.

SOIL CAPABILITY ANALYSIS

Soil or land capability classification is one of many methods for evaluating soils. Such classifications are not new. One of the first was developed over 40 years ago by the United States Department of Agriculture (USDA). This classification grouped soils into eight classes on the basis of soil type, slope and erosion. For many years, modifications of the USDA system were used by the Canadian provinces to evaluate land for agriculture. In 1964, however, increasing pressure for a systematic national inventory of land resources made it necessary to devise a Canadian system. The first component of this system to be developed was the soil capability classification for agriculture. Capability classifications for forestry, wildlife and outdoor recreation soon followed. These classifications, along with a capability classification for sport fish, data on present land use, a socio-economic land classification system, an agroclimatic classification system, inventory data — geo-information system, together with information generated from pilot land use projects collectively comprise what is known as the Canada Land Inventory Programme (CLI).

Each of the land capability classifications have certain common characteristics. Soils or land types are grouped into one of seven classes depending on their capability for production. In each, class 1 is best and class 7 is worst. The classes are subdivided into subclasses, the number of which varies according to use. Each classification system is designed to be compatible with the others. Brief descriptions of the four basic land capability classifications in the CLI system follow.

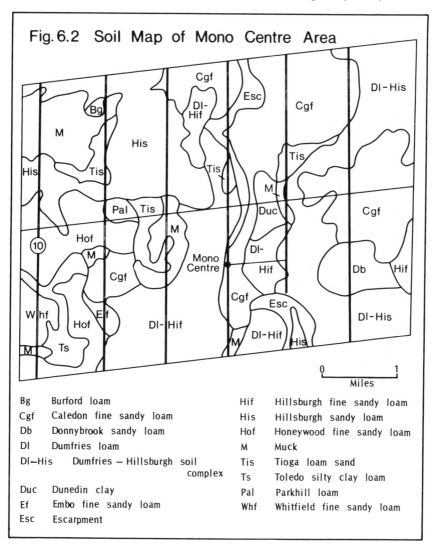

Fig. 6.2 Soil Map of Mono Centre Area

Bg	Burford loam		Hif	Hillsburgh fine sandy loam
Cgf	Caledon fine sandy loam		His	Hillsburgh sandy loam
Db	Donnybrook sandy loam		Hof	Honeywood fine sandy loam
Dl	Dumfries loam		M	Muck
Dl—His	Dumfries — Hillsburgh soil		Tis	Tioga loam sand
		complex	Ts	Toledo silty clay loam
Duc	Dunedin clay		Pal	Parkhill loam
Ef	Embo fine sandy loam		Whf	Whitfield fine sandy loam
Esc	Escarpment			

Soil Capability for Agriculture

The agricultural inventory provides information in the form of maps and statistical tables on the location, quality and extent of land suitable for the production of annual field crops, forage, improved pasture and native grazing. The data are used at municipal, provincial and national

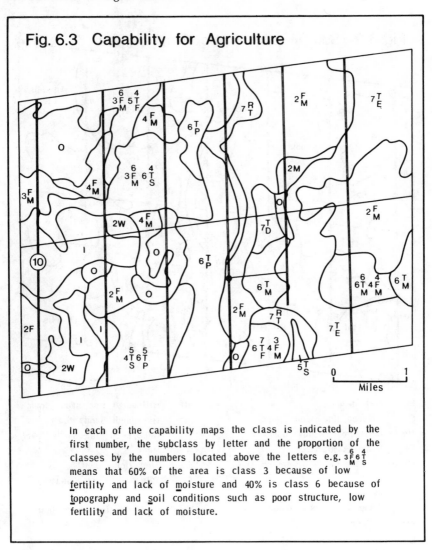

Fig. 6.3 Capability for Agriculture

In each of the capability maps the class is indicated by the first number, the subclass by letter and the proportion of the classes by the numbers located above the letters e.g. $3^{6}_{F}6^{4}_{S}$ means that 60% of the area is class 3 because of low fertility and lack of moisture and 40% is class 6 because of topography and soil conditions such as poor structure, low fertility and lack of moisture.

levels for planning the efficient use of agricultural resources. The information is particularly useful to: 1. delineate agricultural lands, 2. identify submarginal farmland, 3. consolidate farms into viable units, 4. establish an equitable assessment base and 5. to indicate where urban and industrial expansion might take place without unduly reducing agricultural production.

The capability inventory is based on the interpretation of the data provided by systematic soil surveys, generally at the scale of one or two inches to the mile. Through interpretation, the soils are ranked according to their general suitability for the production of common field crops, taking into account the effects of climatic and soil limitations in a system of mechanized farming.

In the classification, the mineral soils are grouped into seven classes depending on the degree of limitation and into thirteen subclasses, according to the kinds of limitation.[4] Class 1 soils have no significant limitations and, together with classes 2 and 3, are considered capable of sustained production of common field crops. Class 4 soils are physically marginal for sustained arable agriculture. Soils in class 5 are unsuitable for annual field crops but suitable for forage production and improved pasture, while those in class 6 are restricted in their use to native grazing. Class 7 soils are unsuitable for agricultural use. Organic soils are not included in the classification but are shown as a separate category on the maps.

Land Capability for Forestry

The classification of land capability for forestry was developed to provide an improved technical basis for land use planning. Fully compatible with the other sectors, the classification serves to indicate the lands on which intensive management practices might be justified. As major commitments in the allocation of forest lands are planned, and as forest management is a long term proposition, dedication of land to this use should be undertaken only after careful consideration of alternative uses.

The objective of the land capability inventory for forestry is to describe the potential capability of the land under indigenous tree species growing at full stocking and assuming good management. Capability is measured in terms of mean annual increment per acre expressed in cubic feet.

Development of the national classification system was completed through pilot projects in each province, followed by regional and national meetings of provincial, federal and university specialists. Basic data for classification were available in most provinces in the form of soil survey and forest inventory maps and reports. Interpretation of these data, together with new field survey data, permitted the system to be established.

The maps are being used for the intended purpose, namely in forestry capability rating for regional planning. Other applications include preliminary appraisals for designated timberland lease areas, for land assessment purposes, for wildlife and recreation land use planning and in teaching of forest land management.

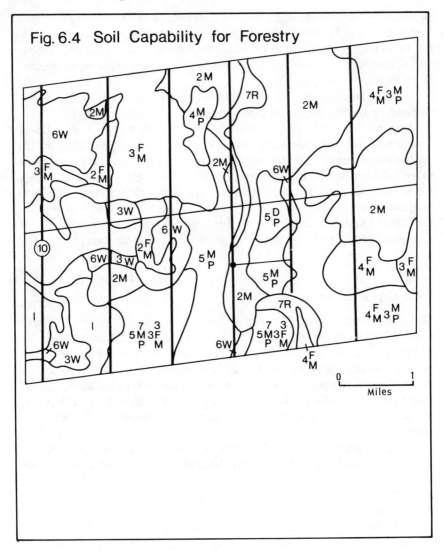

Fig. 6.4 Soil Capability for Forestry

Land Capability for Recreation

The objectives of the recreation land classification programme are to provide a reliable estimate of the quality, quantity, type and distribution of outdoor recreation resources within settled parts of Canada, and to supply the basic information necessary for the formulation of policy and plans by the levels of government involved. Compatibility with other sectors of CLI is mandatory to facilitate inter-sector comparisons in integrated resource management planning.

The recreation sector's initial task was to develop a national classification system acceptable to all provinces and, in conjunction with the provinces, to apply the classification to all lands within the inventory area. The classification system has been developed using seven classes to rank land for its capability for outdoor recreational use, bearing in mind present popular preferences.

The basis of the classification is the quantity of recreation land use which may be generated and sustained per unit area of land per year, under perfect market conditions. A high class land unit, therefore, has a high index of attraction in terms of popular preferences and a "use tolerance" which permits intensive use without undue degradation of the resource. For purposes of uniformity, perfect ranking does not take into consideration present use or accessibility.

The information is being used in outdoor recreation planning for identification of potential park and recreation areas, ranging from intensive day-use sites for urban populations to national parks. The information is useful for preliminary zoning for various recreation uses within large parks, for the designation of lakeshore cottage lots and for the reservation of water frontage for public use.

The recreation sector has conducted an inventory of outdoor recreation facilities, which, together with the capability inventory and demand studies presently underway, should give a more complete picture of the outdoor recreation market demand and supply situation so necessary for the formulation of more adequate policies and programmes.

Land Capability for Wildlife

Wildlife constitutes a separate resource with its own values. Decisions on land use for wildlife will generally be made in the context of recreational requirements. Because of their mobility, land requirements for wildlife will differ at different stages of the wildlife resources' life cycles. Areas used for production and those used for viewing, photography, or harvest of the resources may not only be physically separated but may be of a different biological and physical nature.

A nationally accepted system of evaluating and describing land capability for wildlife use has been developed for each of two general headings, Ungulates and Waterfowl. The system was developed in full realization that many other kinds of wildlife are important. These two groups were selected because of their broad appeal to the public and their wide national distribution.

The land capability classification developed for wildlife reflects the physical characteristics of land units, meteorological and other factors

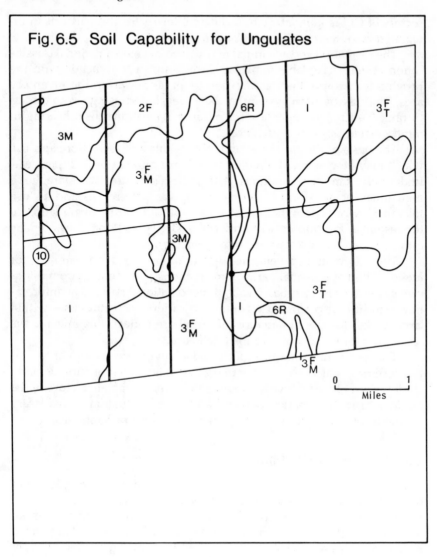

Fig. 6.5 Soil Capability for Ungulates

which influence wildlife. The classification includes seven categories of capability, ranging from very good to very poor. In the printed maps for public use, land capability is indicated by map colouration and suitable symbols. Factors which limit the production of the resource are designated by letters.

The foregoing capability classifications have proved useful in pinpointing areas that are better than others for defined purposes. Maps of

Land Capability for Recreation, Wildlife, Forestry and Agriculture have been prepared on base maps of the National Topographic Series 1:250,000 scale.[5] These are available from Information Canada, Ottawa. It must be noted that the classifications do not indicate best use or profitability. They are simply inventories of our soil and land resources and a guide to planning (see Figures 6.2, 6.3, 6.4 and 6.5).

Among these classifications, only one contains information which indicates productivity in terms of actual yield. This is the land capability classification for forestry. According to this classification system forestry class 1 land produces more than 111 cubic feet per acre per annum; class 2, 91 to 110 cubic feet; class 3, 71 to 90 cubic feet; class 4, 51 to 70 cubic feet; class 5, 31 to 50 cubic feet; class 6, 11 to 30 cubic feet and class 7, usually less than 10 cubic feet per acre per year.[6] None of the other national classification systems attempt to quantify productivity. However, some research which provides a quantitative relationship to the agricultural soil classes has been conducted in Ontario. Multiple regression analysis was used to determine the correlation between the yield of selected common field crops and certain characteristics of the land in each soil capability class.[7] Yields of grain corn, oats, barley and forage by class are shown in Table 6.3.

Grain corn, oats and barley are arable crops and are not grown on class 5, 6 and 7 soils which, by definition, are non-arable soils. For this reason no values could be obtained for grain corn, oats and barley yields on class 5, 6 and 7 land. However, values were obtained for yields of forage on all classes of land except class 7.

TABLE 6.3

**Mean Yields of Grain Corn, Oats, Barley and Forage
by Soil Class**

Soil Class	Grain Corn	Oats	Barley	Forage
	(bu./ac.)	(bu./ac.)	(bu./ac.)	(lbs./ac.)
1	136	90	81	6420
2	105	73	67	5136
3	80	62	52	4173
4	59	52	38	3531
5	no value	no value	no value	3210
6	no value	no value	no value	2568
7	no value	no value	no value	no value

Because yields for each genotype vary within each class some means of establishing equivalents is needed. This has been done by developing a performance index. The index has been prepared by assigning a value of 1.00 to class 1 for each crop and determining a comparative ranking for the remaining classes. Performance indices for corn, barley, oats and forage are shown in Table 6.4. The performance indices for corn, barley and oats on class 2 sites are similar, but 10 percent differences occur on classes 3 and 4. In spite of the range in values within a class it is possible to develop one set of performance indices which can be applied to all common field crops. This can be done by calculating the mean and standard error for each class. Performance indices for all common field crops are shown in Table 6.5. These indices can be used to amplify the definitions of classes 1, 2, 3 and 4 of the soil capability classification for agriculture. Indices for classes 5 and 6 can be obtained from those calculated for forage crops (Table 6.3).

TABLE 6.4

Performance Indices for Soil Classes 1 to 4 Based on Yields of Corn, Barley, Oats and Forage

Class	Performance Indices			
	Grain Corn	Barley	Oats	Forage
1	1.00	1.00	1.00	1.00
2	.77	.83	.81	.80
3	.59	.64	.69	.66
4	.43	.47	.57	.55

It seems evident that the allocation of a soil or land class to a site, no matter what the use, is made by value judgement in most instances. Experience is needed by researchers in making value judgements that are unbiased and uniformly applicable to similar sites across the country. On occasion, the required experience is not available and some modification of the analysis by value judgement is needed. One such modification is the "penalty point method" in which arbitrarily selected points are assigned to the major soil limitations and are subtracted from 100 to provide a rating. Some idea of how this technique is used can be determined from the soil capability classification for organic soils which follows.

TABLE 6.5

Performance Indices for Soil Classes 1 to 4 for Common Field Crops

Class	Index	Range
1	1.00	. . . . .
2	.80	.80±.03
3	.64	.64±.04
4	.49	.49±.06

A Guide for the Capability Classification of Organic Soils

This system was developed in Ontario to be used for rating organic soils for their potential production of vegetable crops. It is a simplified version of a much more complex system applicable to organic deposits in the southern part of the province. It is therefore regional in nature and is included in this chapter just to demonstrate a technique.

The features used to determine organic soil class are those of soil and climate (Table 6.6).

The six characteristics listed in Table 6.6 have numbers to the left of each description. As a guide to the proper land class, the numbers which are opposite the descriptions selected are totalled and subtracted from 100. The land class below approximates the value obtained.

1	2	3	4	5	6	7
100-85	80-70	65-55	50-40	35-25	20-10	Less than 10

As in other soil capabilities classifications each class has been defined.

Class 1 – (100-85) Organic soils of this class have no water, topographical or pH limitations and are deep and level. They are located in climate category 1 and are at an intermediate stage of decomposition.

Class 2 – (80-70) Organic soils in class 2 have one limitation which restricts their use in a minor way. The limitation may be woodiness, reaction, flooding, topography, depth or climate.

Class 3 – (65-55) Organic soils in this class have moderately severe limitations that restrict the range of crops or that require special management practices.

Class 4 – (50-40) Soils in this class have limitations which severely restrict the range of crops or which require special development and management practices. Reclamation and management costs will be high.

Class 5 – (30-20) Soils in this class have such severe limitations that they are restricted to the production of perennial forage or other specifically adapted crops. Large scale reclamation is not feasible.

Class 6 – (20-10) Class 6 organic soils are capable of producing only indigenous crops and improvement practices are not feasible.

Class 7 – (under 10) Organic soils of this class have no capability for agriculture.

TABLE 6.6

Capability Classification Criteria for Organic Soils

Decomposition	Wood Content*
	0 None
35 Fibric	5 1-25%
0 Mesic	10 26-50%
20 Humic	20 > −50%

Reaction	Depth	
	0 Deep	(>72″)
20 pH under 5.0	20 Mod. deep	(52″−72″)
0 pH 5.0 to 7.0	35 Shallow	(36″−52″)
20 pH over 7.0	50 Very Shallow	(<36″)

Substratum Texture	Climate
0 Fine	0 Climatic category i
20 Medium	20 Climatic category ii
or coarse	35 Climatic category iii

*Wood Content — expressed as percentage of total material present within the control section (volume)

The rating of organic soils is a relatively simple procedure when the guide is closely followed. First, identify the stage of decomposition, reaction, wood content, substratum texture depth and climate category in the appropriate classes as defined. Next, classify the capability as outlined previously. Brief definitions of the soil characteristics follow.

Decomposition   Refers to the stage of decomposition of the organic materials.

> Fibric — The least decomposed of all organic soil materials. There are large amounts of well-preserved fibre that are readily identifiable as to botanical origin. A rubbed fibre content of more than 40% of the organic volume.

> Mesic — The intermediate stage of decomposition. Has a rubbed fibre content between 10% and 40% of the organic volume.

> Humic — The most highly decomposed. Has a rubbed fibre content less than 10% of the organic volume.

Wood Content — Wood located within 60 inches of the surface will probably interfere with cultivation practices. The limitations posed by woody layers are noted.

Depth — Refers to the depth of organic material over sand, silt, loam, clay, marl or bedrock. Limitations occur when any of these materials occur within 6 feet of the surface.

Reaction — Refers to the acidity or alkalinity of the soil.

Substratum Texture — Refers to the proportion of sand, silt and clay in the underlying mineral material when it is within 60 inches of the surface.

Climate — Refers to the climatic zones. Climatic category i includes the following climatic types: 1G, 2G, 2H, 2F, 3F,3G, 3H and 3K. Climatic category ii includes the following climatic types: 2F, 3F, 4G, 4H and 4K. Climatic category iii includes the following climatic types: 5G, 5H, 5K, 5L, 1C, 2C, 3L, 3M, 4F, 6G and 6H. The climatic types are those developed by Chapman and Brown.[8]

The penalty point procedure can be used for other classifications. One example is the "Development Difficulty Classification" applied to organic soils. It is possible that two separate organic soils may have similar capability for agriculture but one may be more difficult to reclaim than the other. A development difficulty rating from 1 to 7 is proposed for all organic soils in an unreclaimed state. Brief definitions of the development difficulty classes follow.

Classes 1, 2 and 3 — Only minor reclamation is required. Minor reclamation is considered to be those operations which can be carried out by a single operator.

Class 4 — Major reclamation is required but is warranted when soil capability is high. Major reclamation is that requiring cooperation between adjoining operators and/or outside financial assistance.

Classes 5 and 6 — Major reclamation is required and seldom warranted.

Class 7 — Hazards to development are so serious that they can be overcome only by major scale projects. Such development is unwarranted.

Hazards which are considered in arriving at the degree of development difficulty are those shown for the capability classification together with vegetative cover, excess water and flooding, and surface roughness.

To determine development difficulty class follow the features as for capability class, add the appropriate amounts of the following and subtract from 100 as before.

Vegetative Cover	*Excess Water and Flooding*	*Surface Roughness*
0 Light (grasses, reeds, etc.)	0 None	0 None
20 Moderate (brush, small trees)	35 Frequent	35 Holes and Mounds 1 to 2 ft.
35 Heavy (numerous large trees)	65 Extreme	50 Holes and Mounds 2 ft.

The guide for classifying the capability of organic soils for agriculture was prepared for Ontario conditions and was not developed for application to larger, more diversified regions. The technique, however, can be used on a continental basis by increasing or otherwise changing the number of physical features and their penalty points. For example, penalty points could be added for salinity and type of underlying material. Modifications can be made to the guide as it is field tested and more information becomes available.

The technique of soil capability analysis can be applied to many uses in addition to those already described. A soil capability classification need not consist of only seven classes. The number of classes may vary according to the objectives of the classification. For example, the following soil capability classifications for waste disposal and urbanization are five class systems.

Soil Capability for Waste Disposal

The soil capability classification for waste disposal has been devised in order to provide some basic guidelines as to the suitability of soils for the disposal of household waste, mainly by septic tanks. In determining this classification a number of "soil and site" factors have been taken into consideration. These are outlined below:

1. *Depth to Bedrock*
Bedrock near the soil surface effectively limits the volume of soil available for disposal purposes. This is particularly evident in the case of dense rock which acts as an impermeable barrier resulting in soils which become water-logged and develop foul odours. At the other extreme, porous or highly fissured bedrock permits the raw sewage to flow almost directly to ground water, with the distinct possibility that shallow wells or other bodies of water at lower elevations will become contaminated.

2. *Depth to Water Table*
The water table is that elevation at which water will appear in a hole dug for observing soil properties and drainage conditions. Most health authorities consider soils with a depth to water table of less than five feet to be wholly unsuitable as a medium for waste disposal. Sewage effluent quickly saturates wet or poorly drained soils with the result that surface flows of sewage occur. This may lead directly to the contamination of surface streams and water courses.

3. *Slope and Seepage*
The pattern in which effluents are distributed is determined by soil slope. When slopes of greater than four to six percent occur, the tile lines must be laid along the contours to facilitate a uniform distribution of effluent. In the case of slopes above six percent, considerable care is required in trenching, laying tiles and in making proper connections to

prevent a concentration of effluent in the lower tile beds. Areas where natural ground water seepage occurs, and areas along an escarpment, where flowing springs are most likely to occur, are unsuitable either for weeping tile beds or as sites for dumps.

4. *Stoniness and Trees*

The cost of septic system installation increases rapidly as the volume of soil occupied by stones and boulders, especially those greater than four inches in diameter, increases. Weeping tile beds and trees are totally incompatible on the same plot of land. Unless the trees are removed, the roots will permeate and plug the drain pipes. Trees will also interfere with other means of waste disposal and must be removed in areas to be used for sanitary land fill.

The following classification system has been devised to relate degree of stoniness to capability for waste disposal:

Stoniness Class	Description
0	Stonefree
1	Few stones
2	Moderately stony. Sufficient stone to interfere with trenching, digging, etc.
3	Very stony. Sufficient stones to interfere seriously with trenching, digging, etc.
4	Exceedingly stony. Stones so numerous that they often touch one another. Trenching, digging, etc., extremely difficult. Serious problem of stone disposal created.

5. *Natural Soil Drainage*

There are two general types of poor drainage conditions, including soils that are poorly drained most of the year and soils subject to periodic flooding for short periods of high water table. As the natural drainage of soil becomes progressively poorer, the degree of waste treatment and renovation is also lowered. Adequate waste treatment using the soil as a disposal medium requires aerobic conditions where oxidation of the effluents can readily occur.

6. *Soil Texture*

Texture refers to the composition of the mineral portion of the soil in terms of sand, silt and clay, with the classes ranging from coarse gravelly material to impermeable fine clays. In soils that are very permeable, the effluents are not filtered and the materials are not retained long enough for total biodegradation. In the case of impermeable soils, the effluents cannot penetrate the soil layers and are retained at or near the

TABLE 6.7

Soil Capability for Waste Disposal

Soil and Site Factors	Subclass Symbols (used on map)	1	2	3	4	5
Depth to Bedrock	R	>5'	>5'	>5'	>5'	>5'
Depth to Water Table	B	>6'	>6'	4–6'	3–4'	<3'
Slope — percent — pattern	T	0–5% Aa (symbols used on map)	6–9% B	6–9%–b 10–15%–C	10–15%–C	>15%
Stoniness	P	Classes 0,1	Classes 0,1	Class 2	Class 3	Class 4
Natural Drainage	W	good	moderate	imperfect	poor and rapid	very poor
Texture	A	loams clay loams	fine, sandy loams sandy loams clays	loamy sands gravel silt loams	very fine sands silts	any texture with high water table
Structure	D	strongly granular or blocky; porous; water stable	moderately strong granular or blocky; porous; water stable	weakly granular	structureless	structureless, unstable
Impermeable Layers	Y	none	none or more >3 ft. deep	one or more 2-3 ft. deep	one or more 1-2 ft. deep	one or more <1 ft. deep

surface. Soils of intermediate texture — including loams, most silt loams and clay loams — are most suitable for sewage disposal beds. These present a relatively large surface area (due to the clay content) for absorption sites and retain the effluents long enough to facilitate biodegradation. Serious problems in permeability can occur in several types of soil, especially if these occur as lenses or segregated layers in a soil which might otherwise be acceptable. With regard to this problem, particular attention should be paid to very fine sands and silts.

7. Soil Structure
·Structure refers to the arrangement of sand, silt and clay particles to form natural aggregates or structural units. A good porous structure is usually associated with the organic matter in the surface layers. As a result, a highly desirable type of structure is that found under grasses which have been established for several years. A porous type of structure (it should be noted that sand and gravel are structureless) permits water to flow and air to enter the soil to enhance biological activity. Weeping tiles will frequently become clogged when a poor soil structure impedes good drainage. In such cases the soil pores are filled with solids from the effluent, or the soil structural units are disintegrated due to the dispersing action of detergents.

8. Impermeable Layers
Impermeable layers in the soil interfere with soil moisture and root penetration. These, like structure, have some influence on the landscaping of an area; however, they may also interfere with installation of drainage tile, pipe lines or other underground facilities.

The relationship between the factors outlined above and the capability for waste disposal is outlined in Table 6.7.

Soil Capability for Urbanization

The soil capability classification for urbanization provides an indication of which soil characteristics are most likely to have an effect on a site selected for both the "in-soil" and "on-soil" forms of construction. Such things as buildings, roads, pipe lines and landscaping are all affected by various features of the soil. The following section provides an outline of the various soil characteristics and their effects on the soil capability for urbanization.

1. Depth to Bedrock
The depth to bedrock is important in most types of construction. Those areas with little or no soil cover present considerable difficulties to the

construction of certain below ground facilities. Included among these is the serious limitation for house construction. In general, basements cannot be built without considerable additional expense and those that are placed below grade may prove to be wet as a result of the lateral movement of water through the bedrock.

2. *Depth to Water Table*
Soils with a water table close to the surface are usually unsuitable for most forms of below grade construction unless a means can be devised to install drainage.

3. *Slope*
The degree and pattern of slope can affect the cost and difficulty of construction. Soils with steep slopes require cut and fill techniques or levelling for many types of construction. The slope pattern is also important, with smooth slopes being much easier to manage than those which are complex or irregular.

4. *Stoniness*
A limitation is caused by stoniness when stones are prevalent in large numbers. Soils in any planning area are extremely variable in their degree of stoniness. The same classification system devised to relate degree of stoniness to capability for waste disposal is used in the soil capability for urbanization.

5. *Drainage*
Those soils which are saturated with water for most of the year (10 to 11 months) are classified as poorly drained, while those which are saturated for up to eight months are referred to as imperfectly drained. Conditions such as these will affect road construction, building construction, or any construction which is likely to be disturbed by conditions of high moisture.

6. *Texture*
Certain sizes of soil particles will provide a better base for construction than others. Particles which are silt size will erode easily and soils having a high silt content can slip and slide unless carefully managed. Slopes for soils of this texture must never be steep along road sides nor should the soil be exposed to water or wind for any length of time. Gravelly soils often act as aquifers and contain lenses of quick sand which can add considerably to the cost of building if not identified and located. Soils of an organic nature may subside while clays will quickly form into clods if disturbed when wet. The effect of texture on the

162 /

TABLE 6.8

Soil Capability for Urbanization

Soil and Site Factors	Subclass Symbols (used on map)	1	2	3	4	5
Depth to Bedrock	R	>20'	8–20'	0–8'	0–8'	0–8'
Depth to Water Table	B	>20'	>20'	8–20'	0–8'	0–8'
Slope — percent — pattern	T	0–5% Aa, Bb	6–9%—C	6–9%—c 10–15%—D	16–30%—d	>30%
Stoniness	P	Classes 0,1	Classes 0,1	Class 2	Class 3	Class 4
Natural Drainage	W	good	moderate	imperfect	poor	very poor
Texture	A	loams clay loams	fine, sandy loams clays	loamy sands gravels	very fine sands silts	any texture with high water table
Structure	D	strong, granular blocky; porous; water stable	moderately strong granular or blocky; porous; water stable	weak granular or blocky;	structureless	structureless unstable
Impermeable Layers	Y	none	one or more >3 ft. deep	one or more 2-3 ft. deep	one or more 1-2 ft. deep	one or more <1 ft. deep

quality of the soil as a site for urbanization must be recognized in order that the limitations will not result in costly errors.

7. Structure
Although soil structure does not seriously affect most construction techniques, it does have influence on the ease with which landscaping can be conducted. Soils such as unstable clays and structureless sands do not provide a good medium for plant growth and require very careful handling when used for plant production.

8. Impermeable Layers
The rationale for this factor is the same as in the discussion of soil capability for waste disposal.

The soil capability rating system for urbanization is shown in Table 6.8.

LAND RESOURCE DEVELOPMENT IN CANADA

Land capability analysis techniques are used in the planning and management of land resources in Canada but not extensively. For example, while regions in British Columbia, Ontario and the Atlantic Provinces are vigorously pursuing plans which use the soil capability for agriculture analyses to allocate land for farming, the rest of the country is not showing the same degree of interest. Capability analyses have also been used on a limited basis to locate housing subdivisions, parks, waste disposal sites, septic tanks, tile beds, industrial basins, highways and pipelines.

One of the most promising applications of land capability methods has been their employment to appraise the suitability of land for various uses in and around areas subject to high urban growth pressures. British Columbia and Ontario have been the scenes of pioneering efforts along these lines.

In Ontario the most widely applied tool is known as the Land Capability and Development Constraints Map. This map is a composite of the following components.

A. Base Map
The base map, over which land capability and development constraint overlays are placed, consists of a generalized regional land use map. The land use map depicts as land use categories the following: residential, seasonal residential, commercial, industrial, forestry, agriculture, outdoor recreation, quarries, sand and gravel

pits, water bodies, Indian Reserves, airports, railways and major roads.

B. *Overlay Maps*
1. The following overlays are prepared from Canada Land Inventory Capability Maps:
   (a) Land of high soil capability for agriculture
   (b) Land of high recreation potential
   (c) Land of high potential for forest production
   (d) Land of high potential for production of wildlife (ungulates)

2. Land physically unsuitable for intensive urban development as a result of one or a combination of the following factors:
   (a) Excessive slope
   (b) Land liable to flooding or waterlogging
   (c) Water bodies, poorly drained or marsh areas
   (d) Large excavated areas
   (e) Airport noise zones

3. Woodland areas

4. Mineral resource zones

The intention of this analysis is to discover, by means of an elimination process:

1. the intrinsic suitability of the region for certain land uses;

2. those areas regionally suited for urban development.

The form of this elimination procedure essentially involves:

a. a description of the pattern that the capability and restraint areas take;
b. an account of how these capabilities and restraints relate to one another.

The crucial variable, land use, is also incorporated into the analysis. The importance of understanding land use is underscored by its function in delineating the areal extent, distribution and interdependencies of human activity. When capabilities and restraints are superimposed on the generalized land use map, the pattern of potential urban development areas is revealed.

Where the traditional method of urban growth and land use determination may have been annexation and zoning, the direction and type of urban development now become based upon physical and ecological perspectives.

The Land Capability and Development Constraints Map provides a general indicator of land use capability within a region. It assists in formulating a spatial plan for regional investment. For example, it enables the concentration of investment in areas classified as having a high potential for recreation facility development. The actual amount and distribution of regional recreation investment would depend on the scale and range of activities at each potential site.

The environmental evaluation of alternative regional designs is another essential function of the Land Capability and Development Constraints Map. It can assist in the goals fulfilment test of different development patterns. Furthermore, analysis of the map can contribute to the selection of the optimum comprehensive plan of development.

The Land Capability and Development Constraints Map shows what the land and its processes provide for prospective development and its form. It must be emphasized that this does not constitute a plan. The plan can evolve only when there is sufficient information on such factors as:

1. nature of demand;
2. locational and resource characteristics;
3. the capacities to realize objectives;
4. the social and economic goals of the region.

It seems evident that capability analyses do help with the decision-making process but they do not provide the whole answer to the solution of land allocation problems. Much additional economic data are required before adequate answers can be provided.

It is not within the terms of reference of this chapter to discuss all the ramifications of the many forces influencing land use and land use change. However, it might be useful to briefly discuss the external effects of agricultural land use in order to indicate the danger of making land allocation decisions on the basis of soil capability information alone. (External effects are the secondary attributes of a course of action or of a particular product. External effects have been referred to as "externalities", "spillover effects", and "social costs and social benefits.")

Social Costs and Social Benefits

External effects exist when all benefits and costs are not incident on the decision-maker. The private decision-maker considers only those benefits which accrue to him rather than to others, and only those costs which he is required to pay. However, a decision about the use of a resource may also affect the benefits and costs to others. For example: farmers, when applying fertilizers and pesticides to soil and crops, are concerned only with the possibility of increased yield, not with the amount of chemical leached or eroded into open bodies of water. The resulting damage done to lakes and rivers is not borne by the individual farmer who makes the decisions leading to these external effects, but rather, by society. Soil erosion is another example. Soil loss from gently sloping fields left without cover can be high and soil particles washed from fields adjacent to open water can cause siltation. Water reservoirs, ponds and lakes are often filled by soil accumulations and their usefulness is thereby destroyed. Not only is damage done to water reservoirs through siltation, but flood hazards increase. Usually damage to others is inflicted also in those instances where low quality soil particles are deposited atop fertile lands of other owners.

Society cannot reasonably expect a land owner to voluntarily undertake soil or water conservation measures if the primary benefits accrue to someone else. Legal constraints or restraints may be imposed on individual action to eliminate or mitigate external effects. Soil erosion in southern Ontario may not present a great problem insofar as the maintenance of the productive capacity of agricultural land is concerned. However, external effects of soil erosion may be large. For example, about 20 percent of the phosphorous discharged from southern Ontario into the Great Lakes can be traced to rural runoff.[9] The phosphorus is carried in sediments from erosion of streambanks and ditches, as well as from surface erosion of farm fields.

Society pays a price for increased productivity which is not included in the price of the product. Since farmers do not pay the costs attached to spillover effects, their costs are excluded in their decision-making. If all benefits and costs were properly accounted for, it is likely that the level of fertilizer and pesticide use would be lower and the rate of increase of agricultural production somewhat diminished.

These examples all describe negative external effects. However, external effects can also be positive. An obvious example is the provision of open space around cities by agricultural land. Such space performs an important function in air and water management, including air recharge (noxious air of the cities being diluted and cleansed with fresher air provided by trees and green plants) and the recharge of underground water reservoirs by rainwater. Open space plays an important role in maintaining emotional well-being for city dwellers. Farmers providing open space thus render a service to society for which they are not paid. In other words, the value of open space to society may be much higher than the indicated agricultural use value of the land.

Another example of a positive external effect is the benefit that society derives from farm woodlots. The positive effect of trees on the ecology and the scenic amenities provided are not priced in the market. Society cannot expect a farmer to increase or conserve his woodlot if the benefits accrue, not to him, but to others.

Spillover effects are, to a great extent, associated with qualitative aspects of land use. Their values are not incorporated in either output or input prices and where these effects loom large, land prices are the wrong indicator for determining land use and soil productivity estimates are better.

Land use conflicts can be reduced by planning. Land resource development in Canada often proceeds without careful consideration of the consequences. In this respect we are no different than the people of many other countries, but serious attempts must be made to improve our land development process. This will include the development of a "land ethic," the promotion of long term planning and a better understanding of the social costs and benefits of various land development schemes. Indeed, any planning programme should help broaden the political channels for public input on land use questions.

Soil capability analyses are but a step in the search for betterment but each step is worthwhile to the extent that it generates more informed attention to the interactions between land and people.

NOTES

1. Barnes, C.P. (1949). "Interpretive Soil Classification: Relation to Purpose." *Soil Science*, 67, 127-29.
2. Harcourt, R., W.L. Iveson and C.A. Cline. (1923). *Preliminary Soil Survey of Southwestern Ontario*. Toronto: Queen's Printer.
3. Canada, Department of Agriculture. (1974). *The System of Soil Classification for Canada*. Publication 1455, Ottawa: Queen's Printer.
4. Canada, Department of Regional Economic Expansion. (1969a). *Soil Capability Classification for Agriculture*. Report No. 2, Ottawa.
5. Canada, Department of Regional Economic Expansion. (1969b). *Land Capability Classification for Outdoor Recreation*. CLI Report No. 6, Ottawa: A.R.D.A.
   Canada, Department of Regional Economic Expansion. (1970a). *The Land Capability Analysis Component of Ontario's Regional Development Plans*, C.L.I. Report No. 3, Ottawa: A.R.D.A.
   Canada, Department of Regional Economic Expansion. (1970b). *Land Capability Classification for Forestry*. CLI Report No. 4, Ottawa: Queen's Printer.
   Canada, Department of Regional Economic Expansion. (1970c). *Land Capability Classification for Wildlife*. CLI Report No. 5, Ottawa: Queen's Printer.
6. Canada, Department of Regional Economic Expansion. (1970b). *op. cit.*
7. Canada, Department of Regional Economic Expansion. (1969a). *op. cit.*
8. Chapman, L.J. and D. M. Brown. (1966). *The Climates of Canada for Agriculture*. The Canada Land Inventory Report No. 3, Department of Forestry and Rural Development, Canada.
9. Miller, M.H. and D.W. Hoffman. (1970). "The Challenge of the Land: Physical Resource Aspects." In *Environmental Change: Focus on Ontario*, edited by D.E. Elrick, Don Mills: Science Research Associates, 9-29.

7

Soil Properties and Soil Engineering in Canada

O.L. White, Department of Civil Engineering,
University of Waterloo

SOIL — AN ENGINEERING DEFINITION

Soil has different meanings to different people and, of necessity, we must define our usage of the term for the present discussion.

To an engineer, soil is all the material which lies above bedrock and in Canada soil thus becomes synonymous with glacial drift and post-glacial deposits. Residual soils — that is, soils which have developed in-situ on pre-existing rocks — are virtually unknown in Canada because of the extensive glaciation in Pleistocene times and the temperate climate which has prevailed since glaciation. To some the above definition means that soil is ground that can be excavated by earth moving equipment without blasting,[1] but such a concept excludes the cemented glacial gravels or the basal till that is frequently more dense and more difficult to excavate than the bedrock on which it sits.

In pedology, soil is the term applied to the material at the earth's surface which has been altered to such an extent that plant life can be supported. This upper zone can often be divided into three horizons, A, B and C. The uppermost horizon A, commonly referred to as topsoil, usually contains an appreciable amount of organic material. The B horizon, the zone of accumulation, often contains much fine grained material removed from the A horizon. The lowermost or C horizon is relatively unaltered and is referred to as the parent material. In Canada, the A and B horizons combined rarely exceed a thickness of two to three feet. In engineering activities, the A horizon will often be stripped from a site and stockpiled. Not only is the A horizon useful in landscaping after construction but its presence under other material is undesirable because of its low strength and high compressibility.

Soil Properties of Major Concern to an Engineer

Just as data on the strength and deformation properties of steel and concrete are required for the safe design of a structure then so must the properties of a soil be known to permit a safe and economic design. With soils, the engineer seeks to determine the *strength, compressibility* and *permeability* of the material he must use.

Strength The mechanism by which foundation failures occur is governed by the shear strength of the soil so this property of the soil is of prime interest to engineers and may be measured directly by shear tests or, indirectly, through compression.

Compressibility All soils are compressible to some degree. Consequently all structures built on soil experience a certain amount of settlement and although total settlement can be allowed for in design and construction, an excessive differential settlement of one part of the structure with respect to another part could be disastrous.

Permeability The ability of a soil to permit the passage of water through a soil mass is referred to as permeability. When a saturated soil is loaded, compression can only occur as the water in the voids moves out of the loaded area. The removal of the water permits the mineral grains of the soil to move closer together and so settlement occurs. The rate at which the water moves is a function of the permeability of the soil and in turn affects the rate of settlement of any structure placed on the soil. Sands and gravels have high permeabilities thus allowing the rapid escape of water when the soil is loaded. Buildings placed on highly permeable sands and gravels will settle while under construction and virtually no further settlement occurs after construction. In contrast, clays and silts have low permeabilities, the water does not move quickly through these materials and may continue to escape for months and even years after construction is completed. Consequently, settlement of a structure placed on fine grained materials may continue for many years after construction[2].

Variability of Soil Properties

Of equal importance to the engineer in his concern for soil properties is the variability of those properties within a soil mass. Even within the confines of a single site considerable variation in soil properties can be found from point to point as well as in depth. Changes in the type of material and hence soil property can be rapid and sometimes unpredictable but a knowledge of the origin of the deposit will often assist in anticipating the variations.

Glacial deposits are particularly notorious in this respect and Legget[3] suggests that variability of composition is the principal characteristic of glacial soils. Of all glacial deposits, glacial till probably leads to the greatest problems because of its variability. A section cut through till in the vicinity of Cornwall, Ontario during the construction of the St. Lawrence Seaway revealed a situation which although not common is not unusual (Figure 7.1). Difficulties with excavations in till (related to

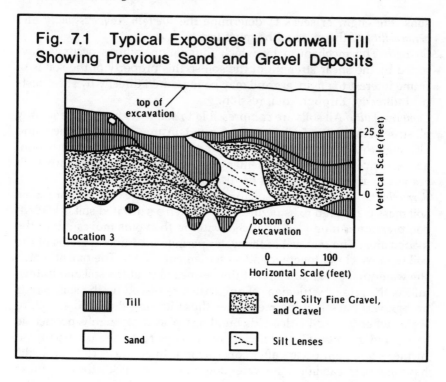

Fig. 7.1 Typical Exposures in Cornwall Till Showing Previous Sand and Gravel Deposits

soil variability) during the construction of the Seaway led to prolonged legal proceedings after the completion of the project[4] and similar problems occurred in the construction of the Welland Canal in the 1920's[5]. Glacio-fluvial deposits are also quite variable in content, especially those formed in ice-contact situations where meltwater conditions undergo rapid changes over short periods of time.

Glacio-lacustrine deposits may be considered somewhat more regular in composition than till, but even some of these deposits may vary rhythmically in depth. Such is the case with varved clay deposits, which consist of alternating layers of essentially silt and clay, each layer ranging in thickness from about one-eighth inch up to three or four inces.

Floodplain deposits of alluvium can be extremely variable, with materials ranging from dirty sands and gravels to lenses and pockets of clay. Variations in the extremes can be as prevalent in depth as on the surface and the changes can be rapid.

Nor are residual soils free from the problem of variability, but in these materials the variability will be, to a large degree, a function of the structure and variability of the pre-existing rock on which the soil is formed.

The inherent variability of soils requires that considerable attention be paid to not only obtaining samples of soils for testing purposes but to obtaining sufficient samples in order to thoroughly characterize a particular site. Naturally, a more intensive sub-surface investigation will be made and usually more samples will be taken when a selected site is located on material suspected or known to exhibit heterogeneous characteristics.

THE ORIGIN OF SOIL PROPERTIES

A soil mass is an aggregate of discrete particles and so the mass might be expected to possess properties related to those of the individual particles. This indeed is the case, but in addition, the properties of the mass are also related to the size and shape of the individual grains, the percentages of the various grain sizes present in the mass and the manner in which the individual grains are arranged or "packed" together. Thus, the origin of a soil, its mode of deposition or the manner in which the individual particles are assembled to form the soil mass can have a considerable effect upon the properties of that soil mass.

In 1776, a French military engineer, Coulomb showed that the shear strength(s) of a soil could be expressed as:

$$s = c + p \tan \emptyset$$
where c is the amount of cohesion between individual particles
  p is the pressure applied normal to the plane of failure and
  $\emptyset$ is the angle of internal friction or, preferably, the angle of shearing resistance.

With cohesionless soils (coarse silts, sands and gravels) the value of c is zero so the shear strength(s) becomes equal to $p \tan \emptyset$ and as p is an external factor applied to the soil mass, the shear strength of cohesionless soils becomes a function of $\emptyset$. Although the applied pressure p is a major factor in the strength of the soil mass, p is not further considered in the discussion.

The parameter $\emptyset$ is considered to have two component parts:

1. $\emptyset_f$ is considered as the frictional resistance to sliding of one particle over another and thus depends upon the composition of the particles and the fluid which occupies the voids between the particles (Horn and Deere, 1962);

2. $\emptyset_i$ which is related to the interlocking effect between the particles and thus depends not only on the shape of the particles (angular, rounded, etc.) but also on the density or degree of packing of the soil particles.

Thus, the internal source of strength of a cohesionless soil is expressed as the angle of shearing resistance $\emptyset$ and this depends to a large degree on:

1. The density of the soil, which is often expressed in terms of the void ratio (e), i.e. the ratio between the volume of voids to the volume of solids in a unit volume of soil. (As the void ratio decreases and the density increases then so will the value of $\emptyset$ increase.);

2. The angularity of the soil particles. (As the angularity increases, the value of $\emptyset$ will increase considerably.);

3. The gradation of the soil, that is, the distribution of the various sizes of particles within the soil. (A well graded soil will have a lower void ratio than that of a similar, more uniform-sized soil and hence a higher value of $\emptyset$ (Figure 7.2).)
as well as on the friction between the soil particles.

Typical values of $\emptyset$ for several types of soils are given in Table 7.1.

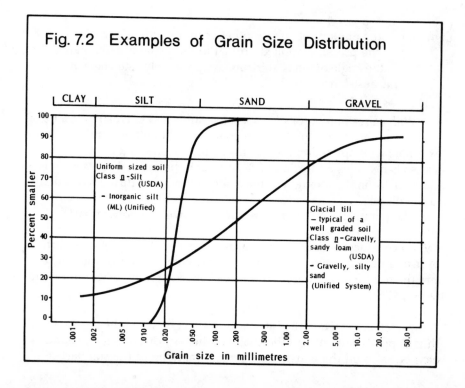

Fig. 7.2 Examples of Grain Size Distribution

TABLE 7.1

Typical Values of $\emptyset$ for Representative Soils

	Loose	Dense
Sand, rounded grains, uniform size	27°	34°
Sand, angular grains, well graded	33°	45°
Sandy gravel	35°	50°
Silty sand	27°—33°	30°—35°
Inorganic silt	27°—30°	30°—34°

With fine grained soil like clay, cohesion between the particles of clay minerals also makes a contribution to the strength of the soil mass. All clay minerals (such as kaolinite, illite and montmorillonite) exhibit the property of cohesion which distinguishes them from the non-clay minerals, although very small size particles (0.001 millimetres (mm)) of non-clay minerals do show a small amount of cohesion.

The strength of fine grained soils depends not only on the amount and kind of clay mineral present but also on the water content. An increase in water content will, for various reasons, usually result in a decrease in strength of a fine grained soil.

In fact, the presence of water in any soil, cohesive or cohesionless, can have a significant effect upon the strength of the soil. The shear strength of a soil was noted above as being a function of the pressure applied to the soil. Later work showed that the *effective* pressure has far more effect upon the behaviour of the soil than the *total* pressure and that the effective pressure (p') is defined as the difference between the total pressure (p) and the pressure exerted by the water in the pores or voids of the soil (u). Thus: p' = p − u. The pore water pressure can be changed by quite a variety of external agents and if increased can produce an appreciable decrease in the strength of the soil. The excessively high pore water pressures may be induced either by applying a load to the soil or by the presence of an upward pressure gradient as a result of particular ground water conditions.

If the pore water pressure increases to a value that equals the normal pressure applied, the soil will become unstable and will lose its capacity to support any load. This extreme condition is referred to by engineers as "quick", a condition that is often referred to by laymen as "quicksand". However it should be noted that there is no such material as quicksand; the layman's "quicksand" merely being ordinary soil in a quick condition.

In summary, the shear strength of a soil depends upon the effective pressure applied to the soil as well as the cohesion and friction which, in turn, depend upon the mineral content (cohesive clay minerals or non-cohesive minerals) and grain shape, sorting and packing, all of which can be related to the way in which the soil was originally formed or deposited.

All soils are permeable to some degree in that they contain voids between the particles which are connected and which thus permit the flow of water through the soil mass. In engineering, it is not the fact of permeability that is so important, but rather the flow rate at which the water may move through the soil mass.

Thus, permeability (k) is a function not only of the amount of voids but the size of the voids and, consequently, of the gradation of the soil and the size of the particles. Mineralogy will also be involved for clay minerals will usually be restricted to a size of about 0.004 mm or less.

A soil consisting of uniform-sized particles (e.g. a sand) will usually have a higher permeability than a similar soil consisting of a variety of particle sizes (e.g. a well graded soil such as a till). In such a circumstance the uniform-sized soil will have a higher void ratio than the well graded soil. But high void ratios do not always indicate a high permeability since a clay with a high void ratio will have a much lower permeability than a sand with a lower void ratio. In this case the absolute size of the voids in the clay are much smaller than those in the sand, and small voids constrict the passage of water through a soil.

Natural soil deposits cannot be expected to have the same permeabilities in all directions throughout the mass. Each layer or stratum could have a different permeability from that of the layer above or below and at the same time even within a single layer the permeability in the horizontal direction could be much greater than in the vertical direction, by as much as a factor of ten.

The compressibility of a soil refers to the ability of the soil to undergo a reduction of volume when subjected to a load. With such loads as may be involved, this reduction of volume is in effect a reduction of the void space in the soil mass, and is achieved by the movement of the solid particles into new positions in what might be called a closer packing arrangement. If the voids are occupied by water, the reduction in volume cannot occur without an expulsion of the water from the voids, and the rate of expulsion which is a direct function of the permeability of the soil will control the rate of the consolidation of the soil. A common situation of soil loading occurs when a building is constructed on a soil foundation. If the soil is compressed when loaded a reduction in soil volume will occur and the building will actually settle below its original elevation, commonly a matter of centimetres, but in some exceptional cases the settlement has been recorded as several metres. With sands, settlement is almost instantaneous with the application of the load, but with clay the settlement may still be occurring several years after the completion of the building.

If the soil particles are loosely "packed" when originally deposited, considerable volume reduction will follow when the soil is loaded. Thus a dense or closely packed soil will be much less compressible than a loose soil. If some kind of closer packing or densification can occur while the soil is being deposited (for example, through glacial pressures) that soil will have a very low compressibility when loaded. A soil consisting of particles covering a wide range of sizes (a well graded soil) will be much less compressible than a soil consisting to a large degree of particles of one size or a very small range in size (a uniform soil).

An important concept to consider when discussing compressibility of soils is that of the over-consolidated deposit. Such soils are those which at some time in their history have been subjected to a greater vertical pressure than is presently acting. These soils will have much lower compressibilities than they had initially and consequently can support a much greater load without appreciable settlement occurring. Over-consolidation may occur naturally or may be deliberately caused by man to improve the properties of the soil. Natural over-consolidation of a soil can be caused by the overriding of a glacier (consider here the possibility of a loading of 10,000 feet of ice), the previous existence of soil overburden now removed by erosion, the lowering of the groundwater level (the soil above the lowered groundwater level will exert a greater pressure on the soil below and the effects remain even if the groundwater level is restored) and by the effects of desiccation or the drying out of the soil (shrinkage stresses set up during drying out have a similar effect as the direct loading of the soil).

Soils which are both highly compressible and highly sensitive are special cases and occur in Canada along the Ottawa River and St. Lawrence River valleys and in the vicinity of Lac St. Jean, Quebec. These soils were deposited in marine or brackish water conditions after the withdrawal of the glacial ice some 10,000 to 12,000 years ago. The soil particles are arranged in a "cardhouse" structure — an edge to face arrangement — which can be relatively stable up to a certain value of loading but once that load is exceeded the cardhouse structure collapses. Not only is the soil highly compressible when the structure collapses, but the strength is considerably reduced (hence the term "highly sensitive" for these soils).

Thus, just as for the shear strength, the other major engineering properties of permeability and compressibility also are dependent both upon the grain size and the grading of the soil and to a lesser extent upon the mineralogy, all of which are functions of the depositional environment of the soil, while the compressibility can be further related to the post-depositional history. The geological history of a soil deposit is therefore an accurate indicator of the potential behaviour of a soil mass as an engineering material.

MEASUREMENT OF SOIL PROPERTIES

Methods used to test soils to determine their engineering performance include both conventional tests used for a variety of materials and in many fields of interest as well as tests which are confined to soils and to civil engineering. Some of the tests measure fundamental parameters of the bulk soils or the individual particles and some tests determine the response to particular procedures which are used to classify the soils into categories of engineering behaviour or which can be used directly for design purposes.

In most cases the results obtained must be interpreted in terms of the conditions by which the samples were obtained and the environment in which the sample was located.

Conventional Tests

GRAIN SIZE ANALYSIS

The grain size analysis is one of the most common tests in soil engineering, as it is in many other areas of science and technology. The test involves the passing of a prepared sample of soil through a series of sieves or screens with progressively smaller openings. Weighing the amount of soil retained on each screen indicates the distribution of the various sizes of particles within the sample. For fine grained soils (silts and clays) the particle size distribution is measured with a hydrometer when a sample of the soil is allowed to settle in a standard sedimentation cylinder. Such a test can involve a period of over 24 hours in order to determine the percentage of clay size particles in a sample (i.e. those particles smaller than 0.002 mm).

Grain size analyses are commonly done on soils because considerable use can be made of the results in identification, classification and evaluation. For coarse grained soils, the grain size analysis can indicate their suitability for use in a compacted earth fill for a dam or embankment, their suitability for use as a filter material and such properties as permeability. With gravels used for concrete manufacture the grain size distribution controls the amount of cement that must be added to the mix to produce concrete with acceptable strength. A well graded gravel, (i.e. with a good distribution of all sizes of particles) will require much less cement to fill the voids between particles than a gravel made up of particles mostly the same size. For fine grained soils, considerable use is made of the hydrometer results in classification, in broad evaluation of the potential behaviour and, with other data, in the determination of the "activity" of the soil (see Figure 7.3).

When different soils are to be mixed to form a base course for a highway or other compacted fills the grain size analyses provide the information for the design of the mix.

WATER CONTENT

The water content has a very great effect upon the working properties of a soil and, as a result, is determined on most samples taken in the field as well as on samples taken, for example, during the construction of a compacted fill. In soil engineering, the moisture content of a soil is expressed as a percentage of the dried weight of the solids, so that with some special types of soils the water content can exceed the weight of the solid materials and in such cases will be reported in excess of 100 percent. For example, soils in the vicinity of Mexico City have natural water contents as high as 300 percent[7] and peat (a special type of soil) in lower British Columbia has been reported with a moisture content in the range of 500-1,500 percent with occasional values of 2,000 percent.[8]

BULK DENSITY

The density of a soil is an important factor in its engineering behaviour, either in its natural condition in–situ or in a situation where the soil has been placed to form an earth structure such as a fill or an embankment. The density will depend upon the arrangement of the individual grains with each other. A soil with a low density or high void ratio — where the volume of voids (Vv) is high compared with the volume of solid particles (Vs) (i.e. $e = \dfrac{Vv}{Vs}$) — will tend to compact or consolidate under load, and will have a much lower shear strength than the same soil in a dense condition (where the particles are more closely packed together.)

The density referred to above (sometimes called bulk density) includes both the solid particles and voids in a unit volume of soil and can be measured in the field or in the laboratory. Very often the in situ density is related to the maximum and minimum states of density that can be determined for the soil.

For example,

Relative Density, DR $= \dfrac{e\ max - e}{e\ max - e\ min}$

is expressed in terms of void ratios

where e $\quad$ = void ratio of the soil in its measured condition

$\quad$ e max = void ratio in the least dense condition

$\quad$ e min = void ratio in the most dense condition

The Standard Penetration Test (discussed below) is the most common method used to evaluate indirectly the relative density of a soil in the field but other, direct methods of measurement of density are used when and where appropriate.

SPECIFIC GRAVITY

The specific gravity of a soil is the ratio of the unit weight of soil particles to the unit weight of water. The specific gravity is not made use of directly in soil engineering but is used to determine other useful properties of the soil.

The soil in a particular area will usually be composed of an assemblage of materials which remain constant over a fairly wide area and an approximate value of the specific gravity will often be assumed for such an area. For instance, Quigley[9] reports that the clay size fraction of the glacial lacustrine soils around Winnipeg contains:

Quartz	10-15 percent
Kaolinite	5-10 percent
Montmorillonite-illite	80 percent

Such a material would probably have a specific gravity of about 2.65 – 2.70. But soils which contain an appreciable percentage of heavier minerals, such as the reddish coloured tills in southern Ontario which have been derived from the iron-rich shale of the Queenston Formation, will have higher values; i.e. in the range of 2.75 to 2.80[10].

Engineering Tests

ATTERBERG LIMITS

Although the Atterberg tests were first devised for use by a Swedish agriculturist, the various tests which give the Atterberg Limits of fine grained soils are widely used in soil mechanics.

The Atterberg Limits are actually moisture contents at which the soil undergoes various changes in behaviour in altering from a liquid to a solid state. The liquid limit is the moisture content at which the soil changes from a viscous fluid to a plastic state; the plastic limit is the moisture content at which the soil changes from a plastic state to a semi-solid state; and the shrinkage limit is the moisture content below which there is no change in volume of the soil with change in water content. A useful index obtained from the results of the Atterberg tests is the plasticity index which is the arithmetic difference between the liquid limit and the plastic limit. The resulting figure indicates the range of moisture content over which the soil behaves plastically.

The liquid limit is determined by placing a soil-water mixture in a specially designed shallow cup. The cup is tapped in a regular fashion on a solid base until the two sides of a groove placed in the soil pat come together. The test is repeated at several different moisture contents and results are interpolated to give the moisture content at which 25 blows will bring the two sides together. The plastic limit is determined by rolling the soil-water mixture by hand into thin rods and noting the diameter of the rods when they break. The moisture content is determined when the soil is at this particular condition. An equally simple test procedure permits the determination of the shrinkage limit. The relationships between the various limits are given in Figure 7.3.

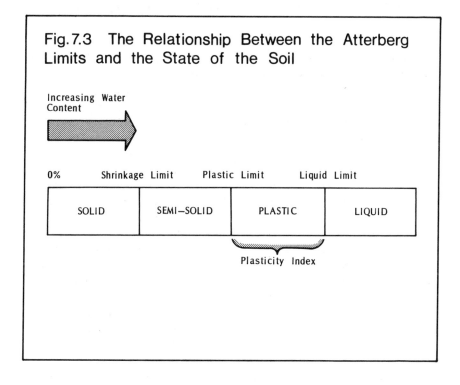

Fig. 7.3   The Relationship Between the Atterberg Limits and the State of the Soil

The Atterberg Limits are used not only to indicate the probable behaviour of soils but are very widely used to classify and correlate different soils from place to place. However, Atterberg Limits, by the nature of the tests involved, are determined on soils in their disturbed condition and so Atterberg Limits may not always be good indicators of the behaviour of some soils which have granular and mineralogical properties which impart special properties to the soil in its undisturbed condition in situ.

Skempton[11] introduced the concept of the "activity" (A) of a soil and this is given as the ratio of the plasticity index (PI) to the percentage of the soil particles finer than 0.002 mm $\left(A = \dfrac{PI}{(\% \, 0.002 \, mm)}\right)$. Thus the activity number of a soil relates the plastic behaviour ot the clay size fraction of the soil; whereas the presence of a small percentage of a highly plastic clay mineral can produce a large PI, the same PI could also result from a large percentage of a much less plastic clay mineral. The activity number will clearly show the difference between the two soils which have similar PI's but which owe such values to different clay minerals. Soils from a similar geologic deposit will generally have the same activity number regardless of the percentage of clay-size particles present in the soil.

MOISTURE-DENSITY RELATIONSHIPS

The determination of the moisture-density relationship of a soil is very important in situations where earth fill is being placed under a building or roadway or where an embankment or earth dam is being constructed. Under such circumstances, the condition of the soil to provide maximum strength and minimum compressibility is crucial. For materials to be used in these circumstances the maximum dry density and optimum moisture content must be first found in the laboratory and then be constantly checked while the soil is being placed in the field.

When water is added to a dry soil the density of the mixture increases to a maximum before diminishing with further additions of water. The amount of water present in the maximum (dry) density condition is known as the optimum moisture content and after this has been determined in the laboratory the earth fill being placed in the field will be constantly checked to ensure that the field water content is within limits (95-100 percent optimum) to ensure a maximum dry density.

In the initial laboratory testing, water is added in stages to the soil. At several different water contents, the wetted soil is compacted into a standard size metal cylinder using a standard method of compaction and the bulk density determined. This is repeated a number of times until the density has diminished with the addition of excess water. Ultimately the optimum moisture content corresponding to the maximum dry density is found. This procedure is known as the Proctor Compaction test (Figure 7.4).

When the soil is being placed in the field numerous checks are run to see that the densities and water contents are within specified limits. Field methods used include the physical measurement of the volume of a weighed amount of excavated soil, or the determination of the density of the soil by nuclear density meter.

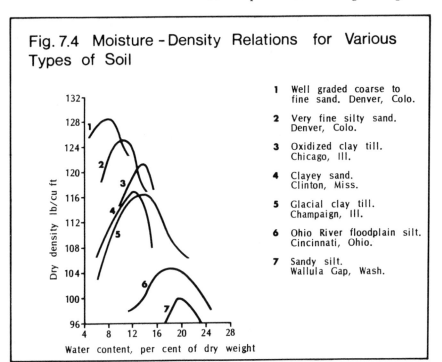

Fig. 7.4   Moisture - Density   Relations   for   Various
Types of Soil

1 Well graded coarse to fine sand. Denver, Colo.

2 Very fine silty sand. Denver, Colo.

3 Oxidized clay till. Chicago, Ill.

4 Clayey sand. Clinton, Miss.

5 Glacial clay till. Champaign, Ill.

6 Ohio River floodplain silt. Cincinnati, Ohio.

7 Sandy silt. Wallula Gap, Wash.

STRENGTH TESTS

Although the shear strength of a soil is of prime interest to an engineer, the correct determination of shear strength is one of the most difficult tasks facing him in the testing of soil. Shear strength is not a constant property of a soil for it varies according to conditions of moisture, density, drainage and the degree to which the soil has been consolidated as well as to the method of testing. Thus, the engineer seeks to determine the shear strength of the soil under the worst probable condition that the soil will be subjected to in service.

Two main methods are involved in the evaluation of the shear strength of soil: the direct shear test and the triaxial shear test.

1. *The direct shear test*

In this test, the soil is placed in a shallow, metal box which has separate top and bottom portions. During the test the bottom portion is fixed and the top portion is moved across the bottom part to shear the soil contained within the box. The load required to shear the soil is measured and the shear strength of the soil can be calculated.

The soil sample may be prepared by careful trimming to shape for insertion into the metal box or the sample may be placed in small, successive amounts directly into the box, each amount separately and systematically compacted to produce a test specimen as homogeneous as possible. Samples are loaded vertically and the shearing force is determined for several different vertical loads.

2. *The triaxial shear test*

In the triaxial test, cylindrical samples are used in sizes from about two inches diameter by four inches long up to four inches diameter by eight inches long or even larger. The sample is usually encased in a rubber membrane and then placed in a transparent, plastic cell. This procedure permits the sample to be subjected to an "all-round" pressure before and during the application of the vertical load. The vertical (compressive) load is then increased until the sample fails, although this process may be done in steps with the "all-round" pressure increased at each step.

Each type of test has its advantages and limitations. The triaxial test permits a variation of the sample environment during the test and also permits the measurement of the pressure developed within the pore-water of the soil during testing and especially at the moment of failure (pore-water pressure). A variation of the triaxial test, used commonly because of its simplicity and speed, is the unconfined compression test in which a small sylinder (e.g. 1½ inch diameter) of cohesive soil is tested in compression without first being encased in a membrane or being placed in the cell. In this circumstance, the "all-round" pressure is taken as zero and the shear strength as one-half of the compressive strength. The direct shear test is preferred if large samples have to be tested.

Cohesive soils are often tested both in their natural undisturbed condition (as found in situ) and in a remoulded condition. In the remoulded condition the original soil will be broken down and remade into a new sample at a density and moisture content close to the original condition. The ratio of the undisturbed shear strength to the remoulded shear strength is known as the "sensitivity" of the soil and may be as great as eight for normally sensitive soils. For very sensitive or "quick" clays, such as occur in the landslide areas in Quebec and eastern Ontario, the sensitivities can be as high as from 15 to 100.

CONSOLIDATION TESTS

When a load is applied to a mass of soil by, for example, the construction of a building or an embankment, the individual particles which comprise the soil will tend to move closer together or consolidate. All soils will consolidate to some degree when loaded. This leads to a reduction in volume of the soil mass and, consequently, the settlement of any structure which might be founded on such soil.

Thus the engineer is concerned with the consolidation or settlement characteristics of the soil he has to use and will conduct consolidation tests on soils whenever appropriate to determine the amount of settlement which may occur under a proposed structure. In most cases the maximum loads applied to a soil are restricted more by the consolidation characteristics of soil than by the strength characteristics.

The test itself involves the preparation of a sample of soil in the shape of a flat cylinder about two to four inches in diameter and one to two inches thick. The soil is placed in a closely fitted brass ring and seated on a porous metal plate (made from sintered metal powders). Another porous plate is placed on top of the soil and the whole assembly placed in an oedometer (a machine for measuring consolidation of soils). Loads are applied vertically through the porous plates and as the volume of the soil is reduced and as the upper porous plate settles, the amount of settlement is measured and the load required to produce the particular settlement recorded. Each load is allowed to act for 24 hours or until most settlement has occurred before the load is increased and this procedure is continued until the maximum test load has been applied. The load is then progressively reduced back to the initial load or to zero load. This allows the soil sample to expand or swell and although the amount of rebound can be considerable, the soil rarely returns to its original thickness.

The use of porous metal plates top and bottom of the sample is to permit water to drain from the soil during loading and to re-enter the soil during unloading. If water is unable to drain from the sample during loading, the soil will not consolidate and hence no settlement will occur.

In such circumstances (of no drainage) excessive pressures are developed in the water contained in the pores of the soil, and as excess pore water pressure leads to lower effective strengths, any condition in the ground which tends to produce excess pore water pressures must be allowed for in design.

Consolidation tests are usually restricted to fine grained soils such as clays. Some clays will continue to consolidate for many years after the initial loading so the total settlement and the time involved in that settlement are both important[12]. Total settlement itself is not always as important as differences in settlement between several parts of the structure. If one part of the structure settles more than other parts, the stresses developed within the structure may cause considerable damage to the structure itself.

THE STANDARD PENETRATION TEST

The Standard Penetration Test is widely used in North America both as a means of obtaining sub-surface soil samples at a site and to provide data for the design of foundations.

After a hole has been augered or bored to the desired depth, an open-ended cylindrical tube is lowered to the bottom of the hole and driven into the soil a further two feet. The tube is commonly two inches in outside diameter and is supplied with a three-inch-long cutting shoe at the bottom and a coupling at the top to attach to drill rods. The tube itself is split longitudinally and when brought to the surface can be opened to permit the sample to be removed.

When used to provide design data through the Standard Penetration Test, the sampling tube (or split spoon) is driven into the ground with a 140 lb hammer and allowed to drop through a distance of 30 inches. The number of blows required to drive the split spoon a distance of 12 inches is recorded as the N-value and these results can generally be correlated with the physical properties of the soil, especially the relative density. The correlation is fairly reliable with sands but rather unreliable with clays. Modifications to the correlation are necessary in circumstances where the sands are particularly dense, saturated or located a considerable depth below the surface. Even though such modifications are not infrequently required, the test procedure is widely used for foundation design.

SOIL ENGINEERING IN CANADA

Soil Engineering for Foundations

The design and construction of the foundations for buildings and similar structures provide, probably, the most common circumstances involving soil engineering. As indicated above, the soil must have both its strength and compressibility characteristics evaluated before the applied unit loads can be determined and the foundations designed. Most commonly, the structural loads applied through the foundation to the soil are limited by the compressibility of the soil. Theories and appropriate test procedures are available to the soil engineer to determine what loads should be applied to the soil in question, but much also has been learned about the behaviour of soils by observing the performance (i.e. settlement) of buildings after construction and in some cases by thoroughly studying the occasional foundation failure which has occurred.

Time-settlement relationships are obtained in the laboratory from consolidation tests on soils, but similar relationships can be obtained on actual buildings by accurately noting the elevation of fixed points (bench marks) in the buildings. Figure 7.5 indicates the maximum settlement which occurred for three buildings in the Ottawa area over a ten-year period.

These buildings were all constructed with a special type of foundation designed to produce as little settlement as possible and in fact the

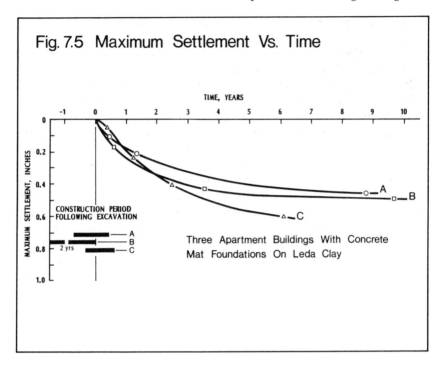

Fig. 7.5 Maximum Settlement Vs. Time

Three Apartment Buildings With Concrete Mat Foundations On Leda Clay

settlement was less than two centimetres over the ten-year period. The buildings, all seven or eight storey apartments, were constructed in the early 1950's so that the total load of the building was placed on a large slab which extended over the entire area covered by the structure. The structure was designed so that the total weight of the building was equal to or was very little more than the weight of the soil removed during excavation of the site. Hence very little settlement was expected, for the building was not likely to stress the soil beneath the foundation much more than the excavated soil which previously existed at the site. The net increase in pressure due to the structures varied between 0.54 and 0.73 tons per square foot.

These loads are far less than the loads which are calculated to have been transmitted to the soil by another Ottawa building on similar soil. The National Museum Building was constructed in 1910 with heavy sandstone walls resting on "spread" footings. Unit loads in excess of 4.0 tons per square foot are believed to have been exerted on the soil by the structure[13]. Total settlements in excess of 1.5 feet and considerable differential settlements have been recorded. So severe were the differential settlements that the internal basement walls were severely damaged and the tower over the entrance was removed in 1916 to prevent a complete failure of the tower. Little settlement occurred after the tower was re-moved.

One of the best and perhaps the longest time-ranging record of the settlement of a building is that of the Empress Hotel, Victoria, B.C.[14]. Built over 60 years ago, on a 50-foot-thick deposit of clay, records show that the south end of the building settled some 4 feet in the first 10 years after construction and then only an additional 0.6 inches in the following 55 years. The average increase in vertical load on the soil was approximately 2 tons per square foot. Good correlation was noted between the measured amounts of settlement and the amounts calculated in recent years on soil samples taken near the hotel site.

But engineers have also made use of studies of actual failures and one of the most spectacular foundation failures in Canadian engineering history is that of the grain elevator at Transcona, Manitoba in 1913.

The actual structure remained intact when the soil on which the elevator was founded failed and allowed the structure to tilt over at an angle of almost 27° to the vertical. The 20,000 ton weight bin-house of the elevator was subsequently restored to its design position by jacking piles to bedrock after 875,000 bushels of wheat were removed and the elevator remains in use to the present day. The restoration itself was no mean engineering feat and remains, to this day, a credit to the engineers and contractors (The Foundation Company, Limited) responsible for the restoration.

The whole structure was founded onto a 40-foot-thick deposit of glacio-lacustrine clay typical of the glacial Lake Agassiz deposits in the Winnipeg area. Based on field load bearing tests conducted before construction, the ultimate bearing capacity was calculated as 6,600 lbs per square foot. Failure occurred a few weeks after the filling of the elevator commenced and although the structure was shortly put back in service, detailed site investigations were not conducted until about 40 years later. In 1952 several investigators[15] took a number of sub-surface samples, and after laboratory testing was completed determined both the recommended bearing pressures and the ultimate bearing capacity of the soil, using the current theories available to the engineer for the design of foundations. After all calculations were completed, pleasure was noted that the conditions leading to failure verified the theories by which a foundation design is currently determined and which were not generally available to the original designers.

The Construction of a Dam

In the construction of a dam, be it for the impounding of water to generate hydroelectric power, to provide a reservoir for a water supply or to provide for flood control, the engineer has to design the embankment or impounding structure not only to remain intact and in a stable

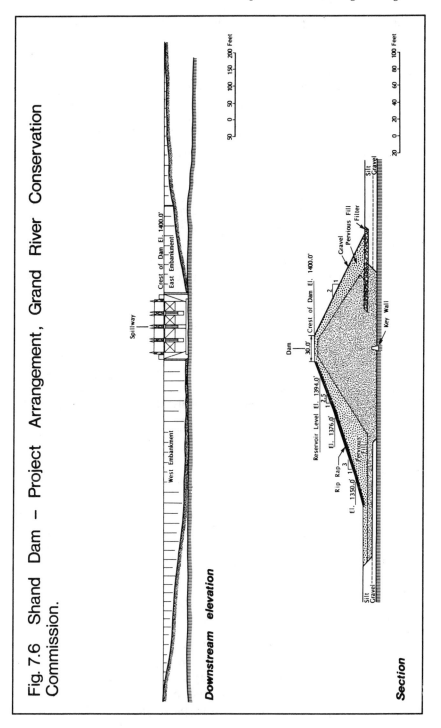

Fig. 7.6 Shand Dam – Project Arrangement, Grand River Conservation Commission.

condition but also to prevent excessive leakage of water from the reservoir.

Embankments may be constructed from concrete, rock fill or earth fill or from a combination of the various materials. The choice of material depends upon the site conditions, such as the foundation material and the valley profile, but very often is a function of the availability of suitable materials. With 95 percent of the area of Canada subjected to glaciation and with 75 percent of all the glacial drift composed of till,[16] it should not be surprising to learn that many Canadian dams have been constructed of this ubiquitous material. And yet the first Canadian dam to be built from glacial till was not completed until 1941.

The Shand Dam, located on the Grand River in south-western Ontario, three miles north-east of Fergus, is 78 feet high and extends 2,100 feet along the crest. The central control section of the dam is a concrete gravity structure founded directly onto the dolomite bedrock of the Guelph Formation. But the major part of the dam is a 537,000 cubic yard earth fill embankment constructed from glacial till obtained in the immediate vicinity of the dam site (Figure 7.6).

Extensive testing of samples of the fill taken from numerous boreholes and test pits preceded the selection of embankment material and the design of the embankment[17]. As is usual for many tills, a wide range of particle sizes were present in the local materials to give a well-graded material which compacted well to form an impervious core for the embankment. The clay-size material (<0.002 mm) ranged between about 8-20 percent but apparently did not include any (or very few) clay minerals, the clay-size particles consisting essentially of non-clay minerals. Nevertheless, despite the absence of clay minerals, the compacted till provided an adequate impervious material from which the embankment was constructed.

Since the completion of the Shand Dam numerous Canadian dams have been constructed from glacial till, including many to heights of 200 feet or more. Although glacial tills can vary in texture from a clay-rich material to what is essentially a sandy material, the grading of glacial tills usually permits them to be compacted to a reasonably high density to provide a high-strength, impermeable material suitable for dam embankments.

Landslides in Eastern Canada

Landslides occur widely throughout Canada but in recent years their frequent occurrence in parts of eastern Ontario and Quebec has drawn wide attention. A landslide may be triggered by the action of man or by natural forces in the normal development of the face of the earth. They occur in a great variety of soils and particularly in clays but the landslide-prone soils of the valleys of the Ottawa and St. Lawrence Rivers are special cases of "quick clays." Many geological and engineering studies on these clays have been initiated in recent years in order to more thoroughly understand the behaviour of these materials which on failure have frequently caused loss of life and considerable property damage.

The clays were deposited in the valleys of the two major rivers as well as in the valley of the Saguenay River and in the vicinity of Lac St. Jean shortly after glaciation when the land was still depressed from the effect of the weight of ice and when the sea waters entered the valleys after the glaciers had melted. Subsequently, these marine clays were raised high above present sea level as the surface on which they had been deposited "rebounded." This temporary invasion of the sea along these valleys has been designated the Champlain Sea (the Laflamme Sea in the Saguenay valley) and the material deposited therein is known as Champlain Sea clay (previously, Leda clay).

Engineers are concerned with designing stable slopes cut in these materials, with evaluating the stability of buildings and other structures (embankments) placed on them and with evaluating the stability of natural slopes with the intention of ensuring their stability.

The Champlain clays are believed to have a somewhat special arrangement of the individual soil particles such that the plate-like particles are oriented to each other in an edge to face arrangement in the undisturbed condition, i.e. "cardhouse" structure. This structure is fairly rigid and strong if it remains undisturbed but if the soil should be stressed beyond an upper limit, the "cardhouse" structure is destroyed and the strength of the soil is considerably reduced. Where the ratio of undisturbed strength to the strength of the soil in its disturbed or remoulded condition is high, the soil is said to be sensitive and as this ratio for Champlain clays is of the order of 20, such clays are readily seen to have this property.

When field conditions change (such as the erosion of the toe of a riverbank, or the overloading of the upper part of a slope) and the original "cardhouse" structure is destroyed, the soil changes to an almost liquid-like material which flows readily on disturbance. This is apparently what occurred in the spring of 1971 when the undercutting of a slope triggered a slide at St. Jean Vianney in which 31 lives were lost and 40 houses were destroyed. The clay with its structure destroyed and a high moisture content moved as a viscous fluid down the stream channel at an estimated speed of 14 mph, en route to the Saguenay River.

Methods of stabilizing existing slopes generally involve the control of groundwater, the flattening of the slope or the protection of the foot of the slope to prevent the occurrence of toe erosion. Drainage of the soil mass which forms the slope could result in the reduction of pore pressure and consequently the increase in strength of the mass. Flattening of the slope would result in the reduction of the magnitude of the force which tends to produce instability, and the prevention of toe erosion again reduces the magnitude of the driving force.

NOTES

1. Hunt, C.B. (1972). *Geology of Soils*. San Francisco: Freeman.
2. Crawford, C.B. and J.G. Sutherland. (1971). "The Empress Hotel, Victoria, British Columbia, Sixty-five Years of Foundation Settlement." *Canadian Geotechnical Journal*, 8 (1), 77-93.
3. Legget, R.F. (1974). "Glacial Landforms and Civil Engineering." In *Glacial Geomorphology*, Proceedings of Fifth Annual Geomorphology Symposium, Binghampton, New York.
4. Engineering News Record. (1958a). "St. Lawrence Blues." May 15th, 25.
   Engineering News Record. (1958b). "Just How Much Has It Really Cost?" June 13th, 31-3.
5. Legget, R.F. (1974). *op. cit.*
6. Horn, H.M. and D.U. Deere. (1962). "Frictional Characteristics of Minerals." *Geotechnique*, 12, 319-35.
7. Lo, K.Y. (1962). "Shear Strength Properties of a Sample of Volcanic Material of the Valley of Mexico." *Geotechnique*, 12(4), 303-18.
8. Lea, N.D. and C.O. Brawner. (1963). "Highway Design and Construction Over Peat Deposits in the Lower Mainland of British Columbia." *Highway Research Board, Research Record*, No. 7, 1-33.
9. Quigley, R.M. (1968). "Soil Mineralogy, Winnipeg Swelling Clays." *Canadian Geotechnical Journal*, 5(2), 120-2.
10. Hegler, D.P. (1974). *Lake Ontario Shoreline Erosion in the Regional Municipality of Niagara*. Unpublished M.A.Sc. Thesis, University of Waterloo.
11. Skempton, A.W. (1953). "The Colloidal 'Activity' of Clays." *Proceedings of Third International Conference of Soil Mechanics and Foundation Engineering*, 1, 57-61.
12. Crawford, C.B. and J.G. Sutherland. (1971). *op. cit.*
13. Crawford, C.B. (1953). "Settlement Studies on the National Museum Building, Ottawa, Canada." *Proceedings of Third International Conference of Soil Mechanics and Foundation Engineering*, 1, 338-45.
14. Crawford, C.B. and J.G. Sutherland. (1971). *op. cit.*
15. Baracos, A. (1957). "The Foundation Failure of the Transcona Grain Elevator." *Engineering Journal*, 40 (7), 973, 977 and 980.
    Peck, R.B. and F.G. Bryant. (1953). "The Bearing Capacity Failure of the Transcona Elevator." *Geotechnique*, 3, 201-8.
16. Scott J.S. (1975). "Geology of Canadian Tills." Paper presented at Glacial Till — An Interdisciplinary Conference, Ottawa.
17. Leggett, R.F. (1942). "An Engineering Study of Glacial Drift for an Earth Dam, near Fergus, Ontario." *Economic Geology*, 37(7), 531-56.
    McQueen, A.W.F. and R.C. McMordie. (1940). "Soil Mechanics at the Shand Dam." *Engineering Journal*, 23(4), 161-77.

PART 5
ECOLOGY AND
NATIONAL DEVELOPMENT
IN CANADA

Introduction

The two papers which comprise this section of the book appear, on the surface, to be concerned with quite unrelated topics. Theberge's study deals with what he feels are needed changes in the ways we manage our national park system in Canada. Kitchen is concerned about the ways we manage, or rather fail to manage, the process of development in and around our urban areas. There is, however, at least one clear, unifying link between these two seemingly disparate concerns. Both authors adopt a common approach. Together they see in the philosophy, concepts and methods of ecology the basic tools needed to combat the problems we encounter even in such contrasting environmental settings as the city and the wilderness.

Theberge provides us with a great deal of background information on the concept and history of national parks in general, and on the nature and evolution of Canadian national parks policy in particular. He also includes in his paper a short account of the development of ecological ideas and methods of analysis. His main object, however, is to critically examine the current state of the planning process as it applies to the national parks system in Canada, and to provide an agenda for needed action in this area.

Coming from an academic, Theberge's recommendations are perhaps predictable. They fall into two general categories — the need for more research and the importance of using national parks as educational vehicles in a war against "ecological illiteracy" among the public at large. Predictable or not, these are obviously crucial components of any strategy aimed at the fulfillment of the primary goal of Canada's national park system as set out in official policy: ". . . to preserve for all time areas which contain significant geographical, geological, biological or historic features . . . ."

Kitchen's paper divides neatly into two parts. In the first part, he develops a rationale and methodology for the conduct of what he terms "ecoplanning": the introduction of ecological values and knowledge into the urban planning process. In the second part he provides us with the evidence to support his theoretical propositions. This takes the form of three case studies of urban development projects in which the author participated as a research consultant.

Ecology, for Kitchen, is not a slogan in any campaign advocating a no-growth society. He acknowledges the necessity for growth and development. What he does not acknowledge is the necessity for the environmental degradation which seems always to accompany the development process in Canada. This he feels can be amelioriated, if not completely avoided, by means of ecological monitoring and assessment techniques at all stages in the development process.

Both Kitchen and Theberge point out the many difficulties facing the advocate and practitioner of an ecological approach to solving planning problems. Some of these difficulties include the lack of basic information on the structure and function of ecosystems "threatened" by development and the relatively primitive state of the arsenal of available techniques. Both men agree, however, that these essentially technical problems pale to insignificance compared to the constraints which arise when ecological values come into conflict with other interests and objectives.

This, of course, is the stuff of politics, not ecology. In the long run, ecological values will begin to be consistently accorded the consideration they probably deserve only if and when they become institutionalized. There are some signs in Canada indicating that such a process is underway. There are, however, just as many signs which point in the other direction. Economic growth is likely to retain its priority status over environmental quality as a national objective for a long time yet.

8

Ecological Planning in National Parks

John B. Theberge, Department of Man-Environment Studies and School of Urban and Regional Planning, University of Waterloo

WHY ECOLOGY IS CENTRAL TO NATIONAL PARK PLANNING

National parks are respiring, energy trapping, oxygen producing, nutrient cycling, gigantic living organisms. Enmeshed in them is life in thousands of forms, woven together by intricate threads of functional relationships that man only dimly perceives; the same threads that made life on earth possible, and, if not torn apart, will allow life to continue. National parks are living treasures of unestimable value, not just for man, but all life.

For man, national parks are other things too: economic entities, with local, regional and sometimes national significance; social creations, drawing people from thousands of miles; at times even political pawns, the subjects of heated negotiation and debate. No wonder guidelines for managing national parks are difficult to formulate and apply.

Despite the many obvious benefits to be gained from managing national parks to realize socio-economic, recreational or political goals, preservation of intact, naturally-functioning ecosystems should be the overriding objective of national parks policy. In no other way can either their special contribution to the needs of man be assured, or indeed their very survival be guaranteed. To achieve the goal of preservation, the principles and approaches of applied ecology must guide national park planning and management.

What Are National Parks? — An Historical Perspective

The world's first national park, Yellowstone, was established in the United States in 1872 as "a pleasure ground for the benefit and enjoyment of the people."[1] Recreation, not preservation, was stressed. Forty-four years later, however, the U.S. National Parks Act of 1916 gave greater weight to the protective role of national parks:

> *to conserve the scenery and the natural and historic objects and wildlife therein and to provide for the enjoyment of the same in such a manner and by such means as will leave them unimpaired for the enjoyment of future generations.*

The official attitude in Canada to national parks underwent exactly the same kind of change in emphasis between the founding of the first national park and the passage of the first true national parks act. Thus, Banff was created in 1887 as "a public park and pleasure ground for the benefit, advantage and enjoyment of the people," almost precisely the same wording as used for Yellowstone, while Canada's National Parks Act passed in 1930 contained almost the same wording as used in the U.S. National Parks Act 14 years earlier:

> *The Parks are hereby dedicated to the people of Canada for their benefit, education and enjoyment . . . and such parks shall be maintained and made use of as to leave them unimpaired for the enjoyment of future generations.*

In theory, both countries recognized that long term public benefit depended on maintaining the land "unimpaired." In practice, however, recreation, often backed by large commercial interests, dominated national parks. It remained this way in Canada for 34 years after the passage of the 1930 National Parks Act during which period no official national parks policy under the act was ever drawn up. As a result, Banff townsite was decked out with bowling alleys, car washes and wax museums, and provision of urban services consumed much of the annual maintenance budget of the National and Historic Parks Branch in Ottawa.[2] Townsites also grew in Jasper and Riding Mountain, while summer resorts sprang up in Prince Albert. At the same time Point Pelee became overrun with cars and people (see Figure 8.1 for locations of Canadian National Parks).

Obviously the words "benefit, education and enjoyment" were being interpreted "according to the economic needs of the times and a large degree of public misunderstanding developed as to the real and unique purposes of national parks."[3] Canada's National Park Policy, when it finally came in 1964, pointed out this misunderstanding:

> *The popular interpretation of the general purpose section of the National Parks Act has been to permit, in fact encourage, artificial recreations and to develop parks to quite an extent along summer resort lines. This interpretation has not completely ignored the value of nature. That value has, however, taken a decisive second place.*

The National Parks Policy attempted to correct this. It states that

> *since benefit, education and enjoyment apply not only to the present but also to future generations, our obligation to protect the areas against impairment implies not only protection against private exploitation, but also guarding against impairment by over-use, improper use and inappropriate development.*

Fig. 8.1 Canada's National Parks

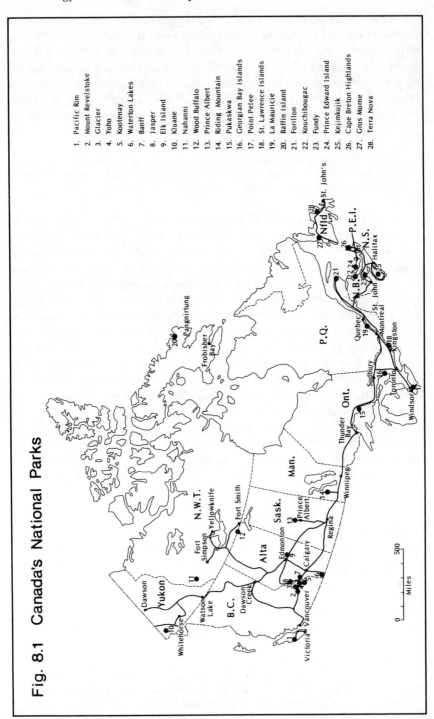

1. Pacific Rim
2. Mount Revelstoke
3. Glacier
4. Yoho
5. Kootenay
6. Waterton Lakes
7. Banff
8. Jasper
9. Elk Island
10. Kluane
11. Nahanni
12. Wood Buffalo
13. Prince Albert
14. Riding Mountain
15. Pukaskwa
16. Georgian Bay Islands
17. Point Pelee
18. St. Lawrence Islands
19. La Mauricie
20. Baffin Island
21. Forillon
22. Kouchibougac
23. Fundy
24. Prince Edward Island
25. Kejimkujik
26. Cape Breton Highlands
27. Gros Morne
28. Terra Nova

The need for greater emphasis on protection was underlined by the consequences of the U.S. "Mission 66" project.[4] After close to ten years of building roads, lodges, campgrounds, public buildings and utility systems costing almost one billion dollars, some U.S. parks faced major urban problems, such as rapidly increasing crime rates, traffic jams and smog.[5] The essential character of parks such as Yosemite and Yellowstone was being lost. By 1964 it was clear that "Mission 66" was aggravating, not solving, many park problems.

Canada had a chance to benefit from the U.S. experience and in part did so. The two guiding statements in Canada's National Parks Policy are:

1. *The basic purpose of the National Park system is to preserve for all time areas which contain significant geographical, geological, biological or historic features as a national heritage for the benefit, education and enjoyment of the people of Canada.*
2. *The provision of urban type recreational facilities is not part of the basic purpose of National Parks. Such recreation facilities in harmony with the purpose and preservation of a park may be introduced as required to meet recreational needs but always so as to minimize impairment and not at all if substantial impairment is inevitable.*

While the first statement gives priority to preservation, the second one is contradictory. How can provision of "urban type recreation" help accomplish preservation? Can it do other than cause "substantial impairment"? Thus, while it professes the goal of preservation, the policy falls into the trap of intensive use. This leads to incongruities in the rest of the document. For example, after safeguarding the national parks against the real but relatively minor problem of controlling scientific research, the policy leaves a loophole for a multi-million dollar recreation development in Banff, with no regard for protection, with the statement:

If a park area is particularly suitable or has necessary characteristics which are not available elsewhere, the development required by, for example, the Winter Olympics should be permitted in the national interest.

By coincidence, at the time this policy was written, Canada was already preparing a bid for the 1972 Winter Olympics in Banff. This bid was squashed largely by concern voiced at the international level over the negative impact such violation of national park ideals might have on national parks around the world.

Has the concept of preservation, as the primary function of national parks, been strengthened since the policy statement was initially written? Village Lake Louise suggests it has. In 1971, the federal government, in consort with the commercial enterprise Village Lake Louise Ltd. and Imperial Oil, again proposed a multi-million dollar development for skiing in Banff. Public debate was intense. Credit card holders mailed back their cards to Imperial Oil. Hundreds of briefs were received. The outcome — the Minister responsible for National Parks, J. Chrétien, cancelled the proposed development.

Parks managers today are even questioning camp grounds and the traditional interpretive centres within national parks. As people-pressures on parks grow, even the minimal facilities of the past have the potential to be destructive. "By 1985 we will likely have about four times the national park visitation we had in 1967, and perhaps five times as many campers if they can be accommodated."[6]

In 1969, the International Union for the Conservation of Nature and Natural Resources recommended a definition of national parks to all world governments. The definition emphasized preservation. It included five basic conditions:

1. large areas where one or several ecosystems are not materially altered by human activity;
2. contents of outstanding plant, animal or geomorphological features of value for special scientific, educative and recreative interest;
3. managed by highest competent authority of the country;
4. no exploitation or occupation;
5. visitors allowed to enter for educative, cultural and recreation purposes.

Furthermore, the definition made a special point of requesting that governments *not* designate national parks "where public outdoor recreation takes priority over conservation of ecosystems." Expert world opinion today, then, clearly endorses the primacy of preservation.

In summary, the concept of the purpose of a national park has changed markedly in the last 100 years. There has been a progressive decrease in emphasis on intensive urban type recreation and, conversely, an increasing stress on preservation. The more preservation is emphasized, the more essential is an ecological approach to park management. This basic change in the concept of national parks provides the first important evidence of the significance of ecology to their future.

What Is Ecology? — An Historical Perspective

In the past decade the meaning of the term *ecology* has become unclear. There are at least three main reasons for this. Ecology is broad. It encompasses all levels of biological knowledge (cells to ecosystems); it overlaps with chemistry, physics, mathematics and other disciplines; it has suddenly become a popular term with the media. Even text-book definitions of ecology vary: "the structure and function of nature"[7]; "the scientific study of the relationships of living organisms with each other and their environment"[8]; "the scientific study of the interactions that determine the distribution and abundance of organisms."[9]

As a science, modern ecology has evolved from diverse origins. Chief among these were plant geography, natural history, population demography and physical geography. From an early stress on the structure of nature, it has moved to a concern with function. More recently it has become applied.

As an applied science, ecology is characterized by activities such as monitoring environmental quality, assessing environmental impacts of proposed developments and simulating future human environments based on computer models. These applications are the fruits of seeds planted in a host of books published since the end of World War II warning of the consequence of mismanagement of natural resources[10]. By 1968, "ecological crisis" had become a household phrase, and in 1969 the U.S. passed the landmark National Environmental Protection Act. Similar legislation is now being prepared in Canada at the federal and provincial levels.

The U.S. Environmental Protection Act requires all federally-funded construction projects to undergo environmental impact assessments. After the Act was passed, the U.S. Geological Survey published a guide on how to prepare impact statements.[11] This was largely a checklist of ecological components (geomorphology, soils, plants, animals), with the suggestion that each item be rated for the "magnitude" and "importance" of any possible disturbances that might be caused by the project. Subsequent improvements have led to the development of a number of new techniques, some giving greater stress to the functional characteristics of ecosystems than did the original.[12] Now more than ever before national park managers using these new techniques have an opportunity to apply ecology, particularly to help them predict the impact of humans on park environments.

Ecology also has a philosophical heritage of great significance to national parks. Before the word ecology was even coined, this philosophy was expressed in the early pleas of naturalist-philosophers to preserve natural environments for both religious and practical reasons. Thoreau's words "in wildness is the preservation of the world," appear increasingly prophetic as today's "technological fix" threatens to let us down. John Muir[13] expressed the religious significance of wild land when he fought to preserve California's Hetch Hetchy valley in the second U.S. national park, Yosemite: "Dam Hetch Hetchy! As well dam for water-tanks the people's cathedrals and churches, for no holier temple has ever been consecrated by the heart of man." In more recent times Aldo Leopold[14] wrote, "That land is a community is the basic concept of ecology, but that land is to be loved and respected is an extension of ethics." Dubos expressed it in different words:

> We may be about to recapture an experience of harmony, an intimation of the divine, from our scientific knowledge of the processes through which the earth became prepared for human life, and of the mechanisms through which man relates to the universe as a whole. A truly ecological view of the world has religious overtones.[15]

The message has changed very little over the years. Many people, including myself, believe that if we embark on a voyage to conquer all of nature, we will sever our evolutionary life-line. Man will drown in a sea of technological gadgetry that will have swallowed up our resources, regimented human life and strangled the human spirit.

Where do national parks fit in? They are the breeding grounds of a philosophy that will insure the perpetuation of life, a "love and respect" for the land. If ecology can help protect parks, there is no more vital application of its principles to the welfare of man.

ASSESSMENT OF THE PRESENT STATE OF ECOLOGICAL PLANNING IN NATIONAL PARKS

Barriers to an Ecological Approach

Ecological park planning means basing planning and management decisions on the philosophical premises and scientific principles of ecology. The need for this approach has been evident for many years to many people involved in park management and to many park users. Yet one continually comes across statements by knowledgeable people deploring the lack of ecology in park planning. "Until quite lately to raise the subject of ecological studies and facilities for conducting them with most park managers was to encounter reactions of blank ignorance."[16] "Thus it is essential that park master planning reflect serious ecological thought in determining the location of initial development. We certainly have not done well enough in this respect."[17] "It has become evident that little or no concern has been shown in the past in planning for the continuation of natural populations of larger mammals in national parks . . . ."[18]

Furthermore, why is it that one can still so easily find examples of unwise management decisions where the integrity of the land was sacrificed in favour of other objectives? The fact that Village Lake Louise was even considered for a moment has seriously shaken the faith of many ecologists in the managers of national parks. Boundaries for recent national parks were drawn on the basis of political criteria. In the case of Kluane in the Yukon Territory, the boundaries do not reflect natural boundaries of ecosystems[19] or, as at Pacific Rim, their application has resulted in valuable park features being left out.[20] Pacific Rim has been subjected to logging since its establishment in 1971, a condition of agreement with the Province of British Columbia. The examples are numerous, each one an isolated case of political compromise that collectively make up a non-ecological approach to national park management.

It is safe to say that most of the ills that beset our national parks have an ecological component, and arise from proceeding in the absence of policy objectives framed in ecological terms and from decisions made in ignorance of ecological alternatives and consequences.[21]

I submit that there are two reasons why the job is not being done well. One is that decision-makers are often forced to over-compromise. The compromise they initially have made is to provide a national system that covers a mere 1.5 percent of Canada, and when fully developed will still only take in perhaps four or five percent of the national territory. But, in almost every national park, further compromises have been made to lobbyists for private holdings, chambers of mines, power authorities and forest industries. Park values are lost in local squabbles with vested interests. At a grander political scale, early in 1974 the Parks Act was used for an entirely different end. An opposition M.P. attempted to alter the bill before the House of Commons that was to provide legal status for all ten national parks declared since 1968, in an effort to gain greater constitutional powers for northern territorial councils. This almost resulted in a political stalemate denying legal status for over half the supposed national park holdings.[22] When national parks become political playthings all ecological considerations vanish.

The second reason that ecology is not playing the leading role it ought to may be easier to correct than the first. Even though recent research into methods of conducting environmental impact studies has placed some tools in the hands of park planners, we still lack systematic approaches proven over time in parks. Literature on parks is full of general statements on ecology. There remains, however, a great dearth of specific information on techniques.

Problem of Defining an Ecological Approach

In an ecological approach, the *ecosystem* becomes the unit for management, and the techniques of ecology the tools for learning about and manipulating the environment if necessary.

"The ecosystem is the major ecological unit."[23] It consists of a community of living things plus its non-living component such as soil, bedrock and climate. It "results from the integration of all of the living and non-living factors of the environment for a defined segment of space and time".[24] It is similar to the term *landscape* as used by geographers, but stresses biological rather than chronological and physical characteristics.[25]

Smith[26] characterizes ecosystems in nine discreet, descriptive sentences that embody the following ideas:

1. Ecosystems have structure and function.
2. The more complex the structure, the greater diversity of species.
3. Function of ecosystems include flow of energy and cycling of materials.
4. Energy needed to maintain an ecosystem depends on its structure.
5. Succession takes place with orderly changes in energy capture and diversity.
6. Exploited ecosystems decline at maturity.
7. Populations occupy functional niches in ecosystems which are discreet and unique for each species.
8. Regulatory mechanisms control population sizes.
9. Changes in selection pressure of an evolutionary nature are ongoing.

The study of what is embodied in these nine statements makes up most of the science of ecology. The problem is: how do you make the whole broad field these statements encompass applicable to specific parcels of land you wish to manage?

Ecological Approaches as Presently Practised

The extent to which ecological considerations are taken into account in national parks can be seen by reviewing the planning process. This is broken into three phases — system planning, master planning and site planning. Finally there is ongoing management of the "developed" park.

System Planning

System planning is deciding where parks should be. It is guided by the *National and Historic Parks Branches' System Planning Manual*[27], which divides Canada into 39 "natural regions," with an objective of including samples of all regions in a completed system (Figures 8.2 and 8.3). This approach replicates one used by the U. S. National Park Service[28]. The natural regions are derived from a physiographic classification of Canada[29], with further subdivision of one of these classes, the Canadian Shield, based on Rowe's *Forest Regions of Canada*[30].

Fig. 8.2 National Park Natural Regions

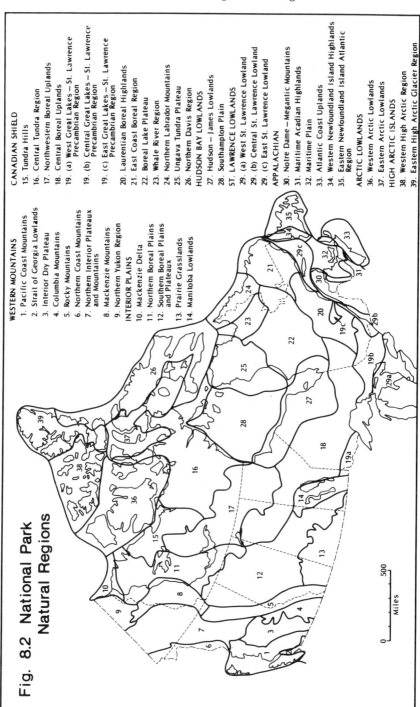

WESTERN MOUNTAINS
1. Pacific Coast Mountains
2. Strait of Georgia Lowlands
3. Interior Dry Plateau
4. Columbia Mountains
5. Rocky Mountains
6. Northern Coast Mountains
7. Northern Interior Plateaux and Mountains
8. Mackenzie Mountains
9. Northern Yukon Region

INTERIOR PLAINS
10. Mackenzie Delta
11. Northern Boreal Plains
12. Southern Boreal Plains and Plateaux
13. Prairie Grasslands
14. Manitoba Lowlands

CANADIAN SHIELD
15. Tundra Hills
16. Central Tundra Region
17. Northwestern Boreal Uplands
18. Central Boreal Uplands
19. (a) West Great Lakes – St. Lawrence Precambrian Region
19. (b) Central Great Lakes – St. Lawrence Precambrian Region
19. (c) East Great Lakes – St. Lawrence Precambrian Region
20. Laurentian Boreal Highlands
21. East Coast Boreal Region
22. Boreal Lake Plateau
23. Whale River Region
24. Northern Labrador Mountains
25. Ungava Tundra Plateau
26. Northern Davis Region

HUDSON BAY LOWLANDS
27. Hudson – James Lowlands
28. Southampton Plain

ST. LAWRENCE LOWLANDS
29. (a) West St. Lawrence Lowland
29. (b) Central St. Lawrence Lowland
29. (c) East St. Lawrence Lowland

APPALACHIAN
30. Notre Dame – Megantic Mountains
31. Maritime Acadian Highlands
32. Maritime Plain
33. Atlantic Coast Uplands
34. Western Newfoundland Island Highlands
35. Eastern Newfoundland Island Atlantic Region

ARCTIC LOWLANDS
36. Western Arctic Lowlands
37. Eastern Arctic Lowlands

HIGH ARCTIC ISLANDS
38. Western High Arctic Region
39. Eastern High Arctic Glacier Region

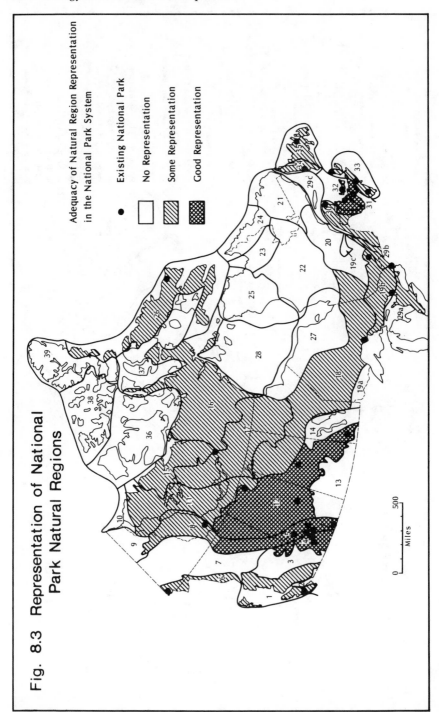

Fig. 8.3 Representation of National
Park Natural Regions

Locating parks within natural regions is done by describing "natural history themes" which "bring out the essence of the natural region". These themes include land forms, geological history and land and water ecosystems that are significant in each region. The planning objective is to preserve all of the themes identified in each particular natural region.

This procedure for system planning is decidedly ecological. Political boundaries between provinces and territories are ignored. Both U.S. and Canadian national parks officials deserve credit for adopting this approach.

Its success within any natural region, however, depends upon the adequacy of resource inventory and knowledge of all potential natural history themes. Presently, detailed inventories of landforms, flora and wildlife precede the selection of boundaries for some parks; for others, existing literature is relied upon to a greater extent. But for no region has adequate information or analysis of the functional aspects of its ecosystems been collected before the establishment of park boundaries.

Master Planning

Once a national park is established, it is "master planned" — decisions made on what and where activities should be carried out, what facilities are necessary and how protection of the environment should be accomplished (Figure 8.4). The master plan is shaped by a team which includes an array of expertise and is coordinated by a park planner.[31] Zones are established according to the following classification system: 1. special unique or sensitive area, 2. wilderness recreation, 3. natural environment, 4. general outdoor recreation (highway corridors, campgrounds), 5. intensive use (urban, even though such may violate park policy).

Information leading to zoning comes from a number of sources. The most pertinent are the resource inventories, which are conducted under the supervision of the "Applied Research Division." These inventories cover physical (soils, bedrock, water) and biotic features (plants and animals, both at the species and community levels). They identify and locate unique, representative and sensitive features and those worthy of interpretation for park visitors. Most of this work is carried out under contract by other government departments such as the Canadian Wildlife Service, or by universities and private consultants. The inventories result in the production of a "resource atlas" for each park, which leans heavily on graphics and is designed to be useful to non-ecologically trained planners.

Information leading to zoning also comes from a "guidelines" statement based partly on the resource inventories and partly on park

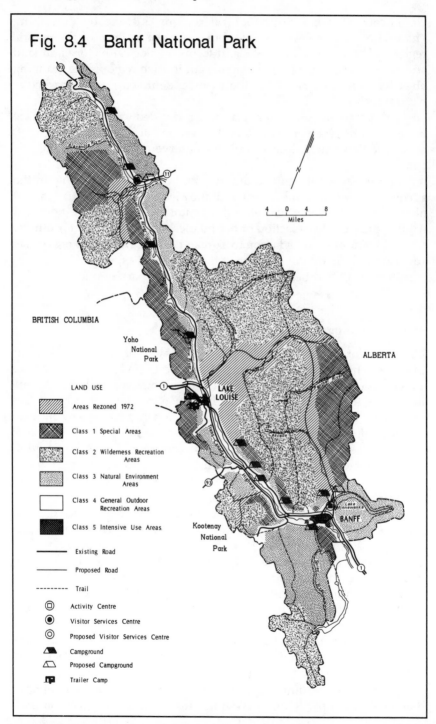

Fig. 8.4   Banff National Park

policy regarding such things as wildlife preservation, access and campground restrictions. These guidelines identify the purpose of the park, activities that are compatible with one another and alternative zoning possibilities.

From the resource inventories and the guidelines, a provisional master plan is drawn, after which public input sought through hearings and modificationss are made if necessary.

In theory, this approach to master planning should ensure a central role for ecological considerations. However, operational weaknesses still allow ecological values to sometimes slip out of sight. The "Applied Research Division," coordinator for the all-important resource inventories, effectively signs off once the resource atlas is completed. It should retain a central advisory position through to the end, with master planners directly accountable to it. Otherwise even the best resource data can simply be wasted through lack of understanding or appreciation.

Even with this well-defined procedure, the need for speed in planning has caused what should be successive steps to be telescoped. In one case, a full provisional master plan was drawn before completion of the resource inventories.

Site Planning

Site planning involves "designing with nature" wherever human impact may be great. Here is where environmental impact assessment techniques developed in relation to other land uses can help park planners. In a Parks Canada publication[32], three different approaches to land use planning and environmental impact analysis are discussed and their applicability to national parks commented upon. The three approaches to land use planning have some value to master planning: one in helping identify ecological units (Hills); one in helping identify "linear natural and cultural resource corridors" such as waterways (Lewis); and one in displaying results of ecological inventories for analysis on transparent overlays (McHarg). The three approaches to environmental impact assessment include Leopold's matrix (discussed earlier), another approach that displays ecological information on limited sites by use of computer drawn maps (Steinitz) and a third that attempts to quantify impacts of alternative developments (Stover). No single method has been adopted by Parks Canada, as all have strengths and weaknesses. Rather, each problem is tackled by whatever means seems suitable, which is usually up to the discretion of consultants. Recent site planning studies done for Parks Canada include: twinning the trans-Canada highway through Banff, possible routes to the glaciers at Kluane and a major campsite at Pukaskwa on Lake Superior.

Management

At the management level, once parks are operational, ecological problems will always appear. Ecosystems are dynamic, visitor preferences and demands change and cumulative effects of people on the land all require a flexible approach to management. Parks Canada has only recently revised its administration to allow ongoing ecological "troubleshooting." In the past, such activities were only carried out sporadically, under agreement with the Canadian Wildlife Service, and mostly in the western parks. In the last year, the "Applied Research Division" has decentralized, with biologists now assessing ecological research priorities in each of five regions. Studies such as the probable future numbers of deer and their impact on the vegetation of Point Pelee National Park (Ontario), the role of fire on the ecosystem of Kluane National Park and the distribution and limiting factors to woodland caribou in Pukaskwa National Park are underway or planned. All will have implications to managing park ecosystems.

An ecological approach to park planning has been conceived, perhaps even born. But it is weak, helpless and still susceptible to infant mortality. How can we ensure its survival?

HOW TO DO IT BETTER — A PERSONAL VIEW

The Ecologist as Physician

The first measure to better implement an ecological approach involves standing back, asking again what ecological information is vital to park planning, then taking new steps to collect this information and transform it into management. This task is analogous to that of a doctor. The patient is the ecosystem. Its anatomy is the structure of the ecosystem — the vertical and horizontal distribution of its living elements, its intra-community relationships within and between both plants and animals. Its physiology is the functions of the ecosystem: circulatory system — the hydrological cycle, digestive system — its energy pathways, nervous system — the regulatory mechanisms that control population growth, respiratory system — its oxygen, carbon dioxide and other biogeochemical cycles.

Like a human patient, an ecosystem has vulnerable parts; any malfunction there is potentially fatal. Remove predators and it may suffer a cancerous growth in herbivore populations. Alter ground water supply or capacity and the ecosystem may die of thirst. Reduce species diversity and the ecosystem is susceptible to fatal disease.

And just like a doctor, the ecologist has a body of knowledge and a set of instruments to help him diagnose the patient's illness. Thermometer, stethescope, syringe are replaced by binoculars, soil auger, tree tape.

The main value of this analogy is that like the doctor, an ecologist must, from a general knowledge and a specific set of symptoms, ask the right questions, test the right characteristics and prescribe the right medicine quickly. Upon this ability rests the real success of an ecological approach to park planning.

Here then, is a medical guide to quick diagnosis of the health of park ecosystems:

Test 1.

Determine if the ecosystem has its normal complement of wildlife — small and large mammals, furbearers, birds, fish, amphibians, reptiles. The significance of this test is that wildlife populations will reflect any alterations or changes in any abiotic characteristic of ecosystems (climate, water, soil); in conditions of the vegetation; in inter-relationships among different species; in the existence of disease (plant or animal) or in the levels of pollution in air or water. In other words, wildlife inventories, if interpreted carefully, measure more than wildlife; they measure a vast array of characteristics of ecosystems.

Three examples back this up. The serious decline of waterbirds in Everglades National Park in Florida reflects man-caused changes in the hydrological regime of the park.[33] Ungulates in Banff and Jasper (Alberta) are suffering from reduced amounts of early succession forests because of unnatural forest fire protection.[34] White-tailed deer and beaver have disappeared from Yellowstone, where the removal of predators placed them in direct competition with elk.[35]

At present, wildlife inventories are used in master planning only to locate animal populations so that appropriate zoning and interpretive plans can be made. This is not sufficient. Inventories should be interpreted against some norm — either historical records or comparison with nearby and similar ecosystems. Only then will inventories tell us anything about the health of the ecosystem and lead to identification of any symptoms of illness.

A second change in present procedure involving wildlife inventories is to conduct much more intensive inventory and analysis at the system planning level before boundaries are delineated. Otherwise, the cause of ecosystem problems in a national park may lie outside, beyond the control of park authorities. There are many examples of this problem some of which are easier to remedy than others. A particularly difficult problem is posed in Wood Buffalo National Park (Alberta and Northwest Territories) where the unnatural water regime caused by the W.A.C. Bennett Dam upstream on the Peace River has resulted in the widespread replacement of sedges, important food for buffalo, by less palatable grasses.[36] Easier to correct are the boundaries of Kluane National Park which as presently drawn only protect the park's single caribou herd for a few weeks each year.[37]

A third necessary change is the need for periodic monitoring of wildlife populations. At present, monitoring involves only occasional observations of big game by the warden staff. Monitoring should cover all wildlife and should be carried out on a long term and systematic basis.

A fourth necessary change involves personnel. Field inventories of wildlife should be supervised and the results analyzed by qualified ecologists. Parks Canada has recently broadened the responsibilities of its warden staff to include "resource conservation." While these parks personnel are well equipped to gather certain kinds of field data, they are rarely well enough versed in ecological literature to fully interpret the results. Many natural phenomena act to change wildlife numbers: genetic polymorphism, intra-specific stress, succession, social behaviour. Compensatory mortality often makes seemingly important causes of mortality irrelevant at the population level. Changes in numbers caused by such agents are acceptable; preservation must include all natural ongoing processes. But separating these effects from man-induced changes is often exceedingly complex. I agree with the comment of Sheard and Blood[38] that the role of park naturalists must go beyond that of "entertainers," to "provide a scientific input to park management." It is ironic that many parks have on staff people fully trained in the biological sciences, but "resource conservation" falls outside their terms of reference.

Test 2.

Determine what biotic associations existed historically. Historical research must include the study of vegetation in order to gain understanding of plant succession. It should document, as well, the successive impacts of man, such as has recently been done for Point Pelee National Park.[39]

Historical associations are important as baselines for park management. U.S. National Park Policy states that "biotic associations within each park be maintained, or where necessary recreated, as nearly as possible in the condition that prevailed when the area was first visited by the white man." (This does not necessarily imply holding succession back, but rather accepting different stages so long as they have been created by natural forces.) While no such policy exists for Canadian National Parks, it is implicit in our first objective of "preservation." It should be made explicit for each park.

Test 3.

Determine what species and abundance of predators are in the ecosystem, and what functions they perform. The significance of this test lies in the fact that predators, which occupy third and fourth trophic levels at the summit of food chains, are sensitive to a vast array of ecological conditions below them. Most species of predators have substantially different food webs, so by monitoring all the predators, you are monitoring much of the animal and plant life in the ecosystem. For example, studies of predators by T. Cottrell and the author in Kluane National Park have shown that the numbers and distribution of wolves are closely dependent upon the size and distribution of both the moose and Dall sheep populations. These in turn can be expected to mirror stages of plant succession — the extent of willows and poplars (moose) and open bunchgrass communities (sheep). Coyotes reflect snowshoe hare and Arctic ground squirrel populations, which in their turn depend upon succession in both forest and grassland ecosystems. Red foxes depend on small mammal (microtine) populations as well as snowshoe hares and ground squirrels.

Studies of predators must obviously go beyond distribution and abundance to include food habits. Ecosystems may change, but if buffer food species are available, predator numbers may remain constant. That has happened in Algonquin Provincial Park in Ontario, where, in the late 1960's moose and beaver replaced deer as a major component of the diet of wolves. Deer numbers in Algonquin decreased largely because of changes in logging practices that reduced the extent of deer browse at feeding height.[40] By monitoring predators and their food habits over a span of almost 15 years in Algonquin, ecological relationships altered by logging could be identified.

Predators are also important in their own right. Until 1959, they were persecuted in Canadian National Parks. Wolves have just recently increased in Jasper National Park where they were previously almost eliminated.[41] Their removal resulted in an imbalance between ungulates and vegetation.[42] Similarly, removal of predators in Grand Canyon National Park in Arizona resulted in part in an explosion of mule deer numbers, range deterioration and ultimately a crash in the deer population.[43] National parks policy in both Canada and United States now protects predators, as it should. The next step is to use predators to monitor park ecosystems and to understand the significance of predation as an agent of both homeostasis and change.

Test 4.

Determine what components in park ecosystems are vulnerable to human activities. The significance of this test is self evident, both for master and site planning.

Running this test involves cataloguing broad soil conditions such as organic versus non-organic (the first being less suitable for any intensive human use), cataloguing sensitive plant associations and nesting or denning areas of wildlife (such as is presently done in resource inventories to identify Class I land) and cataloguing species diversity. It is axiomatic in ecology that the greater the species diversity in an ecosystem, the greater its stability. Alpine tundra in Yosemite National Park, where both species and structural diversity are low, shows much more excessive wear than its pine forests. Grazing by cattle threatens extensive destruction of vegetation and wildlife in desert parks such as Organ Pipe National Monument in Arizona, whereas its impact in more temperate latitudes is less severe.

Species diversity of plants and animals is important beyond assessing vulnerability. It helps provide a baseline for long term management. "One possible management objective for national parks is the maintenance or promotion of high biological diversity, and this probably comes very close to the goal of conserving *natural* ecosystems."[44] Figures for both wildlife and plant diversity for each park ecosystem should be extracted from inventories and historical data.

Test 5.

Determine what are the processes of change, their causes, their rates and their locations. Included are: succession, fire, erosion, flooding, avalanche, glacier movement.

Succession, identified from plant inventories and historical studies, must be understood for each ecosystem. Adequate understanding must include the effect of subsidiary processes: influence of grazing, browsing, disease. These, if significant, may require separate studies.

Understanding the influence of fire is particularly important, since strict control in Canadian National Parks has been a form of mismanagement for many years. Extensive stands of climax vegetation may result that are simply botanical anomalies. Most biomes in Canada were greatly influenced by fire both in short run successional changes and long run evolutionary adaptations. Every discourse that touches on ecology in parks criticizes this policy of strict fire control. Recent ones include Van Wagner[45] Sheard and Blood[46], Carbyn[47] and Theberge.[48] U.S. National Parks policy directs that:

> Fires in vegetation resulting from natural causes are recognized as natural phenomena and may be allowed to run their course when such burning can be contained within pre-determined fire management units. . . .

In contrast, Canadian park policy is "to limit fire."

The historic rate of natural fire, an important guideline for establishing a natural fire regime policy, can often be determined by aging rates of succession through aerial photos, tree borings, scars on trees and sediment analyses.

In summary, placing the stethescope in these five places will allow a more thorough understanding of function and processes and assure continuous monitoring of park ecosystems. This much additional ecological research is mandatory; from it other relevant questions will undoubtedly arise that require further diagnosis and may lead into such studies as behaviour in ungulates, wildlife diseases and plant genetics. Together with present approaches outlined previously, a truly ecological approach to park planning and management may emerge. This will require a longer bookshelf of ecological studies for each park; but if this shelf is shorter than the shelf for policies and administration there is something wrong.

The Need for Education

In the final analysis, the realization of a truly ecological approach to the planning and management of national parks is dependent upon the sustained support of an informed public. This, in turn, implies much expanded educational programmes both in and about national parks across the country.

The knowledge gained from the scientific endeavours enumerated above can and must be used to combat "ecological illiteracy"[49] in the general public. Nature interpretive programmes must broaden their base to go beyond park boundaries, to confront problems such as over-population and resource depletion. Almost all parks are ecologically bound to adjacent land; concern for total environments, not just parks themselves, is vital. Parks are better suited, in some respects even more than are schools, to act as springboards to a land ethic, without which more than just parks may be in peril. This was emphasized over and over at the Second World Conference on National Parks in 1972:

> Unless we succeed in showing mankind as a whole how he is dependent upon a complex system of natural chemical cycles and use of solar energy for his food and much else, there may be no future ahead of us after a few more decades. Parks are an integral factor in improving awareness of the serious situation we have come to.[50]

and, "There are no greater resources for education and social change in the world than national parks and reserves."[51]

The educational value of national parks is not perceived by the vast majority of park users in Canada, revealing the almost total failure to date of our park educational programmes in getting across any ecological message. Our parks policy on education is wholly oriented to "encourage and assist the public to understand, appreciate and enjoy all forms of nature which are preserved in these sanctuaries." In contrast, the administrative policy of the U.S. national parks on education (1970) is to communicate "an environmental consciousness both within and beyond the park." Zion National Park in Utah in 1970 was screening films in its interpretive centre such as "Multiply and Subdue the Earth" with its glaring portrayal of the consequences of unchecked growth. To ponder this, surrounded by yet undefiled red rock canyons hundreds of millions of years old, historic foundations of our world that survive even without underpinning by man must bury conceit even among the most arrogant believers in our bulldozer culture.

Educational values of parks also encompass simple intellectual satisfaction. This is more than a frill; our brains are too highly evolved to leave us satisfied with the mere physical necessities of life. Pimlott, in a paper entitled, "Education and National Parks" wrote:

> When all the cost-benefit analyses have been computed, when all the arguments have been argued about the uses of parks, inevitably the real values of parks come back to the simple things – the opportunity to observe, to study and to learn about ourselves and our environment, and to feel the simple enjoyment of the beauties of the natural world. [52]

Recreational and psychological values of parks are difficult to separate. "Physical rejuvenation is so closely allied to the spiritual as to be almost inseparable."[53] While the subject of considerable literature, little can be added to the expressions of one of the founders of the national park movement, John Muir, who in 1901 began his book, *Our National Parks* with,

> The tendency nowadays to wander in wilderness is delightful to see. Thousands of tired, nerve-shaken, over-civilized people are beginning to find out that going to the mountains is going home; that wildness is a necessity; and that mountain parks and reservations are useful not only as fountains of timber and irrigating rivers, but as fountains of life. Awakening from the stupefying effects of the vice of over-industry and the deadly apathy of luxury, they are trying as best they can to mix and enrich their own little ongoings with those of Nature, and to get rid of rust and disease.

Now even more applicable are Muir's words in today's world! Now even more applicable in the future, when parks are the sum of land that is 'natural, wild and free' in Canada.

Only if the integrity of park ecosystems is sacred will our future parks be "natural, wild and free." Only then will they remain as benchmarks for measuring man's impact on his world, as temples for spiritual satisfaction, as schools for acquiring a land ethic and experiencing the pleasures of learning, and as retreats from "over-civilization." All these demand that ecology take precedence over socio-economic and political considerations, that preservation come before use, that the rights of other species come before man. These are the reverse of principles that guide the management of all the rest of Canada. These are what make national parks unique.

NOTES

1. Harroy, J.P. (1972). "A Century in the Growth of the National Park Concept Throughout the World." Second World Conference on National Parks. Washington, D.C.: U.S. National Park Service.
2. Fraser, B. (1965). "Unspoiled Parks or Neon Jungles?" *Maclean's* magazine, 78(20).
3. Nicol, J.I. (1969). "The National Park Movement in Canada." In *The Canadian National Parks: Today and Tomorrow*. J.G. Nelson and R. C. Scace, (eds.), University of Calgary, 33-52.
4. Wirth, C. L., (1966). "Today in Our National Parks: The Mission Called 66." *National Geographic*, 130(1), 7-46.
5. Cahn, R. (1968). "Cars, Crowds, Crime." In *Will Success Spoil the National Parks*. Reprinted from Christian Science Monitor.
6. Nicol, J. I. (1969). *op. cit.*
7. Odum, E.P. (1959). *Fundamentals of Ecology*. (2nd ed.). Philadelphia: W.B. Saunders.
8. Southwick, C.H. (1972). *Ecology and the Quality of Our Environment*. Toronto: Van Nostrand Reinhold.
9. Krebs, C. J. (1972). *Ecology: The Experimental Analysis of Distribution and Abundance*. New York: Harper and Row.
10. Carson, R.L. (1962). *Silent Spring*. Boston: Houghton Mifflin.
    Osborn, P. (1948). *Our Plundered Planet*. Boston: Little Brown.
11. Leopold, L., F. E. Clarke, B.B. Hanshaw and J.R. Balsley. (1971). *A Procedure for Evaluating Environmental Impact*. Washington, D.C.: U.S. Geological Survey Circular 645.
12. Kreith, F. (1973). "Lack of Impact," *Environment*, 15(1), 26-33.
13. Muir, J. (1912). *The Yosemite*. New York: Century.
14. Leopold, A. (1949). *A Sand County Almanac*. Oxford: Oxford University Press.
15. Dubos, R. (1972). *A God Within*. New York: Scribner's Sons.
16. Nicholson, E. M. (1972). "What Is Wrong with the National Parks Movement?" Second World Conference on National Parks. Washington, D.C.: U.S. National Park Service.
17. Reid, N.P. (1972). "How Well Has the United States Managed Its National Park System? The Application of Ecological Principles to Park Management." Second World Conference on National Parks. Washington, D.C.: U.S. National Park Service.
18. Geist, V. (1972). "On the Management of Large Mammals in National Parks, Part II." *Park News*, 8(5), 16-24.
19. Theberge, J. B. (1972). *Kluane National Park: A Perspective from the National and Provincial Parks Association of Canada*. Toronto.
    Theberge, J. B., (1973a). "Kluane National Park: Victory and Defeat Among Our Highest Peaks." *Ontario Naturalist*, 13(2), 5-12.
20. Nelson, J.G. and L.D. Cordes. (1972). *Pacific Rim: An Ecological Approach to a New Canadian National Park*. University of Calgary.
21. Cowan, I. McT. (1968). "The Role of Ecology in the National Parks." In *The Canadian National Parks: Today and Tomorrow*. J.G. Nelson and R. C. Scace, (eds.) University of Calgary, 931-39.
22. Theberge, J.B. (1974). "Parliamentary Committee Blocks Legal Status for 10 National Parks." *Nature Canada*, 3(1), 34.
23. Smith, R. L. (1966). *Ecology and Field Biology*. New York: Harper and Row.
24. Van Dyne, G.M. (ed.), (1969). *The Ecosystem Concept in Natural Resource Management*. New York: Academic Press.
25. Major, J. (1969). "Historical Development of the Ecosystem Concept." In *The Ecosystem Concept in Natural Resource Management*. G.M. Van Dyne, (ed.), New York: Academic Press, 9-22.
26. Smith, R.L. (1966). *op. cit.*

216 / Ecology and National Development

27. Canada. National and Historic Parks Branch. (1971). *National Parks System Planning Manual*. Ottawa.
28. U.S. National Park Service. (1972). *Part Two of the National Park System Plan, Natural History*. Washington, D.C. Government Printing Office.
29. Bostock, H.S. (1970). *Physiographic Subdivisions of Canada*. Geological Survey of Canada.
30. Rowe, J.S. (1959). *Forest Regions of Canada*. Ottawa: Forestry Branch, Department of Northern Affairs and National Resources, Bulletin 123.
31. Taylor, G.E. (1971). *An approach to interpretation planning within a master planning framework*. Unpublished Mimeograph. Ottawa: Parks Canada.
32. Canada. National and Historic Parks Branch. (1973). *Environment Analysis: A Review of Selected Techniques*. Ottawa.
33. McCluney, W.R., (ed.). (1971). *The Environmental Destruction of South Florida*. Coral Gables, Florida: University of Miami Press.
34. Flook, D. (1964). "Range Relationships of Some Ungulates Native to Banff and Jasper National Parks, Alberta." In *Grazing in Terrestrial and Marine Environments*. G.D. Grispe, (ed.) Symposium, British Ecological Society, No. 4, Oxford, Blackwell.
35. Wagner, F.H. (1969). "Ecosystem Concept in Fish and Game Management." In *The Ecosystem Concept in Natural Resource Management*. G.M. Van Dyne, (ed.), New York: Academic Press, 259-307.
36. Peace-Athabasca Delta Project. (1972). *Report for Federal Department of the Environment*. Ottawa.
37. Theberge, J.B. (1972). *op. cit.*
    Theberge, J.B. (1973a). *op. cit.*
38. Sheard, J.W. and D.A. Blood. (1973). "The Role of National Parks in Canada and Criteria for Their Management." *The Canadian Field-Naturalist*, 87, 211-24.
39. Nelson, J.G. and J.G. Battin. (1974). *Man's Effects on Point Pelee National Park, Ontario*. Unpublished Report, Parks Canada, Cornwall.
40. Runge, R.A. and J.B. Theberge. (1974). "Algonquin: Decline of the Deer." *Ontario Naturalist*, 14(2), 7-10.
41. Carbyn, L.N., (1974). "Wolf Population Fluctuations in Jasper National Park, Alberta, Canada". *Biological Conservation*, 6(2), 94-101.
42. Flook, D. (1964). *op. cit.*
43. Trefethen, J.B. (1967). "The Terrible Lesson of the Kaibab." *National Wildlife*, June-July, 4-9.
44. Lamprey, H.F. (1972). "On the Management of Flora and Fauna in National Parks." Second World Conference on National Parks, Washington, D.C.: U.S. National Park Service.
45. Van Wagner, C.E. (1973). "Forest Fires in the Parks." *Park News*, 9(2), 25-31.
46. Sheard, J.W. and D.A. Blood. (1973). *op. cit.*
47. Carbyn, L.N. (1971). "Description of the *Festuca scabrella* Association in Prince Albert National Park, Saskatchewan." *The Canadian Field-Naturalist*, 85(1), 25-30.
48. Theberge, J.B. (1973b). *Considerations for Fire Management in Kluane National Park*. Report for Canadian Wildlife Service, Edmonton.
49. Curry-Lindahl, K. (1972). "Projecting the Future in the Worldwide National Parks Movement." Second World Conference on National Parks. Washington, D.C.: U.S. National Park Service.
50. Kuenan, D.J. (1972). "Creative Park Use for Science, Education and Public Betterment," Second World Conference on National Parks, Washington, D.C.: U.S. National Park Service.
51. Gilbert, V.C., Jr. (1972). "A Widening Horizon — the Role of Parks and Reserves in Education." Second World Conference on National Parks. Washington, D.C.: U.S. National Park Service.
52. Pimlott, D.H. (1968)."Education and National Parks." In *The Canadian National Parks: Today and Tomorrow*. J.G. Nelson and R.C. Scace, (eds.) University of Calgary, 262-82.
53. Olsen, S.F. (1962)."A Philosophical Concept." First World Conference on National Parks, Washington, D.C.: U.S. Government.

9

Ecology and Urban Development: The Theory and Practice of Ecoplanning in Canada

Cameron M. Kitchen, Department of Geography,
University of Glasgow, Scotland

At present, decisions about urban development are made primarily on the basis of engineering, economic and political criteria. These are unquestionably important factors. But they are not the only grounds upon which urban development decisions should be based when so many projects, which are perfectly viable in engineering, economic and political terms, turn out to be ecological disasters.

ECOPLANNING: NATURE, STRATEGY AND TACTICS

If we assume that maintenance of a diverse, functional and quality environment is an increasingly important social goal these days, then it follows that an understanding of the physical and biological nature of the landscape is an indispensable prerequisite for the proper planning of any area subject to urbanization. The ecological approach to planning (Ecoplanning) is an attempt to integrate this type of environmental understanding into the management of the development process. Ecoplanning is a positive approach to the management of the environment. Many forms of urban development are susceptible to the ecoplanning approach. It is an attempt to influence development in such a way that both long and short term impacts on the environment are anticipated, avoided or reduced where possible. It also introduces into the decision-making process values such as ecosystem function, aesthetics, wildlife, etc., which, in the past, have seldom been considered. The overall goal is to identify, articulate and evaluate those environmental factors which may be affected by or affect (positively or negatively) various forms of development. This requires that the ecologist participate in the decision-making process leading up to a development proposal.

At present, urban development is, to some degree, inevitable, but the level of degradation which it creates is not. Much destruction occurs as the result of ignorance of the potentialities and constraints inherent in the environment. Thus, the prime objective of ecoplanning is to replace the present destructive superimposition of urban form on the landscape with a process of urban development which is sensitive to the inherent qualities and potentialities of the landscape. The information which will provide this sensitivity must come from the expert in environmental sciences: the applied ecologist.

Ecology is a science which deals with the relationships between living things and their environment. It is also a body of knowledge and an approach to attaining further knowledge. Ecology has been traditionally an integrating science. It has relied and will continue to rely heavily on other sciences. In developmental or applied ecology, this tradition continues. Information from relevant disciplines must be brought to bear on understanding environmental relationships as they relate to a proposed development (e.g., what effect will interruption of drainage have on vegetation in a proposed park area). To attain this goal the ecologist must be something of a generalist, for in ecoplanning he must bring together relevant knowledge and expertise to enable a full evaluation of the impact of any proposed use on land, water and air.[1]

In practice, no single person can usually evaluate all the impacts of any large project. A team approach to environmental analysis is more often than not an absolute necessity. A research team has the distinct advantage of having a greater range of talents and professional viewpoints with which to evaluate a given project. It also provides the detailed, specialized information which is often required.

Many "team" studies are not carried out in an integrated fashion. At best, they are multidisciplinary in that they represent the separate findings of various experts which are then correlated (post-correlation). The need in environmental research, however, is for pre-correlation.[2] The various participants must have a clear understanding of the purposes of the study and the type of information that is required of them. Too often, in post-correlated studies, data have not been collected or presented in a form which can readily be adapted to the overall study objectives. All participants in a study must have a clear understanding of the objectives of the study and the technical requirements of the project at the very beginning. Apparently simple decisions, such as a common scale of mapping, are more readily made in a pre-correlated approach to a study.

To achieve effective pre-correlation in such teams considerable effort must be taken in selecting personnel, structuring the research programme and encouraging communication and interaction among team members. Only such interdisciplinary groups can adequately cope with the complexities of urban environmental management.

In this type of effort considerable responsibility is placed on the team leader or coordinator. It is this person who must assemble the team, ensure that the proper questions are asked of the members, encourage team interaction and facilitate integration and communication of the environmental information to the client. Increasingly, it is the team leader who must then represent the environmental viewpoint in the larger project team that generates the ultimate design and investment decision. Obviously, this person must be a scientific generalist as well as being familiar with the design and engineering disciplines.

Environmental assessment has yet to receive the unqualified support of all those involved in the urban development process. There are, however, several locations in Canada where comprehensive environmental data banks have been made available to decision-makers. One of these is Saskatoon where an important inventory was recently published.[3] This particular study, embracing an area within a 20-mile radius of the city centre, dealt in turn with bedrock, surficial geology, pedology, climate and geotechnology. Further subsections focused upon groundwater resources, slope stability and engineering properties, among others.

Another example of a comprehensive environmental information system is that presently available in the Regional Municipality of Waterloo.[4] Environmental information for the municipality was collected and placed in a computerized information bank. The computer mapping technique employed in this study is a positive tool to aid the planning and decision-making process. The computer application is useful because of the analytical capabilities it possesses. The computer also allows for the clarification of issues of urban and regional planning in an environmental context. Conflicts between existing and proposed urban forms and the spatial patterns of resources can be determined very quickly using the computer system.

The most comprehensive environmental appraisal undertaken in Canada to date was recently completed for the new Montreal Airport in the Sainte Scholastique area of Quebec. The study area was approximately 88,000 acres in size of which 18,500 acres were designated as the operational zone, where actual airport facilities, including runways, terminals and hangars have been constructed. The remainder of the area (approximately 70,000 acres) will be affected to varying degrees by the airport facility. The total acreage has been expropriated by the federal government. The purpose of the study was to analyse, in considerable detail, the natural resource patterns of the area and to develop a management programme for the total area.[5]

Finally, it might be useful to indicate the role of the ecological appraisal at various stages in the developmental process. The process begins with the site selection and, ideally, ends with a monitoring programme of the built environment. More realistically, the implementation or construction phase ends the sequence. Ecological inputs are relevant at several distinct stages in the process. Too often, the environmental appraisal is considered as a one time input. Table 9.1 presents a simplified model of the development process. Throughout the process, the environmental team must interact with the other participants in the overall project team (architects, planners, engineers and sociologists).

The ecological input can be very influential at each of the stages indicated in Table 9.1. Ecology should be involved at each step to ensure a better handling of the environment. Too much has been lost by inadequate involvement, particularly at the implementation stage.

TABLE 9.1

DEVELOPMENTAL SEQUENCE (ENVIRONMENT)

1. *Site Selection*
   (a) Establish selection criteria for particular use
       (airport, new town, zoo, etc.)
   (b) Locate areas which meet the criteria
   (c) Select site or study area.

2. *Feasibility Study – Conceptual Planning*
   Generation of alternative approaches or plans for study area.
   (a) Inventory of resource base
   (b) Interpretation of resource data
   (c) Integration of environmental considerations with other
       aspects of study (planning, design, engineering, etc.)
   (d) Develop conceptual plans.

3. *Evaluation of Alternative Approaches*
   Selection of preferred alternative.
   (a) Determine relative merits or constraints of each alternative
   (b) Approval of preferred alternative.

4. *Master Plan – Functional Design – Site Plan*
   Detailed planning and design of selected alternative.
   (a) Detailed appraisal and evaluation
   (b) Detailed environmental design
   (c) Management guidelines for environment
   (d) Master plan approval.

5. *Implementation – Construction*
   Site management to ensure management guidelines are followed.

6. *Monitoring Built Environment*
   Observe operations of environment — success of total operation.

THE PRACTICE OF ECOPLANNING: THREE CASE STUDIES

The purpose of the three case studies described on the following pages is to demonstrate how ecology and the ecological appraisal can be used in an urban developmental context. The first case study deals with a "typical" urban subdivision, a form of urban development familiar to most people. The second study might be described as a "special" type of urban generated development. It will describe an ecological input into a major recreational development (the Metro Toronto Zoo Project). The final study is also urban generated, although it is not always found in an urban area. The example described here is the ecological appraisal as it relates to a proposed highway development. These case studies demonstrate the flexibility and utility of the ecological appraisal across a wide range of urban development types. Although none of the case studies involve all of the developmental stages previously discussed, they demonstrate some of the problems treated in an ecological framework. They also indicate the need for continuing ecological involvement at all stages of the developmental process.

Subdivision Design in Kitchener, Ontario

The subdivision site, a 220-acre land holding located in Kitchener, Ontario, was assembled by a local developer in the late 1950's and early 1960's. An initial development plan was submitted to the city in 1963. This proposal was rejected on the grounds that the site was somewhat separated from on-going development at that time. The city suggested that a staging policy be adopted with house construction possibly commencing in 1968, but preferably in 1969 or 1970. During the interval between 1960 and 1972 when physical development finally commenced, the land remained partially in agriculture, while the rest reverted to a semi-wild state (weeds, shrubs).

The developer actively recommended planning and designing in 1968, hoping for plan approval in 1969. As it turned out, the first part of the draft plan was not approved by the Minister of the Department of Municipal Affairs until June, 1971. Minimal preparatory work, such as road layout and initial house construction, began in the winter of 1971-72. The delay in starting construction on the site reflects the fact that the developer submitted his second plan at a time (1968-69) when the city planning board and the planning department were beginning to acquire an environmental awareness. As a result the site was destined to become the "guinea pig" for environmental design in the Kitchener area.

Increased environmental awareness on the part of decision-makers resulted in the rejection of the submitted plan, which incorporated a standard design approach displaying little sensitivity to the landscape and to the inherent natural qualities and potentials it contained. The members of the city planning board felt that the area could be handled in a manner which would utilize and preserve, to some extent, the environmental quality of the site. At the time neither the developer nor the city had people on their staffs with the necessary skills to formulate ecologically satisfying design alternatives; hence my involvement as a member of the consulting group hired to provide this expertise. The work done on this project can best be described in three distinct phases. These phases demonstrate the practice of ecoplanning at three scales: 220 acres, 20 acres and 1 acre (Figure 9.1).

Phase I

In Phase I the group was concerned with the ecological character of the site as a whole. In terms of the model of the development-planning process outlined in Table 9.1, the work done was of the type described under step 2 — feasibility and conceptual planning.

In an initial survey, wooded areas were examined quantitatively and qualitatively. On the basis of this examination, the stands were evaluated with respect to a number of urban-oriented factors such as: ecological uniqueness; open space potential; capability to survive drainage change; capability to survive opening of canopy as a result of residential development and mosquito production. Twelve distinct wooded areas were identified. Most of these were either lowland types or upland types occupying rough topography. The relative quality, history of use and adaptability of the woodlands were found to be quite variable.

On the basis of the analysis, several recommendations were made. One of the more important of these concerned the area to be dedicated for park uses. The group felt that the area proposed by the developer as the central park was inappropriate. It was a woodland area that had a long history of pasturage, cutting and general misuse. The understorey was very open, reproduction was poor and the topography was relatively flat. From a design point of view, it had only one thing in its favour — centrality to the development. The area which the group recommended as a more suitable alternative exhibited greater species diversity, a more viable age structure and reproduction and a more variable landscape. Also, it could absorb and sustain the type of impact anticipated in an urban park. The developer's plan had designated this area as residential. Apparently from a two-dimensional design point of view the area was considered as less than desirable for park usage because it was located in the northwest corner of the development, so on the plan it looked asymmetrical. The relocation recommendation was accepted and this resulted in a major reallocation of land uses in the development area.

Fig. 9.1 Schematic Maps Illustrating Increasing Detail of Analysis.

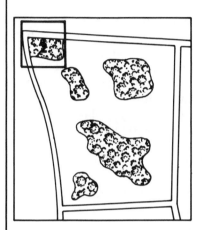

Phase 1 : Development area (220 acres) with woodland areas indicated ⚇⚇ Phase 2 area also outlined.

Phase 2 : Buildings ▢ , Parking lots ▨ . Phase 2 is 200 acres; ridge and Phase 3 area also outlined.

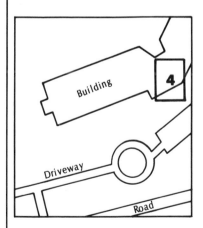

Phase 3 : Small area (1 acre) with buildings and driveway and road indicated.

Phase 4 : Detailed vegetation analysis and management in relationship to apartment building.

Another major recommendation involved the preservation of an aesthetic resource along a perimeter road south of the development. At the time of development, this road was canopied by trees (mature wooded areas along both sides). From an aesthetic point of view, this was considered to be significant. A management programme was required in order to preserve this resource during and after urban development. One side of the road was bordered by a wooded city park. Thus, there was no problem in maintaining this edge. On the development side of the road, however, the anticipated land use was single family residential with yards backing on to the perimeter road. Several issues had to be resolved. The first related to possible road widening. If the city had decided to go ahead with road widening, it would have made preservation very difficult. The city at this point decided not to widen this particular road. The next issue was ecological in nature. The determination of the minimum depth of trees required to maintain the road edge trees was crucial. Based on the analysis, it was felt that a buffer strip of approximately 100 feet in depth would guarantee survival.

The city agreed with the group's management proposal and took measures to control and manage this strip of trees. By not widening the road, the municipality was able to maintain a part of the buffer on the undeveloped road allowance. Beyond this allowance, control will be established by attaching covenants to the deeds of the future home owners. These convenants will prevent tree cutting without specific permission. Unfortunately, the city subsequently changed its policy and proceeded with a road widening programme. A part of the buffer was lost.

Other vegetation recommendations included the reservation of flood-plain clusters of white cedar; planting of trees to screen an industrial area (in advance of construction); the location of an entry road in a gap between two wooded areas rather than through the edge of one of the woodlots and the handling of other wooded areas (clear cutting, impact of wetland drainage) under urban conditions.

A detailed geomorphological and soils survey was not completed, but our preliminary study did indicate a number of problem areas requiring special attention. Areas of high soil erosion potential, organic soil deposits, steep slopes and excessive stoniness were identified. No special management approaches to these problem areas were reflected in the plan as originally submitted. In particular, the problems in utilizing the organic areas were vastly underestimated. The group recommended that a much more detailed analysis be conducted in these problem areas. As a result of the group's "flagging" of one such problem area, a detailed study was conducted and a relatively sophisticated engineering solution was developed and instituted.

Part of the development is underlain by a gravel deposit which may be acceptable for commercial aggregate production. The group was of the opinion that the feasibility of extracting the gravel prior to development should be considered. A reasonable urban landscape could be created during the excavation. A dual value would result: a commercial product and a landform adaptable to urban development. This recommendation, however, was not acted upon.

In essence, these were the recommendations made for the 220-acre site. They related to land use allocation (park), management of vegetation (tree canopy), preservation and planting programmes (white cedar, screens), potential hazard areas (organic soils) and multiple use of resources.

Phase II

Phase I recommended that the major parkland area be moved. This recommendation was followed in subsequent design work (Master Plan). The recommended forest area was approximately 20 acres in size and under present planning regulations the developer could not be forced to dedicate it completely to open space use. It therefore became a question of adapting a proposed development form to this existing woodland area while preserving the open space value articulated previously. Although the unit had been identified as an entity in the previous study and recommended as open space, we now had to allocate areas within the unit to different uses.

As in the previous phase, the ecological input resulted from conflict between the developer and the city. The developer had evolved a design approach utilizing a high rise building, walkup apartment, dedicated open space, easement open space and floodway dedication. It was relatively generous in respect to open space, but it was ecologically disastrous.

The city, in the initial stage, wanted the whole of the area in some form of open space — an expensive and unrealistic proposition. The city could not legally force the developer to dedicate the land, nor could it afford to purchase the land. This proposal was abandoned relatively quickly, and so the question of allocating urban components within the unit became critical.

Based on further analysis of the forest unit, the group was able to identify five vegetation subsectors. Each of these was examined with the following criteria in mind: susceptibility to urban impact; aesthetics; potential for survival; carrying capacity for park use and long term management implications. The several subsections were variable in terms of ecological quality and vulnerability to urban stress. The problem therefore was to place the urban components in the least damaging location.

The developer wished to locate a high rise apartment building on a small ridge running centrally through the unit (Figure 9.1). Locating the building here would have resulted in the cutting of forest cover into relatively small blocks. No subsector of the larger unit would have escaped significant impact. From an ecological point of view, the ridge community was adaptable to change surrounding it — but very susceptible to construction within the community. In other words the ridge community, if left intact, would survive change in surrounding land use. Maintaining the ridge community became a priority in preserving the values which had caused this area to be designated as open space. This argument was finally accepted as the subsequent approved plan shows a relocated apartment building away from the ridge.

The ridge community occupied approximately four acres of land out of the 20 acres in the block. At this scale, ecological inputs assisted in making decisions concerning components within a relatively small urban area. It was not possible to preserve the whole of the area as park. Therefore, it was necessary to make trade-offs between the various subsectors of the unit. The decisions were based on maintenance of quality and potential for survival of the sub-units under high levels of urban impact.

Phase III

The final phase involved the location of a driveway serving two parking lots adjacent to three-storey walkup apartment structures. This small area is located in one of the forested areas discussed in the previous phase.

The developer wanted two entry ways, as opposed to the combined driveway system proposed by the city, and justified the two entry ways on the basis that it would save trees. The area under discussion was approximately 100 feet long and 50 feet wide — a relatively small block of land. It contained approximately 100 trees, and upon examination, it became obvious that the preservation of trees could not be used as justification for a design alteration in favour of the developer. This rather unusual ecologically based decision was taken for a number of reasons relating to the ecologic condition of the site as well as to the impacts likely to result from the development of the site.

The soils underlying the trees were organic in nature (six to seven feet in depth). Soils of this type are very susceptible to alterations in drainage, surface compaction from foot traffic and increased light penetration. The urbanization of the surrounding region will expose the area to these types of stress. In combination, these impacts are likely to create significant alterations in the soil and subsequently, significant impact on the tree vegetation. Secondly, the trees presently occupying the site did not indicate a high potential for surviving urbanization. The tree cover was predominantly white cedar, yellow birch and black ash and since such trees are rooted completely in the upper few inches of organic soil, any compaction or reduction of this upper layer would almost surely spell death for the trees. A fair number of windfall and potential windfalls showed that the process had already commenced. It would not have taken long as urban development and usage intensified (drainage ditch to improve drainage, opening the edge of the stand by road and building construction and higher intensity of foot traffic) for the process to have run its course.

Organic soils require special treatment in an urban area. Frequently they are simply buried under fill and forgotten until settling and compaction create surface problems with sidewalks, driveways and even buildings, if foundations are not deep enough. The safest solution is to remove these soils and replace with fill, or recognize the inherent instability and control use on such areas. Any vegetation occupying such areas rates very low in their capability to survive urbanization.

In the context of ecoplanning strategy, this case study has one important lesson to teach. The ecological input was requested only at points of conflict, when the developer and the city could not agree. In other words, the ecoplanners were not involved in the evolution of any of the design approaches. This created some difficulty. By the time the group became involved, certain emotional and financial commitments were attached to the proposals and the persons holding these commitments were less than willing to retreat from their positions. This could have been avoided by earlier and more continuous involvements. Despite the constraints under which the project evolved, the influence of the ecological appraisal is apparent in the present urban landscape.

The Metro Toronto Zoo Project

The zoo site, located in the northeastern sector of the Municipality of Metropolitan Toronto, is a unique and varied piece of landscape. From the old shorelines of Lake Iroquois to the high quality forest stand on the upland and in the valley of the Rouge River, considerable geological and biological diversity is evident.

The mandate for an ecological appraisal included the following:

1. Inventory the conditions and uniqueness of the tree cover on the site;
2. Inventory in each vegetative landscape unit the plants potentially poisonous to grazing animals;
3. Appraise the impact of construction (roads, pathways, sewers, waterlines, parking lots, buildings and ponds) on the survival of existing forest stands;

4. Inventory the soil characteristics as they relate to erosion, bank stability, construction routes for servicing and subsurface water movement;
5. Appraise the historic factors which initiated the erosion on portions of the valley walls;
6. Recommend suitable measures to preserve existing forest and soil resources and to restabilize banks which are presently without vegetation.

The study[6] attempted to integrate the analysis of soils and geomorphology and the composition of various forest communities into a systematic appraisal of the processes operating on the site and their relationship to the proposed land use. At the same time, an attempt was made to determine the relative influence of human activities (logging, burning, drainage, pasturage) as opposed to natural influence of slope, drainage and exposure on the relative structures, stability, quality of forest communities and slope areas.

The site contains considerable diversity of woodland units. Some excellent climax stands persist in the area (southern deciduous on south and west facing slopes). These stands, which deserve special care, offer unique visual and educational potential. These areas, and others, were designated as special interest zones, requiring management. The less significant woodland areas were also examined and evaluated in the context of the proposed land uses (grazing susceptibility, slope control and aesthetics), and this information was integrated into the design process.

The analysis also demonstrated that the valley walls along the Rouge River are very fragile. Increased water flow and increased traffic along the slopes are likely to generate increased gully erosion and slumping. The forest stands occupying the slopes are, in general, marginally stable but are important in maintaining what stability there is. These two factors indicated that access by humans and animals be controlled in these locations.

The pros and cons of river channelization as a means of attaining bank stability were examined. Although river undercutting probably initiated the erosion, a closer examination indicated that drainage over the bluff and seepage from interbedded sand and silts prevented them from becoming revegetated and, hence, stabilized. The river has in many places moved away from the base. The major conclusions drawn from analysis of the river banks were: 1. that surface drainage control was a critical element in stabilization; and 2. that further thought ought to be given to the question of channelization as a method of bank stabilization.

Despite this concern about the wisdom of river channelization, a decision was made to "improve" the river channel in the Rouge Valley. However, special measures were taken to ensure that the removal of surface water from the upland area did not upset the stability of the slopes as it was delivered to the river.

The soils vary considerably throughout the site. Several areas had limiting characteristics which had to be considered in the zoo design. Boulder pavements, high water tables, erodibility, slope, ponding potential and the inability of some soils to grow forage crops (animal paddocks) were designated as limiting factors of various soil units. These may require the selection of an alternative design or the adoption of appropriate management techniques to overcome the constraint.

Several areas were designated to be avoided in servicing. Two such areas were identified as boulder pavement areas. The boulder pavements are related to old beach lines of Lake Iroquois. A major service line was initially designated in one of these areas. The laying of services in these areas would greatly increase the cost of servicing. Four additional areas were "flagged" as service problem areas because of high water tables during the spring and early summer. The soils in these locations were well sorted sands and, when saturated, required shoring and pumping to maintain trench walls. More general soil information indicated clay areas susceptible to compaction, organic areas and high erosion areas on the site.

The ecological perspective provided by this study allowed the study team to make a number of recommendations with respect to environmental management on the zoo site.

Management of the slopes was a major area of involvement. For the slopes which were actively eroding, it was recommended that a planting programme be initiated. The recommended programme, although experimental in nature, would hopefully accelerate the restabilization of these extreme environments. Plants, which are adaptable to relatively harsh conditions (temperature, fertility, surface mobility) must necessarily be used. Experimental ecological work of this nature is quite compatible with the overall objectives of the zoo.

Related to the issue of slope stability was the location (design) and construction (implementation) of a major transportation facility within the zoo site. The "ride" is an experimental system which required the construction of a raised concrete right-of-way. At two locations this transportation mode had to traverse the steep valley slopes. If poorly executed, this could have caused major disruption by upsetting the balance of the slopes and the vegetation, generating major slope problems. Fortunately the ecoplanning team was able to designate an area and construction approach which reduced the possibility of major disruption. Location of support beams, construction techniques, geological stratigraphy, seepage areas, vegetation and season of construction were all relevant inputs into the decision. Late summer construction was strongly recommended. Late summer construction would avoid the period of greatest instability resulting from bank seepages.

Another example of environmental management during implementation was the restriction of impact to a 40-foot right-of-way. On site control and management during construction was instrumental in keeping the impact of construction within this narrow right-of-way. This was remarkable, considering the size of machinery used in the construction.

In facilities such as a zoo, the location of services and buildings can have serious effects on biological communities. The impact may be generated by alteration of drainage patterns, increased erosion and microclimatic alteration. Unique or sensitive floral areas can be protected by controlling access. This process can be used with organic soils and steep slopes also. Once the areas are identified, pathways and roads can be laid out so as to avoid the sensitive or unique areas.

Construction techniques can also be adapted to existing ecological conditions. For example in the core (main pavilion) area of the zoo site, a relatively significant forest area, important to the overall design concept, was maintained by downhill subsurface drainage of water. Any interruption of the flow would have led to the deterioration of the relatively unique characteristics of the stand, an ecological as well as a design loss. The conflict related to an access roadway across the slope. No alternative location for the roadway was available. The normal hillside construction method involves a slope cut technique where the roadbed is placed in a notch cut into the slope. Such a technique would have interrupted the downhill drainage and led to the destruction of the forest ecosystem. The recommended solution to the problem was to raise the road level with sand fill rather than cutting into the slope. The required drainage pattern could thus be maintained beneath the roadbed. This may appear to be a relatively simple solution, but it is not an obvious one in purely engineering terms. It required an ecological understanding of both the forest involved and the impact the proposed development would have had on the forest's support system.

This study, unlike the previous one, was not generated out of a necessity to resolve a conflict. The ecological team in this case was involved early enough in the process to influence design decisions while they were still flexible. In general, the sooner the ecological team becomes involved the better. Although the ecological study group had no part to play in site selection, the positive role of environmental input from the conceptual plan stage through the implementation stage is well demonstrated in this project (Table 9.1).

The Highway 8 Bypass: Cambridge, Ontario

The final case study deals with a quite different form of urban generated development. The previous studies dealt with land areas most of which will ultimately be used for the anticipated land use. In this study we are dealing with a linear facility and a study area of which only a small percentage of the land area will be allocated to the particular use. This condition is common to studies associated with transportation, communication and utility systems.

Considerable controversy often surrounds any proposal for major highway routing and construction. No longer is the highway engineer able to make a decision based primarily on economics for highway location. It is now commonplace to require the submission of an extensive report including information justifying the project (need for the highway), corridor alternatives, environmental impact, social impact and land use implications of the facility before approval is given. The evaluation as presented in such a report is necessary to separate fact from emotion and provide a framework for evaluating the various corridors and/or alignments.

The philosophy behind the environmental appraisal for highway studies is similar to that described previously. Environmental appraisal provides a means of determining the potential environmental conflict that will occur if a particular route is chosen. This impact must then be weighed against other variables involved (traffic service, social impact).

The project described herein is designated as a feasibility study. A feasibility study, in terms of the stages in the development process, deals with the conceptual design stage and the evaluation stage. The end point of the feasibility study is usually the selection of the preferred alignment. At this point, a recommendation is made to the political decision-making group that the preferred alignment be selected and ultimately constructed.

Normally, the area subjected to an environmental appraisal is significantly larger than the area to be built upon. Theoretically, the highway corridor could fall anywhere within this extensive study area. However, different corridors within the area are not equal in their capability of solving a traffic problem. Nor are they equal in the level of environmental conflict they would create.

The specific facility evaluated in this study is the Highway 8 Bypass planned to circumvent the city of Cambridge in southern Ontario (Figure 9.2).

The initial phase of the environmental assessment was the development of a detailed picture of the resource pattern within the study area. This survey included the following components: surficial geology; topography; soils; wildlife; forest areas; historically significant areas;

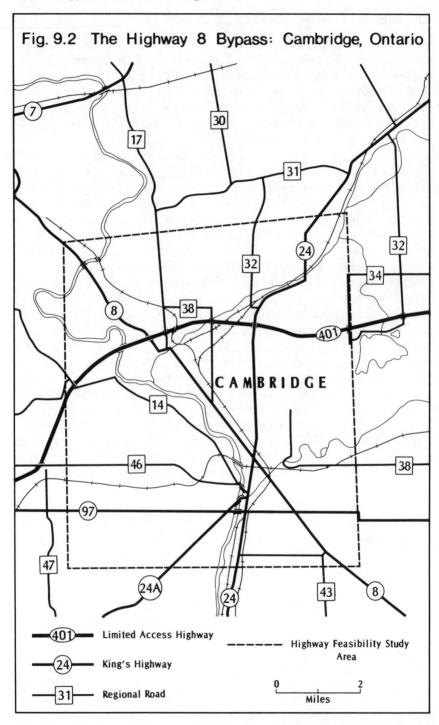

Fig. 9.2 The Highway 8 Bypass: Cambridge, Ontario

CAMBRIDGE

— 401 — Limited Access Highway

— 24 — King's Highway

— 31 — Regional Road

- - - - - Highway Feasibility Study Area

0   2
Miles

water and unique ecological areas. In the study area much of this data was readily available, but it required collation and in some cases re-interpretation to match the special needs of the highway study. Other information, however, was not available and some field work was undertaken.

The data, once collected, must be integrated and interpreted as it relates to the projected highway facility. There are several techniques by which this information can then be presented. Generally, an initial step is the graphic presentation of the information. Initially, maps dealing with forestry area, soils, geology, wildlife areas, historical areas (Caucasian and pre-Caucasian) and aquatic resources, among others, are constructed. The information contained in this variety of graphic displays must somehow be simplified in order to highlight possible resource conflicts. One approach is the preparation of maps showing a combination of resource features. An example is a physical constraints map which shows those features of the landscape which may hinder the construction of a highway facility (e.g. organic soils, slump areas, steep slopes, flood-plain areas and shallow bedrock). With present engineering technology many of these constraints can be overcome but they tend to generate additional cost. "The ideal highway route location is considered to be over level terrain consisting of deep, coarse soils, well-drained internally."[7] The degree of constraint that these features generate is variable. For example, organic soils in excess of 15 feet is more significant than organic soils less than 3 feet in depth. Some form of rating for the level of constraint must also be demonstrated.

A second possible display shows a different interpretation of the resource patterns of the landscape. This might be called an environmental value map. This display identifies those areas considered to have a value which should be considered in the highway decision-making process. As in the physical constraint situation, the relative value of the factors varies considerably. Included on the environmental value display would be historical sites (Caucasian and pre-Caucasian), high quality agricultural land, quality sand and gravel locations, recreation areas, unique ecological and wildlife areas. It is possible that certain areas would appear under several different headings. For example, a bog lake may be described under the following headings: ecologically unique (plants); wildlife production and habitat; aesthetics and organic soil constraints for construction. It is important that these different values be articulated.

The above approach is only one of the possible ways in which the environmental information may be presented. Computer generated maps are another possibility. Common to all approaches is the inventory stage, interpretation of the inventoried data and evaluation of the various resource features identified.

Once this stage has been reached, it is possible to examine possible highway corridors which will, to varying degrees, satisfy the needs for a highway. Each of the corridors will have a different environmental impact, social impact and effectiveness in solving the identified traffic problem. Two approaches can be followed in the generation of possible corridors. The first, unfortunately, is the more common. The traffic engineers draft possible corridors in the study area often before the basic inventory work is completed. The other participants then react to these lines on a map depending on their particular specialities. The second approach involves the total project team in the drafting of possible corridors. This process would eliminate immediately the unacceptable corridor.

In this study, three corridors were designated for further study. They were the West Corridor, "S" Corridor and East Corridor (Figure 9.3). Each of the three corridors and the subsequent refinements of the corridors (alignments) were evaluated against a wide range of general and environmental criteria (Figure 9.4).

The environmental evaluation was done using the data collected during the initial phase. It was often a very difficult process because one must compare the relative value or loss generated by one corridor against that generated by another. Examples of the difficulties involved include the following: does an ecologically unique bog system rate higher or lower than an 1840 mansion; or how does a bald eagle's nest compare with an Indian archeological site? The process is further complicated by a lack of knowledge about the status of many of our natural resources.

Many researchers are attempting to develop more rigorous techniques to facilitate the evaluation problem. It is quite possible that none of the alternative corridors are completely "acceptable" in environmental terms, and this was precisely the case with the initial corridors proposed in the Highway 8 study. It must be constantly remembered that there are factors other than environmental to be considered. An environmentally acceptable corridor (i.e., low environment damage) may create intolerable social impact (i.e., high degree of farm severances, or dislocation of residents), and may not satisfy the traffic requirements. In other words, environment is just one of the factors to be considered.

In this study, there was continual modification of the proposed corridors and alignments. This was a response to the interaction among the various participants in the study. Each of the modified alignments was evaluated in terms of the factors mentioned previously. The stages in the process were the evaluation of three corridors (1,000-foot wide areas), evaluation of five alignments and the evaluation of five modified alignments.

The next step in the procedure following evaluation was the selec-

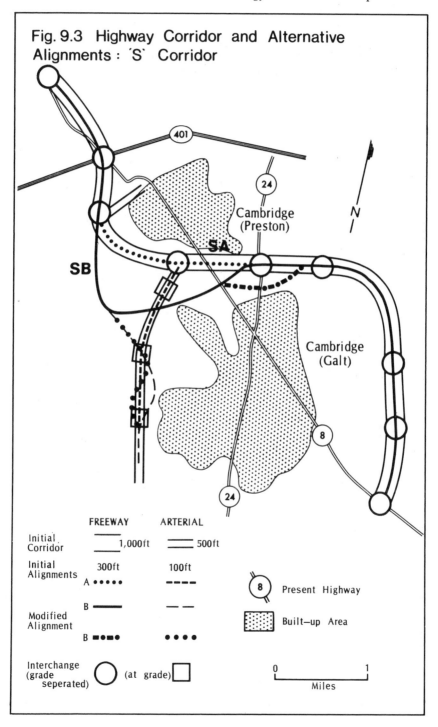

Fig. 9.3 Highway Corridor and Alternative Alignments : 'S' Corridor

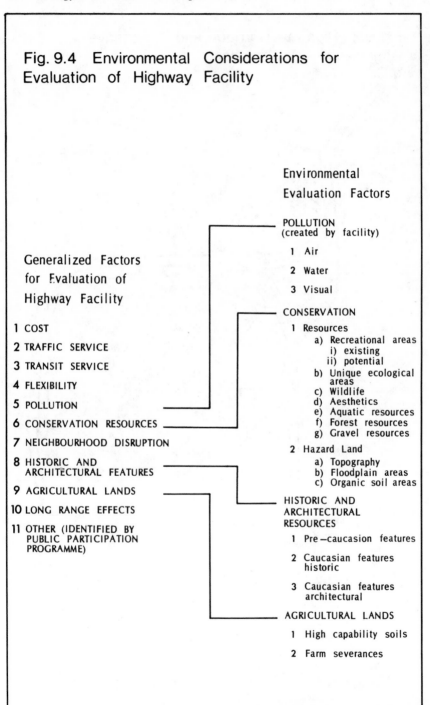

Fig. 9.4 Environmental Considerations for Evaluation of Highway Facility

tion of a preferred alignment. The preferred alignment, in the opinion of the research team, is the one which most adequately fulfills all the factors of evaluation. Once a preferred alignment is selected, a recommendation is made to the effect that the facility be built in the preferred location. Accompanying such a recommendation is a statement detailing the potential impact of the alignment as well as management guidelines to be followed in the functional design and implementation stage.

If the recommendation of the project team is accepted and a decision to build the facility is made, the stage is set for the functional design (Master Plan) stage. The recommended alignment to this point is not a fixed line. It can still be modified in respect to detailed engineering requirements (visual curves, bridges) and to specific environmental situations. It is during this stage that the alignment becomes fixed to a precise location in the study area. Environmental input is relevant at this stage as well. The foci of attention now are specific situations along the alignment. Specific situations would include a river crossing, a forested area, or a lowland wet area. The objective is to design an alignment which does minimal damage to these and other sites along the alignment. Slight shifts in the alignment, sedimentation control during construction, or season of construction, could significantly alter the potential impact. The environmental input is directed at creating a sensitivity to the specific features along the alignment. Additional detailed ecological work will be needed at this stage.

The final stage once again is implementation. Supervision of construction is required to ensure that environmental management guidelines are observed during construction.

In the present study, the feasibility study has been completed and a recommendation for an alignment has been submitted. It is hoped that the environmental involvement will be maintained in subsequent stages.

A FINAL WORD

This paper has attempted to demonstrate the utility and significance of ecology and the ecological appraisal in the planning and design of various forms of urban development.

Ecology cannot, and possibly should not, attempt to achieve the mathematical precision that many sciences such as physics and chemistry are capable of achieving. When dealing with complex environments, there are many variables and many possible results depending on how the variables are managed. However, it is possible that fairly reliable predictions can be made and where such predictions are made, certain probabilities concerning the outcome can also be made on the basis of past experience. One major function of pre-development ecology is to predict damage which will take place resulting from a particular form of action. This may not prevent the action from taking place, but at least we will be aware of the full consequences of the action.

In the realm of urban development and ecology, considerable research is required. Ecology has a considerable body of knowledge which is adaptable to urban development. However, more work is required in fields such as urban forestry, urban wildlife, water impoundments, microclimatic management and energy conservation. This requires a refocusing of the thrust of many scientific, educational institutions and universities. Additional education in urban-oriented fields is to be encouraged, as is additional funding of urban-oriented ecological studies. Similarly, the technocratic decision-makers (planners, engineers, architects and politicians) should also be educated in the basic principles of ecology in order to facilitate communication.

With relation to the previous comments, there is a definite need for more sophisticated evaluation techniques. Placing values on environmental variables is a very difficult process. To a great extent we must rely on expert opinion, educated guess or past experience. There are several techniques which are somewhat mechanistic in nature.[8] These techniques are attempting to represent evaluation techniques as being mathematically precise, but even such techniques must, to some degree, be based on subjective interpretation of the environmental factors. Part of the problem relates to the vast differences in perception and values attached to the various components. An example will illustrate this. The nesting site of a single bald eagle delayed the decision determining the location of a major highway facility. In this particular case, there were several competing values to be considered. If the nest was the only one left in the region, it may have a higher value than if it was only one of a viable population. Another variable involved was the fact that the nest contained only one bird; it did not contain a breeding pair. It may be a very temporary constraint. Ranged against the value of the bald eagle nesting site were a number of other environmental values (impact of alternative alignment), engineering and economic values. The question therefore was: how much value do we attach to the resource of one bald eagle? In reality, there were additional factors involved in this particular case. Firstly, the present status of the bald eagle in southern Ontario is largely unknown. Secondly, many residents in the area reacted very strongly to the situation of the nest, and used its presence as the key to their defence against the highway. In essence, the nest of the bald eagle had a symbolic value to the residents.

Another difficulty with environmental evaluation is the fact that environmental values are ranked against values more widely understood by the decision-makers and the general public (cost, safety, traffic, need for housing, etc.). Also, many of the environmental values can only achieve their full potential over relatively long periods of time.

Unfortunately, many decisons are made in short time frames (4 to 10 years), not in 40 years or more often involved in environmental management decisions.

Other factors of concern regarding ecoplanning and ecological appraisal relate to cost, legal requirements for the survey and timing of the study. Dorney[9] describes the relative cost of the survey on an acreage basis and on a comparative basis with the total cost of the total development. It was his opinion/finding that both the actual acreage cost and comparative costs were low, particularly when cost savings generated by the survey were estimated.

At present, the legal requirement for a pre-development ecological survey varies across the country. It is expected that the ecological appraisal will soon become a required part of the development submission for a greater range of projects, particularly those sponsored by the various levels of government (federal and provincial). Increasingly, private developers are utilizing the ecological approach because they are interested in creating a better development as well as facilitating approval by government agencies who are demanding ecological sensitivity in proposed developments.

The timing of an ecological survey is critical; in general, the earlier in the decision-making process, the better. It takes considerable time to assemble the data base (e.g. base line water quality data may require a year to assemble). The environmental data base should be completed prior to major design and investment decisions. As the project continues, design approaches are generated involving both time investment and personal commitment on the part of the developer/designer. These tend to strengthen as the project progresses, and this makes alterations based on ecological inputs more difficult to initiate. Ecology should be one of the first studies to be undertaken. A related factor is the involvement of the ecologist throughout the design phase. Involvement of the ecologist beyond the stage of report submission is strongly encouraged. He should be part of the overall design team.

Finally, the ecologist working in the urban area must have a good understanding of urbanization and the impacts it has on natural or semi-natural ecosystems. He must be able to answer questions concerning survival or reaction of various systems under the stress created by urban development. He must also understand the requirements of urban development in that certain development forms require levels of service and change which may work against maintaining some elements of the natural environment (e.g. drainage ways). At the same time many of the present practices followed in urban development should be reviewed in an environmental context. It has been my experience that some of these practices viewed as necessary are based on tradition rather than on sound engineering or planning principles.

Like many sciences, ecology can be used for bad as well as good. Unfortunately, we are seeing some of the poorer aspects at the present time. Involvement with ecology has tended to become extremely emotional, irrational, or highly political. To some, it has become a new religion. Ecoplanning must be positive and objective in dealing with urban development. This does not mean becoming a prostitute to the developer.

Ecology does have a positive role to play in urban design and development. Urban development is, to some degree, inevitable, but it does not necessarily have to have the severity of environmental degradation often observed today. Through a better understanding of the physical-biological base, a better adaptation can be achieved, maintaining a more viable natural environment, as well as a better urban environment for human inhabitants.

It is no longer necessary to make major blunders in land use through lack of ecological knowledge. It is no longer necessary to sacrifice long term environmental values for short term economic goals. It is possible to reconcile the conflicting demands upon lands and resources so that irreparable damage is avoided and human population can enjoy meaningful benefits. [10]

NOTES

1. Dorney, R.S. (1970). *"Role of Ecologists as Consultants in Urban Design."* Paper presented at Urban Ecology Today Symposium, AAAS meeting, Chicago.
   Kitchen, C.M. (1971). "Ecological Concepts in Subdivision Design." In *The Waterloo County Area Selected Geographical Essays.* edited by A.G. McLellan, Department of Geography Publication Series No. 1, University of Waterloo, 255-65.
2. Dansereau, P. (1971). "Dimensions of Environmental Quality." *Sarracenia*, 14, 1-1-09.
3. Christiansen, E.A., ed. (1970). *Physical Environment of Saskatoon, Canada.* Saskatchewan Research Council and National Research Council of Canada, Ottawa.
4. Coleman, D. and I. McNaughton. (1971). "Environmental Planning in Waterloo County." In *The Waterloo County Area, Selected Geographical Essays.* Edited by A.G. McLellan, Department of Geography Publication Series No. 1, University of Waterloo, 241-53.
   Coleman, D. (1974). *Ecological Input into Regional Planning.* Unpublished Ph.D. Thesis, School of Urban and Regional Planning, University of Waterloo.
5. Dansereau, P. (1972). "E.Z.A.I.M., An Interdisciplinary Adventure." *National Research Council of Canada Newsletter*, Industry Research Section, Ottawa, 3 (3).
6. Kitchen, C.M., R.S. Dorney, J.W. Wilson and E. MacKintosh. (1970). *Ecological Appraisal of the Metropolitan Toronto Zoo Project Site.* Prepared for the Metropolitan Toronto Parks Commission by Ecoplans Ltd., Waterloo.
7. Bird, S.J.G. (1973). "Environmental Criteria for Recreationally Oriented Highway Planning." *Highway Research Record*, No. 452, 19-26.
8. Leopold, L.B., F.E. Clarke, B.B. Hanshaw and J.R. Balsley. (1971). *A Procedure for Evaluating Environmental Impact.* Washington, D.C.: U.S. Geological Survey Circular 645.
9. Dorney, R.S. (1973). "Role of Ecologists as Consultants in Urban Planning and Design." *Human Ecology*, 1(3), 183-203.
10. Dasmann, R., J.P. Milton and P.H. Freeman. (1973). *Ecological Principles for Economic Development.* New York: Wiley.

PART 6
ENSURING THE FUTURE OF THE CANADIAN NATURAL ENVIRONMENT:
POLICY PRIORITIES

10

Environmental Policy and Environmental Planning in Canada

C.I. Jackson*, Ministry of State for Urban Affairs, Ottawa

A NATURAL ENVIRONMENT OR A HUMAN ENVIRONMENT? THE BASIS OF GOVERNMENTAL CONCERN

By now, the word "environment" has become so much a part of our lives that we seldom ask ourselves what is meant when the word is used. Yet the word does cause confusion, and may mean different things to different people. This confusion is particularly serious when an attempt is made to set environmental priorities; to decide what must be improved or protected first.

For example, is the "environment" the same as the "natural environment"? Is there a difference between the natural environment and the human environment? Both these phrases are used frequently; the natural environment, for instance, appears in the title of this book and the human environment was the subject of the United Nations Conference in Stockholm in 1972, a landmark in the growing worldwide concern for environmental matters.

It seems reasonable to suggest that the word environment is usually used to mean "natural environment" by those whose training and concern is with the non-human aspects of the subject: geologists, climatologists, biologists and others. To them the natural environment is often seen as an ecosystem, or a series of ecosystems, that could exist very largely without man, and that might indeed be in a much better state if man were not around. Those who use the term "human environment" are usually more concerned with the threats to human health and happiness that arise from environmental deterioration; e.g. the toxic effects of pesticides or of mercury, of smog or of polluted water supplies. Such people are not ignorant of the hazards of these and other pollutants to other life forms, but their primary preoccupation is with improving the environment of man. In contrast, those who use the term "natural environment" may be more inclined to search for ways to minimize man's harmful influence on the environment.

There is, incidentally, a third group for whom the term "environment" is much more narrowly related to man's needs and man's activities. For example, the recent report *New Perspective on the Health of Canadians*, published by the Department of National Health and

Welfare[1], draws a clear distinction between those health hazards that are caused by *life-style* and those that are caused by *environment*. Used in this sense, the environment is simply something over which the individual has little or no control. A person may die of a lung disease caused by excessive smoking; this is clearly related to his or her own life-style. He or she may also acquire lung disease because of more widespread air pollution that can be avoided only by moving somewhere else; this is a matter of environment.

We are not concerned here with so broad a contrast as is implied in this last example, but the distinction between the natural and the human environment *is* one that is often important for public policy. It seems fair to say that it is the view of the environment as a *human* environment that prevails in Canada and in other countries as an issue deserving priority attention by governments; the notion of a natural environment is one that is more common among scientists and more useful to them.

Although this distinction is important and useful, it is not absolute. There have been many instances where environmental conservation measures have been instituted, with overwhelming public approval, to assist the preservation of the landscape or of endangered species even though the impact on human life is either neutral or, in a narrow sense, disadvantageous, because the measures cost money, or restrict individual freedoms. Perhaps the most obvious example is the coordinated international effort by Canada and the U.S.A. to maintain the whooping crane in a wild state, despite the fact that only a few dozen specimens exist at present, and are very vulnerable to elimination, especially during their long annual migrations between Wood Buffalo Park and Corpus Christi on the Texas Gulf Coast. As the present writer has remarked elsewhere, however, the measures to protect the whooping crane are based on a human and sometimes quirky code of ethics.[2] As Canadians or Americans we do not object to these measures because the bird is visually interesting, because we are impressed by the enterprise and the dangers involved in its migrations and because, after all, the cost of the conservation measures is relatively small. We may flatter ourselves that we also protect the whooping crane because of a basic concern for the preservation of endangered species, and this feeling may be justified to varying degrees: total in the case of the wildlife biologists most involved in the project, less than total in the case of a politician or official who, like the general public, would not recognize a whooping crane if he trod on one, but who realizes that a negative attitude towards whooping cranes will generate more public opposition than a positive attitude.

Whooping cranes are too easy; there may be more difficulty in generating similar public support for the protection of other life forms that have a less attractive public image. We may write a letter to our Member of Parliament urging the protection of whooping cranes, baby

seals or peregrine falcons; we may then seize an insecticide, or occasionally a rifle, and go off to do battle with other creatures that are attacking
our garden. We may applaud the gentle attempts to dissuade polar
bears from ransacking the trashcans at Churchill; at the same time we
may not do much to save the Ipswich sparrow on Sable Island because
we value the area's oil resources more, or because we tend to feel that
the sparrows of the world can look after themselves.

THE ENVIRONMENT: ONE PRIORITY AMONG MANY

The examples just quoted are still rather straightforward when compared to many of the dilemmas faced by governments when establishing
policy and programme priorities. For example, three main approaches
may be taken by the federal and territorial governments in the management of the Yukon and Northwest Territories, a land that encompasses
40 percent of the area of Canada, and that is both ecologically rich and
ecologically fragile. From the viewpoint of the natural scientist, or even
of the ordinary Canadian citizen who is concerned about the quality of
the natural environment, the first priority for government in the North
may well appear to be the preservation of this magnificent wilderness
and the wildlife that it contains. However, from another standpoint, in a
world where energy and other crises arise or threaten from time to time,
and in a country where the improvement of the standard of living is
taken for granted as a national objective, the mineral and other
economic resources of the North may appear a vast reservoir that should
be tapped as rapidly as possible. Yet again the North is the home of
Canadians, relatively few in total numbers perhaps, but Canadian citi-
zens nevertheless. It is an area with a high proportion of Inuit, Indian
and Métis, whose per capita income, employment, health, education
and other indices of human welfare are normally well below the national
average. Should not the principal priority be the improvement of the
material condition and opportunities of the northern population?

It will not do to respond simply — and probably truthfully — that in
fact these are not real alternatives; that the North is vast enough to
accommodate all three of these approaches without disastrous conflict.
In the first place, such a middle ground is often unpopular, and is often
rejected as a defeat by those who believe strongly that the preservation
of the quality of the natural environment should be the overriding concern. Secondly, the choice among these three approaches often has to be
made, if not in overall terms, then certainly in the case of specific projects, large or small, in specific northern situations and locations. Lastly,
it has to be recognized that the mutual accommodation of all these (and
perhaps other) objectives usually requires substantial time for careful
planning, and this may be thwarted by the pressure of events and of

public opinion. In Alaska, for example, the building of the oil pipeline from the North Slope to Valdez was successfully delayed for several years, during which time native land claims were satisfactorily settled and detailed environmental impact assessments were undertaken. It might be argued that the pressure for a decision generated by the Arab oil embargo came at a time that was right in terms of a reasonable compromise among economic, environmental and residents' interests. Whether this is true or not, it seems reasonable to doubt whether the same prolonged tolerance of non-economic interests would have been shown by American institutions and the American people if the Arab oil embargo had come in the winter of 1969-70 rather than in that of 1973-74. In 1969 and 1970 concern for environmental matters in the U.S. was probably at an all-time high, yet it seems probable that "overriding national concerns" would have led to the speedy authorization of the pipeline. These overriding concerns would have been human concerns, and such a decision would probably have had the overwhelming endorsement of the vast majority of Americans. Had a similar situation arisen in Canada, it is difficult to contemplate a different result.

This view is neither cynical or pessimistic. It is not cynicism to recognize that environmental priorities must compete for attention with many other priorities, and that they will not always prevail. Governments and legislatures are constantly bombarded with proposals for new initiatives, extended programmes and stronger policies that cannot all be accommodated in a crowded legislative programme or adequately funded if they are enacted. Is the environment more important than better housing; than transport for the handicapped; more unemployment insurance; mental health care or aid to the developing countries? There can be no absolute answer to such questions, yet it is this need to choose among a bewildering array of things that are all in themselves "good" which characterizes the role of the policy planner and ultimately the decision-maker in all governments, federal, provincial or local. There is seldom any need to look for cynical reasons if one's personal preference is not shared by the Cabinet, by Parliament or by Treasury Board.

Nor is there any fundamental justification for environmental pessimism — unless one subscribes to the belief that we are already too late to save the environment. Despite the competition among priorities of all kinds, and despite the undeniable fact that some good environmental causes fail to succeed, there seem adequate grounds for believing that Canadians, and their legislators and administrators, recognize the importance of environmental concerns and are prepared to give them adequate attention. Many may be inclined to dispute this, but all too often the basis for their disagreement rests simply on the reality of the environmental hazard, which is seldom in dispute. It is not sufficient to have the right point of view on the environment or to be able to show that environmental damage will result if governments do not act. What are needed are arguments that will convince the decision-maker that the environment has a higher claim on limited resources — of legislative time, of money, of experts — than other equally valid claims. If we examine what has been achieved in the last few years, in the context of all the other things that the governments of Canada are being urged to do, there seem adequate grounds for optimism.

THE GROWTH OF PUBLIC CONCERN DURING THE 1960's

Exactly what set in motion the amazing groundswell of concern for the environment, whether natural or human, in Canada during the 1960's is impossible to determine. Elsewhere[3] the present author has mentioned the impact of Rachel Carson's book, *Silent Spring*, published in 1962. But one book cannot account for a fundamental change in attitude, especially a book that was written for an educated rather than a mass audience. Equally impossible to prove is the influence exerted by more general trends such as the shift from an obsession with economic growth as the sole index of individual and collective happiness, or the phenomenon of a generation of youth and young adults that was unusually large, much better educated than its parents and more inclined to criticize the values of its parents' world. (One advantage possessed by the environment in its claim for attention was its attractiveness to youth; it was difficult to be "against" it as one could be against so many human-oriented things.)

There are probably other, more subtle, factors involved as well. After the national obsession with depression and poverty in the 1930's and with war and post-war recovery in the 1940's, it was perhaps inevitable that the 1950's should be a period when Canadians — and others — were preoccupied with material advances, or at least with the expansion of their horizons, both material and non-material. One of the most important public enquiries of the decade, the Royal Commission on Canada's Economic Prospects, which issued its final report in 1957, was an expression of this preoccupation. In 1961 Canada was still preoccupied with such matters, as the large and influential Resources For Tomorrow Conference testified. Five years later, however, a reaction had set in, and the title of a similar national conference showed a significant change; in 1966 it was Pollution and Our Environment.

Another factor leading to the growth of interest in environmental matters was the influence of television and travel. During the 1950's and 1960's Canadians came to see their country on the television screen, and more and more they were able to explore it, as the construction of the Trans-Canada Highway symbolized the mobility of the car and the camper, and as air travel became normal for large numbers. The Canadian population was ready to listen to those who described the threats to this landscape, especially agencies such as the Sierra Club that had long been preoccupied with wilderness and the preservation of the natural environment.

There were also more immediate influences, which brought environmental matters to the individual in a very direct way. Canadian cities experienced very rapid growth rates during the 1950's and the early 1960's. Annual growth rates of three percent or more were not unusual, so that Calgary, Edmonton, Toronto, Vancouver and a number of smaller centres doubled in size within 15 or 20 years. The growing affluence of these urban populations made a waterfront cottage and a boat a realizable dream for tens of thousands. Gradually, however, they became aware that if very large numbers of people, all similarly prosperous, live close together in an urban society, the distance that one must travel to find a site for that cottage increases year by year. What was worse, the quality of the environment was visibly deteriorating as the economic and urban boom continued. Colour television merely emphasized the revolting character of the pollution that was being dumped into Lake Erie and other waterways; the quality of the air over Canadian cities was decidedly unpleasant, especially in certain weather conditions. Less obvious, but equally direct, were the results of public health tests on water quality. If bathing beaches along the Ottawa River, within sight of Parliament, were closed as a health hazard, residents of Ontario might point an accusing finger at inferior sewage treatment on the Quebec side of the river; but then it turned out that the beaches on the Rideau River had to be closed also. Through such situations, multiplied across the densely inhabited parts of southern Canada, Canadians came to recognize that the Pogo animals had summarized the environmental problem in a single sentence; "we have met the enemy, and he is us."[4]

GOVERNMENTAL ACTION SINCE 1966

Having achieved this state of self-knowledge, Canadians moved quickly to put their environmental house in order. It is, indeed, the speed of this reaction that is one of its most remarkable characteristics. The cynic — or the idealist — may remain unsatisfied, and they may legitimately point out that legislating environmental improvement is one thing; actually improving the environment is something else, and takes much longer. Even after pollution of the Great Lakes is reduced, for example, polluted water may remain in the lakes for a long time before being flushed out into the St. Lawrence, and lake or river bottom sediments may remain contaminated for a much longer period still. Nevertheless, it seems unarguable that in the second half of the 1960's the governments of Canada moved extremely quickly in response to the strong wave of public opinion in favour of environmental action. Almost as significant as the speed of the response is its diverse character. The following summary deals in turn with research, major conferences and intergovernmental liaison mechanisms, new government departments and agencies, legislation, comprehensive planning, international activities and regulation. The taxonomy is incomplete — it tends to omit the very basic task of data collection and monitoring, for instance, and the examples of each type of activity that are described represent only a very small sample of each group. Also, the present account does less than justice to the large volume of provincial government activity in all or most of these fields.

Research

Although the volume of environmental research and the resources made available by government to encourage research expanded rapidly during the 1960's, probably the most tangible research monument is the Canada Centre for Inland Waters which was created in 1967. By 1972 it was located in impressive permanent headquarters under the Burlington Bridge at the entrance to Hamilton Harbour on Lake Ontario, where it had plenty of raw material, pollution included, to occupy the 70 or more professional scientists and their support staff. The Centre's vessels became familiar sights on the Lakes and the Centre itself provided much of the basic data on which the case for a massive clean-up of the Great Lakes was based.

Conferences and Intergovernmental Liaison Mechanisms

Turning to intergovernmental liaison, the federal and provincial governments created, after the Resources For Tomorrow Conference in 1961, a continuing liaison mechanism in the form of the Canadian Council of Resource Ministers (CCRM) with a small secretariat located in Montreal. It was CCRM that organized the 1966 Conference on Pollution and Our Environment, and it was this conference that provided the main stimulus and point of departure for environmental action for administrators and legislators in both federal and provincial governments. It also helped to establish the broad priorities as between air, water and land pollution. A few years later CCRM became CCREM: The Canadian Council of Resource and Environment Ministers.

Government Reorganization

This title — CCREM — would have been impossible before 1970, because there *were* no Ministers of the Environment — or departments to serve them — until that date. By 1975 there were major departments in the federal government and in nine of the ten provinces. Again, the cynic may be inclined to regard this as merely window dressing. At the federal level, for example, he could point out that Environment Canada was initially created by bringing together a large number of pre-existing agencies, including the whole of the former Department of Fisheries and Forestry, the Water Sector from the Department of Energy, Mines and Resources, the Canada Land Inventory from Regional Economic Expansion, and the Canadian Wildlife Service from Indian Affairs and Northern Development. But the effective answer to cynicism of this kind is that it ignores the facts that a credible Department of the Environment must surely contain these units, that new units were also created, including an Environmental Protection Service designed to have power to enforce environmental standards, and also that, until the creation of the new Department, several of the agencies concerned had tended to be on the sidelines of government action. In 1971 they became part of a large department in which the priorities were much more likely to be their priorities and in which they were much more able to influence the key decisions of Cabinet and Parliament.

Legislation

It was in 1970 that environmental action by the federal government reached a peak, especially in regard to new legislation. In that year Parliament passed six bills that either created new environmental statutes or added major environmental amendments to existing legislation. These were: the Canada Water Act; the Clean Air Act; the Northern Inland Waters Act; the Arctic Waters Pollution Prevention Act; and amendments to the Fisheries Act and the Canada Shipping Act.

Although each of these is important, the two Acts that have attracted most attention, for slightly different reasons, are the Arctic Waters Pollution Prevention Act and the Canada Water Act. In both cases concern was expressed about the extension of federal jurisdiction into new areas, one international, the other national. At the time the Arctic Waters Pollution Prevention Act (AWPPA) was passed, the discovery of major oil resources on the North Slope of Alaska was encouraging similar exploration of the Canadian North. The experimental voyages of the Manhattan, an American supertanker of 153,000 tons displacement, through the Northwest Passage were designed to test the feasibility of conveying the oil to market by tanker rather than via pipeline to Valdez. Scientific study, and the more immediately convincing Arrow incident in Chedabucto Bay, Nova Scotia, in February 1970, made it obvious that the hazard presented by oil spillage in cold northern waters was, if anything, more horrendous than further south. The Arrow incident also made it clear that the standards of navigation for tankers had no obvious relation to the hazards of the cargo. The Arrow, it will be recalled, was a relatively small tanker, carrying a particularly glutinous type of fuel oil known as Bunker C, that was holed by hitting Cerberus Rock in Chedabucto Bay. The subsequent clean-up took several months at a total cost of about $3.1 million. The report on the incident, by the Executive Director of the Science Council and his colleagues, commented acidly that;

> . . . we are appalled by the callousness and sloppiness that we find in the operation of the world's tanker fleets, particularly those which sail under flags of convenience. . . . we suggest that Canada protect itself, because under the present sloppy conditions and with the increasing movement of petroleum products in Canadian waters, a second major spill is highly probable.5

In the face of scientific evidence of the potential hazard represented by oil pollution in Arctic waters, and the very practical evidence that accidents were only too likely to happen since operating standards were unnecessarily low, why should the Arctic Waters Pollution Prevention Act have aroused the controversy that it did? The answer again lies in the reconciliation of environmental objectives with other objectives; in this case, the right to free or innocent passage for vessels of all nations on the high seas. For centuries — since the Dutch jurist Grotius first expounded the principle in 1631, in fact — the "freedom of the seas" has been both a watchword and a catchword; like the environment itself, it has a highly desirable ring to it; instinctively one tends to think of it as a "Good Thing."

If instinct is superseded by a little more thought, it soon becomes apparent that this freedom needs some qualification in the modern world. There is presumably a similar freedom of the skies, and in principle we welcome the notion that aircraft of all nations should fly across international borders. Yet we would think at least twice before recognizing that freedom as including the right of supersonic aircraft to fly wherever they like, leaving sonic booms in their wake that disturb the populations beneath their path. We also accept that the right to free air navigation needs careful and close air traffic control if aircraft are to fly safely as well as freely.

In the same way, most people agree that the "freedom of the seas" should not mean freedom to pollute the oceans by deliberate or accidental discharge of fuel or other contaminants, nor should it imply a freedom to disregard navigational standards. Many would also argue that it does not include the freedom to fish some commercial species to near-extinction. What is usually meant by the term "freedom of the seas" is really the right of innocent passage, in which a ship, to adapt a terrestrial phrase to nautical use, takes only a safe course and leaves behind only a wake.

Although such limitations on freedom may seem as uncontroversial as the requirement that ships exhibit navigation lights at night, the "Law of the Sea" is in fact a very complex issue, since it also involves questions of territorial waters (three-mile limits or three hundred miles), the rights of coastal states, rights over the continental shelf and sea-bed, and sundry other matters. Suffice it to say that the provisions in the AWPPA requiring vessels using the Northwest Passage to be certified by Canada as capable of doing so safely, asserting the right of Canada to enforce these and other provisions by boarding the vessels, and requiring heavy financial penalties in cases of pollution generated some lively opposition from other countries. The latter, including the U.S.A., did not for the most part demand a continuation of freedom in the sense of irresponsibility; they were, however, concerned that this extension of Canadian jurisdiction into an international area might encourage other countries whose motives were less altruistic. The right place to seek solutions to such environmental problems, in the opinion of such countries, was in a proper Law of the Sea Conference. The Canadian Government, while recognizing the need to find a more general solution, was more immediately concerned to ensure that the environment should be protected; a satisfactory settlement at a Law of the Sea Conference might have the unfortunate deficiency that it would be reached after the damage was done[6].

In this view, the Canadian Government was supported by Parliament, which took the unusual step of emphasizing its approval of the legislation by taking a vote on second reading of AWPPA that was both recorded and unanimous (198-0). As it turned out, the Manhattan experiment demonstrated fairly clearly that the Northwest Passage was not a feasible supertanker route, yet at any rate, and the Arctic Waters Pollution Prevention Act, although it is still on the Statute Book, is no longer the focus of such strong feelings. It seems probable, however, that it helped to influence the intergovernmental discussions leading up to and during the Law of the Sea Conference held in Caracas, Venezuela in 1974 towards a much greater recognition of the need for such limited jurisdiction to be exercised by coastal states. Since this conference has not yet reached any final decisions, this issue remains in doubt. However, there can be no doubt that the Act demonstrated Canada's determination to find ways to achieve efficient environmental protection, even if this meant that Canada had to act counter to (or perhaps more accurately, in advance of) international convention and approval.

Concern over the Canada Water Act also tended to be concentrated on the legitimacy of federal jurisdiction. Expressed very simply it was argued that water is a resource, that resources are matters within provincial jurisdiction, and that the Canada Water Act therefore represents an invasion of provincial jurisdiction by the federal government. (The

Act is almost wholly concerned with southern Canada; the Northern Inland Waters Act is a complementary piece of legislation that applies to the Yukon and Northwest Territories, where such jurisdictional issues do not arise.)

Against this view, several contrary points could be advanced. In the first place, it is simple fact that many of the major river and lake systems in Canada have international (i.e. trans-border) implications: the Great Lakes-St. Lawrence, the Columbia, the Yukon, Red, Saint John and Saint Croix rivers among them. Other major rivers are interprovincial, including the Saskatchewan-Nelson and the Ottawa. In such circumstances, a federal interest is certainly legitimate. Further, the concern of the Canada Water Act (CWA) is not primarily with water as a resource, but with water as a key element in environmental quality and pollution control. Finally, although the Act does contain some clauses that enable the federal government to act on water quality matters without provincial agreement in certain circumstances, the basis of the CWA rests firmly on the negotiation of federal-provincial agreements leading to the development of comprehensive plans and systems for river basin management. Without the agreement of the provinces concerned, the CWA would be very difficult to implement.

Comprehensive Planning

The rationale for the Canada Water Act rests on the words "comprehensive management." During the 1960's it became evident that the management of water resources could only be effective if it was accomplished within a framework that recognized the immense diversity of water uses. Many of these uses are compatible with other uses; others are not, yet all may in their way be "legitimate." Water is the life environment for fish and other plant and animal life; it is a source of power; a means of transport; an input to industrial processes and domestic life; it is a source of recreation and a means of disposing of waste products. The recognition of these complex interrelationships, and the need to include them all in any comprehensive management system, meant that the Canada Water Act *had* to rest on two assumptions. The first is that major river basins can be managed as comprehensive and complex integrated systems; the second is that federal and provincial government can agree on how this should be done. Neither level of government can be effective alone, since both have jurisidiction over different elements that constitute this complex system.

The Act is therefore not a legal framework that has been superimposed willy-nilly on a natural situation; rather it was the scientific and socio-economic requirements for adequate basin management that shaped the legislation, and the shape is one that is relatively novel. This novelty may account for some of the doubts and even suspicion exhibited by provincial governments; nevertheless it seems reasonable to claim that all or most of this doubt has tended to evaporate as both levels of government have gained experience in the agreements signed as a result of it (together with a few that were signed on an *ad hoc* basis before it came into force). As of January 1, 1975, there are CWA federal-provincial agreements in effect for the development of comprehensive plans for the whole or major sections of the following major basins: Fraser, Okanagan, Peace-Athabasca, Mackenzie, Churchill-Nelson, Lake Winnipeg, Souris, Northern Ontario, St. Lawrence, Richelieu and Saint John.

Others will no doubt follow in future years. Because the physical and socio-economic interrelationships are so complex, and because the earliest agreements justifiably have been concerned with major basins where the problems are most complex, work undertaken through the agreements is still usually at the stage of research and the development of management plans rather than at the implementation stage. This is, of course, not intended as a criticism; the Act is not a crisis-solution measure; it is designed to lead to comprehensive and long term solutions of complex problems.

Although there is not sufficient space to examine other legislation in similar detail, it is worth emphasizing that some of the most effective environmental laws are contained in Acts that are not on the surface concerned with pollution control. The amendments to the Fisheries Act are a good example. Although freshwater fish, when caught, are resources and therefore "provincial", the federal government has the jurisdiction and the responsibility to protect the quality of the water in which they live. Much of the action taken in recent years to decrease the amount of water pollution by pulp mills has used Fisheries Act provisions as a means of enforcement, although humans are probably at least equal beneficiaries.

International Activities and Regulations

At the international level, the Canadian Government has been active both bilaterally and as a participant in various multilateral organizations and ventures.

In a bilateral context, the main achievement has been the agreement with the United States on the clean-up of the lower Great Lakes. There is, it is true, a long list of other items on which bilateral agreement is a requirement or a high priority for environmental quality in Canada: the list includes similar joint action on the upper Great Lakes; air quality in the Windsor-Detroit area; water pollution in the Saint John-Saint Croix systems; movements of supertankers, especially in the Strait of Juan de

Fuca-Strait of Georgia-Puget Sound area; compatibility of regulations on automobile emission standards, and so on. Nevertheless, the agreement on the Lake Erie-Lake Ontario-St. Lawrence system that was signed in April, 1972 by the United States and Canada did tackle what was probably the most important of these concerns, and the work leading up to it again broke new ground in American-Canadian cooperation. This involved the use of the International Joint Commission, an intergovernmental agency that had been created as long ago as 1911 and that until the 1960's had been limited almost entirely to judicial or quasi-judicial interpretation of existing statutes such as the Boundary Waters Agreement of 1909. In 1964 it was entrusted with the management of a joint study of the pollution problems of the lower Great Lakes, and its report, in 1971, provided the basis for the 1972 agreement.

Another distinctive feature of the agreement, so far as implementation of Canadian action is concerned, is the fact that by far the largest expenditures by the federal government are made through another item of legislation that is not normally thought of as an environmental measure, the National Housing Act (NHA). The entire Canadian shoreline included in the agreement lies within the Province of Ontario, and a sub-agreement between the governments of Canada and Ontario provides for federal financial loan assistance of approximately $167 million to Ontario through the sewage treatment assistance provisions of the NHA.

On the multilateral scene, Canada is a member of several intergovernmental bodies that are concerned with environmental matters. These include the North Atlantic Treaty Organization (NATO) and the Organization for Economic Cooperation and Development (OECD). The "non-military" end of NATO includes the Committee on the Challenges of Modern Society (CCMS), which has in recent years organized a series of major "pilot projects," including environmental projects, with different member countries leading each project. One of the Canadian NATO-CCMS projects has been the development of a comprehensive plan for the Saint John River system, in which the U.S.A., Belgium and France have become involved as "co-pilots." In OECD, which is essentially a group of the most highly industrialized nations in Europe and North America, plus Australia and Japan, the Environment Directorate has for several years provided a basis for intergovernmental cooperation in a wide range of environmental matters.

The main Canadian effort on international environmental matters was concentrated on the UN Conference on the Human Environment in Stockholm in 1972, (together with the work of the UN Environmental Programme which originated in Stockholm), and on the preparations for the Law of the Sea Conference, which held its first session in Caracas in the summer of 1974 and was scheduled to reconvene in 1975.

It is characteristic of such international conferences and other activities that their overall effectiveness is extremely difficult to assess, still less to prove. Those outside government who watched the Stockholm Conference during two weeks in June 1972, especially those who were participating simultaneously in the non-governmental "Environment Forum" in the same city, may well have thought the proceedings ponderous, devious and even irrelevant to environmental needs. In fact the Conference did achieve, among some 113 nations, a considerable and even unexpected degree of unanimity, and agreement on matters that would certainly have left many nations far apart even two years earlier. This consensus was presumably achieved mainly because the individual member states of the United Nations recognized the seriousness of environmental quality deterioration. However, this realization was neither automatic nor easy; it required several years of preparations for those two weeks in Stockholm. This preliminary work included several meetings of a 27-nation Preparatory Committee (of which Canada was a member), and the creation of intergovernmental working groups on specific topics such as marine pollution. These meetings were in effect specialized environmental conferences in their own right. The preparations also included meetings of nongovernmental experts, such as those who produced, in 1970 and 1971, the two reports on *Man's Impact on the Global Environment* and *Inadvertent Climate Modification*.

Probably of greatest significance in achieving this general agreement in Stockholm was the long debate during the preceding two years over the apparent conflict between economic growth and environmental protection. This tended to crop up in many contexts; it is, for example, one aspect of the "freedom of the seas" controversy that has been described already. The main expression of this debate, however, took place over the role of environment versus development in the "less developed countries" of the Third World. It was argued, for example, that if there is a choice between avoiding a polluted environment and economic growth, then the governments of the less developed countries would be doing a disservice to their populations if they opt for the former. The low living standards, the short life expectancies, chronic unemployment and all the other characteristics of underdevelopment mean that rapid industrialization has a high priority, and it was argued that if pollution controls increase the cost of such industries (or even deter the establishment of new industry), then the less developed countries should go for economic growth without environmental controls. Indeed, several developing countries looked to gain from the increased environmental awareness in advanced countries: if manufacturing plants and similar production facilities create unacceptable levels of pollution in advanced countries, these less developed countries would be glad to provide an alternative home for them. Following this line of argument even further, several developing countries contended that environmental pollution is mainly a problem generated by the advanced countries; it is the result of industrialization, of societies with high consumption and consequently high waste-producing capabilities, and the prosperity of these countries, it was argued, has historically been based on a rapid advance in living standards achieved at the cost of neglecting environmental standards. Having achieved these high standards, the argument continues, the developed nations have become appalled by what they have created, and the effect of their concern is an attempt to deny similar chances for a rise in living standards to less developed countries. Not merely is this argument immoral, it is also unnecessary; many of the developing countries have ample space to locate polluting industries across their territory so that the pollution will not reach the dangerous levels that have occurred in advanced countries where industries have been crowded together with large urban populations.

This argument may seem exaggerated, but it is certainly true that most of the environmental activists tend to be found in advanced industrialized countries like Canada, and that in the intellectual climate of the late 1960's many of them were also to be found arguing against the notion of economic growth as the primary objective of society. It was neither difficult nor unreasonable for many developing countries to become suspicious of the motives underlying the environmental movement. Nor, it should be noted, was it necessary that the governments of these developing countries should agree fully with the type of argument presented in the preceding paragraphs. If they were left merely with the conviction that environmental action should have a low place in their national priorities, then the principal objective of the Stockholm Conference would not have been attainable.

In the event, this did not happen. A group of experts meeting at Founex, a small village in Switzerland, produced a statement on *Development and Environment* that went a long way towards providing common ground between developed and less developed countries. This was further extended in a series of regional preparatory meetings under the auspices of the UN's Regional Economic Commissions for Latin America, Africa and Asia. By the time of the Stockholm Conference there were few countries that were prepared to maintain the uncompromising attitude summarized in the Cameroun's national report: "The Republic of Cameroun rates 'development' as an absolute priority, whatever the side effects." Far more of them were ready to adopt the position set out in the statement by another African country:

> It is a fallacy to equate economic growth with development, if development is taken to mean the long-term satisfaction of all the needs of the people of Kenya . . . there is no necessity for Kenya to accept new industries which are hesitant to conform to proper environmental control.

It is, indeed, this type of national self-examination — by developed as well as less developed countries — that is probably the most important outcome of the Stockholm Conference, not the international agreements and programmes that were reached and adopted there, valuable though these are. For many, perhaps most, countries of the world, their participation in the Stockholm Conference, and especially in the preparations for it, was the first occasion on which these countries had found it necessary to take stock of their environmental situation, of the levels of pollution and the effectiveness of their pollution control measures, and of the benefits that they could derive from international action to improve the world environment. This is admittedly less true for Canada than for many other countries; as noted already, the environmental wave in Canada crested around 1970. Nevertheless the preparations for Stockholm exerted a strong influence in this country also. Here and elsewhere, it was increasingly realized, for example, that even the direct costs of anti-pollution devices in new manufacturing plants and similar facilities are relatively modest if they are built into new plants from the start. It was recognized also that some of the most serious pollutants can be reduced fairly easily by the use of substitutes, and that in many cases the only solutions have to be international ones. As the present author has written elsewhere:

> *Even a country as large and as powerful as the United States is vulnerable. It can ban the use of a harmful substance within its borders, it can ban the import of the substance from abroad, and it can exert pressure on other countries to take similar measures on a bilateral or multilateral basis. But insofar as the importation of manufactured goods is concerned, how is the United States to be sure that the substances concerned are absent without elaborate testing of a kind which is practically impossible? How can it prevent those substances from washing up its tidal estuaries or falling in rain from an atmosphere which contains them in similar concentrations through the world?* [7]

It would be foolish to pretend that such insights are the result of the Stockholm Conference and its preparatory process, or that they were not known to environmental scientists long before Stockholm, in both developed and less developed countries. There is, however, a great difference between scientific knowledge and government priority. It was the Stockholm Conference that, for the first time, made the environment a priority, temporary or permanent, for the great majority of the world's governments. The same is true, though there is not space here to treat the subject adequately, of the preparations for the Law of the Sea Conference. The environment, including the conservation of fishery resources, was only one element in the agenda for the conference, but without the stimulus of Stockholm and of the growing conflict between the "freedom of the seas" and the wise management of marine resources, environmental concerns would have taken a much lower priority than they now do. Because Canada has a longer oceanic shoreline than any other country; because that shoreline is very vulnerable to oil and other pollution; because the world's fishery fleets are rapidly depleting the resources of the Atlantic and Pacific off Canadian coasts; and because of the similar potential economic importance of the continental shelf off Canada, the Law of the Sea Conference and its objective, a general reconstruction of international law for marine areas in the context of modern problems and modern opportunities, are of vital concern to Canada. So far, the prospects that the conference will reach solutions acceptable to Canada and other nations are reasonably good.

Regulation

There is yet another dimension to the environmental activity of the Government of Canada that is too important to be ignored. This is its power to protect environmental quality by regulatory activity. The various items of legislation passed in 1970, for example, provide for the formulation and enforcement of appropriate regulations to achieve their objectives. Other environmental improvement can be achieved through utilization of the regulatory powers contained in existing legislation. One simple example may be outright prohibition or severe financial penalties on night movements at airports close to residential areas. Of more direct relevance to the geographer, perhaps, are the Land Use Regulations covering the Yukon and Northwest Territories that have been made possible by amendments to the Territorial Lands Act.

These amendments were made to the legislation in 1970, and the main Land Use Regulations were issued in 1971. Essentially they provide a set of ground rules for all economic activity involving the use of land in the Territories, and they apply to every individual and corporation except the native population. As well as general regulations, each specific land-using activity may require a licence, to which special stipulations can be attached. The object of the regulations is primarily environmental protection, based on the premise that the vast majority of economic activity in the Territories at present tends to use land only on a transitory basis; groups pass through an area looking for oil and other minerals, assessing forestry resources or recreation development potential, or for similar purposes. In such situations it is not necessary to indulge in an elaborate cost-benefit exercise to determine whether one barrel of oil is worth ten ducks. For the present we protect the ducks. If more specific development proposals are made — for a mine at this particular site, or for a pipeline along that particular route — then clearly a more elaborate investigation of costs and benefits is necessary.

In order to protect the ducks, however, we need to know that the ducks are there and in need of protection. In order to implement such all-embracing regulations, the federal and territorial governments need as good an information base as possible. It is not enough to say, in effect, "we don't know what is in this particular area, but whatever it is, we think it is more important than what you want to do, and it needs protection." Further, once the decision to adopt this regulatory method of protection has been taken, the governments need the information base as soon as possible, so that the regulations can be implemented as quickly as possible. Lastly, and this is not an unimportant point, the governments' information needs to be both as authoritative as the present state of knowledge permits, and available to all interested parties, including the governments themselves, the corporations or individuals anxious to obtain licences, environmentalists anxious to ensure the protection of the northern landscape, and northern residents. Although some disagreement and scope for different interpretation are inevitable, it would be a severe restraint on the effectiveness of the Land Use Regulations if they were to fall victim to controversy over the facts; "my expert is better than your expert."

This was the background to the initiation of the Land Use Information Series mapping project in what is now the Lands Directorate of the Department of Environment. Acting on behalf of the Department of Indian Affairs and Northern Development (DIAND), as part of DIAND's Arctic Land Use Research programme, a small team of geographers and cartographers began to assemble all the environmental information relevant to land use that was readily available for the Mackenzie valley and the northern Yukon, and to compile this information as an overprint and marginal data on the 1:250,000 topographic sheets of the area. Within 18 months 44 sheets covering some 200,000 square miles had been compiled, printed and published. A second group of 23 maps, covering 106,000 square miles of the southern Yukon, appeared in 1973. A third set, 17 maps of 76,000 square miles of the Mackenzie and Selwyn Mountains appeared in 1974, and the project team is still hard at work.

Two points are especially important in regard to this project. First, although such a scale and speed of production may suggest massive financial and human resources allocation, this has not been the case. The first 44 maps, for example, required only about 11 man-years of professional and technical staff time. The main reason for this has been the emphasis placed on the collection and integration of existing knowledge, rather than on the initiation of new research. Some quick data collection in the field was needed for the first maps, and more is required as the areas covered extend further and further away from the main centres of northern settlement and scientific interest. But there is always far more completed research to be found in libraries and filing cabinets than is effectively used without such a deliberate attempt to integrate it and present it effectively.

The second point can also only be briefly mentioned, but it does have great importance in any consideration of the role of governments in environmental protection, as in other areas of government activity. This is the obvious fact that the time available to produce an effective response bears little relation to the importance of the issue. In a university or other independent research agency, the time taken to investigate a problem normally and rightly bears a close relation to the perceived significance of the problem. In most governmental situations this is not the case: the more important the decision that is taken, the more urgent it is to develop the means by which it can be implemented.

THE FUTURE

Now that this relatively sudden environmental activity by governments has been replaced by a period of implementation and consolidation, what does this imply? What justification is there for the cynical view that the environmental concern expressed by Parliament, the provincial legislatures and public officials was merely a short-lived response to equally short-lived public opinion? Or for the slightly more charitable view that, whatever the good intentions of governments at the end of the 1960's, the energy crisis and the economic conditions of the 1970's have imposed a new set of priorities, one in which environmental matters are fairly low on this list?

The first, cynical view has already been challenged, implicitly and explicitly, in what has been said earlier in this chapter. The magnitude and the varied character of the response of the federal government, and of provincial governments, to the environmental challenges of the 1960's went far beyond mere window dressing. The second type of doubt is more difficult to dispel, and the ultimate proof cannot be provided until towards the end of the present decade. There is no doubt that the environmental movement found the right time to make its appeal. With double-digit inflation and oil at $11 rather than $3.60 a barrel, environmental arguments might have fallen on a much larger number of deaf ears, in Canada and around the world. There are also some signs that the zeal for environmental improvement by governments has slackened, as the trans-Alaska pipeline has finally been authorized and as the raising of the automobile emission standards has been spread over a longer period than was originally planned.

The pessimist can, therefore, probably find some evidence to support the view that the priority of environmental matters is slipping. But there is probably much more to indicate that these are relatively minor setbacks, and that the concern in Canada and the rest of the world that marked the late 1960's has left a permanent and substantial legacy. The sheer volume of legislative change during that period, combined with the creation of major departments of government concerned with environmental matters, should alone ensure that the momentum is maintained. The federal government has now what it did not have before: a large Department of the Environment staffed by scientists and administrators who are not likely to forget environmental imperatives, and who are charged with the implementation of legislation and regulations that affect major areas of national life. A similar situation exists in provincial governments. The Great Lakes agreement is still being implemented, and Canada Water Act comprehensive agreements are being signed with the provinces at a steady rate. Proposals to meet the energy crisis by rapid extension of the transcontinental oil pipeline from Sarnia to Montreal, or by constructing a gas pipeline along the Mackenzie valley, have been met with clear indications that the necessary permissions will only be forthcoming after adequate assessment of the environmental impact of these projects. The conservation of fishery resources and the achievement of major improvements to international law for the marine environment remain high priorities, and there is little reason to believe that the zeal of other countries for such agreement has diminished substantially more than it has in Canada.

It would, indeed, probably be a mistake to regard the changing priorities of the 1970's as likely always to reduce the importance attached to environmental matters. For example, the energy crisis has led to a re-evaluation of the whole structure of oil and gas development and trade in Canada. When oil on the world market cost only $3.60 a barrel, it made good sense to export surplus western crude to the U.S.A., and to import eastern Canadian supplies from overseas. At $11 a barrel there is more concern for the conservation of Canadian resources. This re-evaluation, combined with rapid inflation, has affected the prospects for the development of the Athabasca tar sands and the construction of oil and gas pipelines in the Mackenzie valley. The net effect is not clear at the time of writing but it seems clear that the cause of environmental conservation may gain as well as lose.

THE URBAN ENVIRONMENT IN THE 1970's

Another very important way in which current priorities are likely to reinforce environmental objectives is in regard to urban matters. It may be that the environmental movement will come to be seen as having two distinct phases in Canada and other countries. During the second half of the 1960's, up to about the time of the Stockholm Conference in 1972, the main preoccupation was with the natural environment. Since 1972, however, there has been increased emphasis on the human environment, and especially on the man-made environment of towns, cities and megalopolises, in which the majority of mankind is increasingly to be found.

At the international level, this shift is exemplified by the preparations that are now being made for Habitat, the United Nations Conference on Human Settlements, that will be held in Vancouver in the summer of 1976. Habitat is a direct outgrowth of the Stockholm Conference, where it was realized that, although human settlements were a principal agenda item, the opportunities for agreement and action were more limited than in regard to natural environmental issues such as marine pollution or the protection of endangered species. Urbanization is a world-wide phenomenon, and there is probably little initial disagreement between developed and developing countries about its importance. But it also became clear in the preparations for Stockholm that much more work was needed on urbanization and other human settlement issues.

Canada therefore proposed at Stockholm that a special conference, on the same scale as that on the human environment, be convened to deal with human settlements issues, and offered to provide facilities to enable it to be held in Canada. Habitat is the result. The preparatory process is again likely to be as important as the Conference itself, and there will be an increased emphasis in Vancouver on the demonstration of solutions, by means of audio-visual presentations by individual countries. This recognizes the fact that, although human settlements problems occur world-wide, the main responsibility for action lies with individual governments; the emphasis is therefore on the pooling and utilization by governments of accumulated experience.

Within Canada, the growing importance of the urban environment is evident in a variety of ways. One of the most obvious was the creation of the Ministry of State for Urban Affairs in 1971. In a country where three-quarters of the population are already classed by the census as "urban", it is inevitable that a very large proportion of the activities of all levels of government is directed towards meeting the needs of urban residents. The Ministry is, however, the first agency created by the federal government specifically to deal with urban issues. These issues are not limited to environmental matters; it is not simply a "Ministry of the Urban Environment", but the quality of urban life and the quality of the urban environment are very closely linked.

This concern for the quality of the urban environment is also a high priority of other departments of the federal government, and of other levels of government in Canada. There is, for example, an evident determination to produce during the present decade a better balance between public transportation and the private automobile, especially within urban areas. There is a growing recognition of the role that public agencies can play in revitalizing declining areas of the inner city, not merely through the provision of financial assistance, but by careful integration of new government offices and other buildings with commercial and recreational facilities designed for the urban resident. The Railway Relocation and Crossing Act, 1974, is designed to provide a means by which under-utilized freight yards and other railway facilities that occupy large areas in the heart of Canadian towns and cities can be relocated to the periphery, so that the land may be utilized for other purposes.

Probably the main emphasis during the 1970's, however, will be on what can loosely be termed the management of urban growth. Although some experts would argue that there is a critical size of city — say half a million or so — beyond which further growth inevitably leads to a deterioration in the quality of life, it is the rate at which this growth takes place that is probably of more importance. A city of two million people is not necessarily a more unpleasant place than a city of one million. If, however, it goes from one million to two million in a matter of 25 years or so (i.e. a growth rate of about three percent per annum) the strain on the resources, natural and human, is much greater than if this growth is spread over 50 years (i.e. 1½ percent per annum). In the former situation the city is constantly struggling to keep pace with the growth in population: with providing roads, housing, sewerage, employment, transport, fire protection and all the other basic services. There is little time to ask whether the growth is occuring in the right places, whether good agricultural land is being unnecessarily converted into subdivisions, whether air and water quality could be maintained or improved by a different form of development. There is, in other words, little time to plan and not much opportunity to implement a plan effectively if one is available. Meanwhile, in the centres where such growth is much less rapid or is even absent altogether (usually the smaller towns), there is less incentive to the community or to the entrepreneur to provide new facilities. The contrast between what is available in the big city and in the small town widens, especially in the eyes of immigrants and of a younger generation of Canadians, and growth pressures on the largest centres are maintained.

Having lived through a quarter-century of such rapid expansion, several major metropolitan areas in Canada, and the governments of the provinces in which they are located, have become well aware of the disadvantages of such rapid growth and the need to plan and to manage future growth. The Greater Vancouver Regional District, for example, has been developing its Liveable Region Plan, and the name could be applied also to similar efforts in other parts of Canada such as the Central Ontario Lakeshore Urban Community, from Oshawa to Niagara, and to the planning for the Halifax-Dartmouth metropolitan area.

10g.

CONCLUSION

The present author has been closely involved in the environmental activities of the federal government for the last six years, and he is therefore by no means an independent observer. This chapter has concentrated on what has been achieved, rather than on what remains to be done. There does, however, seem solid ground for satisfaction at what has been achieved by all levels of government in Canada during the last ten years, and similarly grounds for confidence that this momentum will be maintained in the future. The environment was not a temporary preoccupation of governments during the late 1960's. The prominence that it achieved in legislative action and administrative reorganization has certainly diminished, as it was bound to do. But environment will no more disappear from the list of government concerns than did a concern for the reduction of unemployment, for the provision of family allowances, or other matters that were once of little interest to governments but that have long since been taken for granted as matters for continuing concern. In Ottawa, and in the provincial capitals, the environment is here to stay.

NOTES

* The views expressed in this chapter are those of the author and are not necessarily those of the Government of Canada.

1. Canada. Department of National Health and Welfare. (1974). *New Perspective on the Health of Canadians*. Ottawa: Information Canada.

2. Jackson, C.I. (1971a). *The Spatial Dimensions of Environment Management in Canada*. Geographical Paper No. 46. Ottawa: Information Canada. 1.

3. Hare, F.K. and C.I. Jackson. (1972). *Environment: A Geographical Perspective*. Geographical Paper No. 52. Ottawa: Information Canada, 1.

4. Kelly, W. (1970). *Impollutable Pogo*. New York: Simon and Schuster, 128.

5. Canada. (1970). *Report of the Task Force – Operation Oil*. Vol. 1, Ottawa: Information Canada, 2-3.

6. Green, L.C. (1971). "International Law and Canada's Anti-Pollution Legislation." *Oregon Law Review*, 50 (Spring).

7. Jackson, C.I. (1971b). "The Dimensions of International Pollution." *Oregon Law Review*, 50 (Spring), 223-58.

DUE DATE

DUE DATE			
APR 0 6 1992			
OCT 1 4 1996			
OCT 0 2 1996			
DEC 1 7 2003			
DEC 0 9 2003			
	201-6503		Printed in USA